Privatising Old-Age Security

Privatising
Old-Age Security

Latin America and Eastern Europe Compared

Katharina Müller

Research Officer
German Development Institute, Bonn, Germany

Edward Elgar
Cheltenham, UK • Northampton, MA, USA

© Katharina Müller 2003.

Published by
Edward Elgar Publishing Limited
Glensanda House
Montpellier Parade
Cheltenham
Glos GL50 1UA
UK

Edward Elgar Publishing, Inc.
136 West Street
Suite 202
Northampton
Massachusetts 01060
USA

A catalogue record for this book
is available from the British Library

Library of Congress Cataloguing in Publication Data

Müller, Katharina, 1967 -
  Privatising old-age security : Latin America and Eastern Europe compared /
  Katharina Müller.
    p. cm.
  Includes bibliographical references and index.
    1. Old age pensions—South America. 2. Old age pensions—Europe, Eastern. 3.
  Privatization. I. Title.

  HD7105.35.s63M84 2003
  331.25'22—dc21

                                                                              2003051333
  ISBN 1 84376 324 9

Printed and bound in Great Britain by MPG Books Ltd, Bodmin, Cornwall

Contents

Tables

Abbreviations

ADEBA	*Asociación de Bancos Argentinos*; Association of Argentine Banks
AFAPs	*Administradoras de Fondos de Ahorro Previsional*; pension funds in Uruguay
AFJPs	*Administradoras de Fondos de Jubilaciones y Pensiones*; pension funds in Argentina
AFPs	*Administradoras de Fondos de Pensiones*; pension funds in Bolivia, Chile and Peru
ANSeS	*Administración Nacional de Seguridad Social*; Social Security Administration
APRA	*Alianza Popular Revolucionaria Americana*; American Popular Revolutionary Alliance
ATE	*Asociación Trabajadores del Estado*; Union of Public Sector Workers
AWS	*Akcja Wyborcza Solidarność*; Solidarity Electoral Action
BBVA	*Banco Bilbao Vizcaya Argentaria*; Spanish banking group
BCRP	*Banco Central de Reserva del Perú*; Peruvian Central Bank
BOCONs	*Bonos de Consolidación*; consolidation bonds
BPS	*Banco de Previsión Social*; Uruguayan social security institute
BSP	Bulgarian Socialist Party
CC	*Compensación de Cotizaciones*; compensatory pension
CEE	Central-Eastern Europe
cf.	*confer*; compare
CGT	*Confederación General de Trabajo*; Argentine trade union federation
CLAS	Center for Latin American Studies

CNSS	*Caja Nacional de Seguridad Social*; National Social Insurance Fund
COB	*Central Obrera Boliviana*; Bolivian trade union confederation
cont'd	continued
CTA	*Congreso de los Trabajadores Argentinos*; Argentine trade union federation
D.L.	*Decreto Ley*; decree
e.g.	*exempli gratia*; for instance
ÉT	*Érdekegyeztető Tanács*; Hungarian tripartite council
EU	European Union
FCC	*Fondo de Capitalización Colectiva*; collective capitalisation fund
FCI	*Fondo de Capitalización Individual*; individual capitalisation fund
FCR	*Fondo Consolidado de Reservas Previsionales*; Consolidated Pension Reserves Fund
FIEL	*Fundación de Investigaciones Económicas Latinoamericanas*; Argentine research institute
FIT	Frankfurt Institute for Transformation Studies
FONAHPU	*Fondo Nacional de Ahorro Público*; Public Savings Fund
FONARE	*Fondo Nacional de Reserva*; National Reserve Fund
FONCOMs	*Fondos Complementarios*; complementary pension funds
FOPEBA	*Fondo de Pensiones Básicas*; Basic Pension Fund
FSU	Former Soviet Union
FUNDESOL	*Fundación de Desarrollo Solidario*; Foundation for Development in Solidarity
FUS	*Fundusz Ubezpieczeń Społecznych*; Polish Social Insurance Fund
GDP	Gross Domestic Product
gov't	government
HAGENA	*Agencija za nadzor mirovinskih fondova i osiguranja*; Pension Funds and Insurance Supervisory Agency

HDZ	*Hrvatska demokratska zajednica*; Croatian Democratic Union
i.e.	*id est*; that is to say
IDB	Inter-American Development Bank
IFF	individually fully funded
IFIs	international financial institutions
ILO	International Labour Organisation
IMF	International Monetary Fund
incl.	including
INE	*Instituto Nacional de Estadística*; National Office of Statistics
int'l	international
IPD	implicit pension debt
IPSS	*Instituto Peruano de Seguridad Social*; Peruvian Social Security Institute
IT	information technology
KNSB	Confederation of Independent Trade Unions in Bulgaria
KRUS	*Kasa Rolniczego Ubezpieczenia Społecznego*; Polish social insurance fund for farmers
MBL	*Movimiento Bolivia Libre*; Free Bolivia Movement
MNR	*Movimiento Nacionalista Revolucionario*; Nationalist Revolutionary Movement
MP	Member of Parliament
MRTK	*Movimiento Revolucionario Tupac Katari*; Tupac Katari Revolutionary Movement
MSZOSZ	*Magyar Szakszervezetek Országos Szövetsége*; Hungarian trade union federation
MTA	*Movimiento de los Trabajadores Argentinos*; Argentine trade union federation
n.a.	not available
NDC	notional defined contribution
No.	Number
NSSI	National Social Security Institute
OECD	Organisation for Economic Co-operation and Development

ONAJPU	*Organización Nacional de Jubilados y Pensionados del Uruguay*; National Organisation of the Retired of Uruguay
ONP	*Oficina de Normalización Previsional*; Office for Pension Normalisation
OPP	*Oficina de Planeamiento y Presupuesto*; Office for Planning and Budget
OPZZ	*Ogólnopolskie Porozumienie Związków Zawodowych*; Polish trade union federation
p.a.	*per annum*; yearly
PAYG	pay-as-you-go
PIT-CNT	*Plenario Intersindical de Trabajadores-Convención Nacional de Trabajadores*; Uruguayan trade union federation
PR	public relations
PRONATASS	*Programa Nacional de Asistencia Técnica para la Administración de los Servicios Sociales en la República Argentina*; National Technical Assistance Programme for the Administration of Social Services in Argentina
PSL	*Polskie Stronnictwo Ludowe*; Polish Peasant Party
REGOS	*Središnji registar osiguranika*; Central Registry of Insured Persons
Rep.	Republic
SAFJP	*Superintendencia de Administradoras de Fondos de Jubilaciones y Pensiones*; supervisory agency for pension funds
SAFP	*Superintendencia de Administradoras de Fondos de Pensiones*; supervisory agency for pension funds
SLD	*Sojusz Lewicy Demokratycznej*; Left Democratic Alliance
SNP	*Secretaría Nacional de Pensiones*; National Pensions Office
UCeDé	*Unión de Centro Democrático*; Union of the Democratic Centre
UCR	*Unión Cívica Radical*; Radical Civic Union
UCS	*Unión Cívica Solidaridad*; Civic Solidarity Union
UDF	Union of Democratic Forces
UNDP	United Nations Development Programme

US	United States
USAID	US Agency for International Development
UW	*Unia Wolności*; Freedom Union
VMB	voluntary mutual benefit
YPF	*Yacimientos Petrolíferos Fiscales*; Argentine oil company
ZUS	*Zakład Ubezpieczeń Społecznych*; Social Insurance Institute

Acknowledgements

The present volume contains the findings of the research project 'The Political Economy of Pension Reform: Eastern Europe and Latin America in Comparison'. It was conducted from March 1999 to February 2002 while the author was a Research Fellow at the Frankfurt Institute for Transformation Studies (FIT), a multidisciplinary research institute forming part of the European University Viadrina at Frankfurt/Oder. Financial support by the Volkswagen Foundation was crucial to this comparative endeavour and is gratefully acknowledged.

I am deeply indebted to a large number of social policy experts for their generous support before, during and after my fieldwork in Latin America and Eastern Europe. Undoubtedly, their academic interest and practical assistance, as well as the time, information and contacts they shared with me were key for the success of this project. Much to my regret I cannot mention all of them here. Yet I would like to express my particular appreciation to Fabio Bertranou in Santiago de Chile; Carlos Grushka, Jorge San Martino and Walter Schulthess in Buenos Aires; José Busquets, Ernesto Murro, Luis Viana and especially Jorge Papadópulos in Montevideo; Luis Aparicio, César Rivera, Jorge Bernedo and Elio Sánchez in Lima; Alberto Bonadona, Huáscar Cajías, Pablo Gottret and Helga Salinas in La Paz; Mária Augusztinovics, Róbert Gál and András Simonovits in Budapest; Agnieszka Chłoń-Domińczak, Stanisława Golinowska, Zofia Czepulis-Rutkowska in Warsaw and Maciej Żukowski in Poznań; Predrag Bejaković, Katarina Ott, Željko Potočnjak, Snježana Plevko and Siniša Zrinščak in Zagreb; Rosa Chiappe, Plamenka Markova and Hristina Mitreva in Sofia; Johannes Jäger in Vienna and Wolfgang Scholz in Geneva. Robert Holzmann and David Lindeman helped me to find interesting interlocutors in Washington DC, while Winfried Schmähl enabled me to stay in touch with pension experts from Eastern Europe.

I would also like to mention that it was my former colleague Frank Bönker who drew my attention to the ongoing research on the political economy of policy reform several years ago. Throughout the project period, I greatly benefited from stimulating discussions with Barry Ames, Ilean Cashu, Elaine Fultz, Katja Hujo, Stephen Kay, Raúl Madrid, Mitchell Orenstein and Kurt

Weyland on the politics of pension reform. I am also grateful for the comments I received from Zoran Anušić, Elaine Fultz, Manfred Nitsch and Siniša Zrinščak on several draft chapters of the book.

Finally, I would like to express my gratitude to two persons who have supported this project with their enthusiasm and guidance. Carmelo Mesa-Lago invited me to the University of Pittsburgh's Center for Latin American Studies (CLAS), helped me to access the invaluable Eduardo Lozano Latin American Library Collection and shared his personal pensions' archive as well as his thoughts on the Latin American pension reforms with me. Last but not least, Hans-Jürgen Wagener, my former supervisor at FIT, encouraged me to embark on this academic venture, helped me to find the necessary resources and – perhaps most importantly – always ensured that I had the latitude I needed to make my way.

Berlin-Kreuzberg, March 2003 Katharina Müller

1. Introduction

More than two decades have elapsed since Chile's radical departure from the Bismarckian model of old-age security. Today, this iconoclastic pension reform can no longer be considered an isolated event. During the 1990s, many Latin American countries have introduced compulsory individually fully funded (IFF) schemes, run by private pension funds that either compete with, substitute or complement the existing public pay-as-you-go (PAYG) schemes. A similar wave of 'structural' or 'systemic'[1] pension reforms is taking shape in the transition countries of Central-Eastern Europe (CEE) and the Former Soviet Union (FSU). These imply a full or partial shift from an inter-generational contract to individual provision for old age, as well as a shift from the state to the market as the main supplier of retirement pensions. The paradigm change inherent in pension privatisation[2] therefore amounts to a substantial rewrite of the underlying social contract, which does not usually occur in the case of a mere change of the entitlement conditions, commonly referred to as 'parametric' reform.

From a theoretical perspective, the wave of radical pension reforms in Latin America and Eastern Europe is particularly remarkable because old-age schemes were long thought difficult to reform. Established institutional arrangements in the area of welfare provision involve substantial economic, social, cognitive and normative investment and adaptation efforts, turning into sunk costs when these institutions undergo radical change (Pierson 1994; Götting 1998). Pensioners amount to the largest single-issue constituency in many countries, and it has been argued that their power may well increase as populations are ageing (Börsch-Supan 1998). Pierson and Weaver (1993) argue that the elderly are viewed sympathetically by other voters, providing for a large potential of pension reform to generate blame. For all these reasons, political scientists, sociologists and economists focus predominantly on austerity measures and blame-reduction strategies, while doubting that policymakers will engage in fundamental pension reform: 'pay-as-you-go schemes may face incremental cutbacks and adjustments, but they are highly resistant to radical reform' (Pierson 2001: 416).

What accounts, then, for the political feasibility of pension privatisation in Latin America and Eastern Europe? In spite of the striking similarity of pension reform approaches in both regions, no comparative analysis has been presented so far, making this study the first of its kind. Seeking to explore and explain the similarities and differences in pension policy intra- as well as cross-regionally, it analyses the political economy of radical pension reform in Latin America and Eastern Europe. By shedding light on the political viability of radical, market-oriented reforms, it is intended as a contribution to the understanding of the political economy of policy reform. Eight cases of radical pension reform in Latin America and Eastern Europe have been selected: Argentina, Uruguay, Peru and Bolivia, as well as Hungary, Poland, Croatia and Bulgaria. By including cases from the Southern Cone and the Andes, from Central Europe and the Balkans, the choice of countries takes the considerable heterogeneity of both regions into account. The most important differences concern political and economic stability, social cohesion, demography and coverage. Two countries with (semi-)autocratic regimes at the time of pension reform, Peru and Croatia, are included in the sample to account for the difficult balancing act between *dictablanda*, *democradura* and democracy in parts of both regions.[3]

Moreover, all three types of pension privatisation to be observed are represented in the present study: the substitutive, parallel and mixed variants (Mesa-Lago 1998). Under the substitutive model, the former public system is closed down, being replaced by a privately run IFF scheme – such as in Bolivia. The parallel approach implies that a private IFF system is introduced as an alternative to public pension insurance, resulting in two competing pension schemes, e.g. in Peru. Under the mixed model a newly created IFF tier on a mandatory basis complements the reformed public system, such as in Argentina, Uruguay, Hungary, Poland, Croatia and Bulgaria. The predomi- nance of the mixed variant in the present study is justified by the fact that it accounts for more than half of all cases of pension privatisation in both regions.[4] Moreover, it should be noted that all but one of the post-socialist cases of privatisation are mixed. The mixed model also played a major role in the *sui generis* institutional transfer from the South to the East that has occurred.

Taken together, radical pension reform efforts in the eight countries considered here stretched over more than a decade. Due to the number of cases, the simultaneity and lengthiness of some of the reform processes and, last but not least, linguistic constraints, reforms could not be observed directly. Detailed studies of the political economy of pension reform only exist for Argentina, Uruguay and Poland. Shorter accounts on the making of pension privatisation are available for the Bolivian, Peruvian and Hungarian cases, while the Croatian and Bulgarian ones have not been analysed from this perspective so far. Based on extensive fieldwork carried out in both regions in 2000 and 2001, the study attempts a systematic reconstruction of these eight reform stories – if only from an outsider's perspective and with hindsight.[5] To this end, over 300 interviews and background conversations with policymakers, social policy experts, pension fund managers and supervisors, trade unionists, pensioners' representatives and external actors were conducted in Buenos Aires, Budapest, La Paz, Lima, Montevideo, Sofia, Warsaw, Zagreb and Washington DC.[6]

The study unfolds as follows: Part I outlines the conceptual framework of this study. It summarises the basic findings of the multidisciplinary research on policy reform, as well as from the recent studies on the political economy of pension reform. Parts II and III present the Latin American and East European pension reform experience. Each of these parts contains four country studies from two sub-regions that are presented in their regional context and with a focus on the political economy of the pension reform process. In Part IV, the eight reform stories from the Southern Cone, the Andean region, East-Central and South-Eastern Europe are discussed comparatively, while some final remarks conclude this account of the political viability of pension privatisation in Latin America and Eastern Europe.

NOTES

1. In Eastern Europe, the term 'systemic reform' is used for radical pension reform (e.g. Klimentová 1997), while it is usually referred to as 'structural reform' in Latin America (Mesa-Lago 1998).
2. The notion of pension 'privatisation' has been criticised, since the state continues to play a role in the new schemes. Here, the term is thought useful to indicate the scope and direction of the recent reforms in Latin America and the transition countries. For a more detailed discussion see Müller (2002d).
3. Freedom House ratings for all country cases are listed in Chapter 10, Table 10.1.
4. Of all pension privatisations that had been implemented and/or legislated in both regions by 2002, eleven were of a mixed, seven of a substitutive and two of a parallel type (Müller 2003b).
5. Earlier fieldwork was conducted in Poland and Hungary in 1996 and 1997, when these reforms were still ongoing. For detailed findings see Müller (1999).
6. Although pivotal for the understanding of the country cases, these interviews are not quoted here, as many interviewees asked for confidentiality.

PART I

The Conceptual Framework

2. From state to market: explaining policy reform

It is interesting to note that the Latin American and East European pension privatisations occurred in a similar political and ideational setting, as both regions witnessed a recent paradigm shift from a state-led approach to market-oriented reforms (Baer and Love 2000). In the late 1980s, the countries of Central-Eastern Europe and the Soviet Union embarked on a fundamental transition of their economies and societies, abandoning decades of socialist experiments (Lavigne 1995; Havrylyshyn and Nsouli 2001). By this time, neoliberal economic policy had also taken over from the 'import substitution-*cum*-government intervention development model' in Latin America (Corbo 2000: 62), following the debt crisis of the 1980s. Soon, this set of market-oriented reforms came to be known as the 'Washington consensus' (Williamson 1990, 2000).[1]

The political viability of radical reform had long been precluded by conventional wisdom that assumed selfish, rent-maximising bureaucrats and obstructionist vested interests. This apparent puzzle gave rise to a new research programme on the political economy of policy reform. It should be noted that the generic expression 'reform' is often used to refer to a rather specific set of policies in the direction of market opening and liberalisation (Tommasi 2002).[2] Early contributions to the new strand of research centred on the politics of structural adjustment programmes and market-oriented reforms in developing countries (e.g. Bery 1990; Whitehead 1990; Krueger 1993). Soon, its focus of attention was extended to the OECD countries and to the post-socialist world. The growing body of literature is fed by economists, political scientists and sociologists, while the methodology used comprises case studies, cross-national comparisons and formalised explanatory models.[3]

A preceding crisis is a frequently raised argument for the explanation of radical change.[4] A 'benefit of crises' is diagnosed when situations of perceived emergency persuade opposing groups to agree upon unpopular measures (Drazen and Grilli 1993: 598). Although neither a necessary nor a sufficient condition for spurring policy reform, crises can break stalemates and may facilitate the demolition of political coalitions that had previously blocked reform. However, the crisis hypothesis has been criticised as tautological: that 'policy reform should follow crisis ... is no more surprising than smoke following fire' (Rodrik 1996: 27). Moreover, economic crisis is usually associated with a lack of resources to compensate losers and may end up blocking reform, rather than facilitating it. Hence, cases of crisis without reform abound, and there have also been reforms without a preceding crisis (Bönker 2003).

On many occasions the international financial institutions (IFIs) have been identified as vital catalysts for an agenda entailing fundamental change (Toye 1994).[5] Their impact is partially determined by their role as important creditors in many developing and transition countries. By the 1990s almost all programmes included structural conditionality, arousing much controversy (IMF 2001b).[6] While external conditions on an adjustment package may allow local policymakers to avoid the blame for unpopular policy measures, the risk of backlash effects should not be disregarded (Haggard and Webb 1993; Sachs 1994; Williamson 1994). Yet, it is important to point out that the IFIs' leverage is not limited to their own financial involvement. Rather, it is the general level of external indebtedness that matters. The International Monetary Fund (IMF) and the World Bank 'may signal that a developing country has embraced sound policies and hence boost its credibility' (Stiglitz 1998: 27). The IFIs' assistance may thus be interpreted as extra leverage given to reform-minded policymakers.

Several scholars have stressed the importance of leadership in reform initiatives (Harberger 1993; Sachs 1994). In policy reform, agency matters: courageous, extraordinarily committed individuals and their ability to communicate a vision of the 'promised land' ahead have often proved crucial for radical reform (Rodrik 1994). A fundamental change of the agenda has frequently been brought about by market-oriented economists-as-politicians, convinced that the size and role of the state needed to be diminished (Williamson 1994; Grindle 2001). At the same time, the pivotal role of ideas in policy reform has been rightly stressed (O'Neil Trowbridge 2001). Yet, market-friendly reforms have not always been carried out by neoliberal governments, but also by 'unlikely' left-wing or populist administrations (Cukierman and Tommasi 1998a, b; Ross 2000). This phenomenon has been related to the superior ability of left-leaning politicians to communicate the advantages of such policies to their constituencies – or, rather, the lack of political alternatives (Tommasi 2002). When such unlikely administrations are involved in policy reform, this amounts to a 'Nixon-in-China syndrome' reversed.[7]

Yet, a strong, market-oriented change team is often not sufficient to guarantee success against powerful interest groups and political opposition

(Williamson and Haggard 1994; Tommasi and Velasco 1996; Schamis 1999). A carefully planned reform strategy has been considered an important device to mitigate political constraints. Consequently, the appropriate timing, speed, bundling and tactical sequencing of reforms have been much discussed.[8] Advocates of big-bang strategies argue that they will make reforms irreversible before substantial opposition builds up (Sachs 1994). When not all reforms are tackled at once, but the most promising ones are given priority, demonstration effects may be produced and political support created (Nelson 1994). Packaging and design may also be crucial for the feasibility of radical reforms. This includes the politics of compensation that may take five different forms. Exclusionary compensation exempts powerful groups from reform, direct financial compensation tackles groups adversely affected, indirect and cross-compensation imply trading off one policy for another or linking reforms, and political compensation exchanges broader political rewards for support on a specific issue (James and Brooks 2001).

While reform design bears a direct impact on the 'redistributional calculus' of radical reforms (World Bank 1997c: 146), the interpretation of reform costs is also relevant (Bönker 1995). Large policy changes may be tolerated if a newly elected government succeeds in blaming the previous regime for the *status quo*, a phenomenon denoted as 'honeymoon effect' (Haggard and Webb 1993; Rodrik 1994; Williamson 1994). Conversely, radical reforms are less likely to succeed shortly before elections. Moreover, high social costs may not be obstructive to radical reforms if those affected lack political voice and power (Tommasi and Velasco 1996).

Democratic regimes differ with regard to their respective capability of filtering discontent. Hence, many analyses of policy reform consider the design of political institutions, such as the electoral and party system, and institutional veto points.[9] Bresser Pereira, Maravall and Przeworski (1993: 208) have pointed out that radical reform has been pursued in four distinct policy styles: while decretism (reliance on presidential rule by decree) and mandatism (executive use of a legislative majority to short-cut legislation) are two exclusive, technocratic policy styles, parliamentarism and corporatism (or concertation) involve extensive negotiations with opposing forces in the legislature and beyond. The technocratisation of decision-making on policy reform has been criticised (Silva 1999), as it weakens democratic institutions and does not help to build the political consensus required for political sustainability (Bresser Pereira, Maravall and Przeworski 1993; Stiglitz 2000).

It should be noted that the literature on the political economy of policy reform has been criticised for its extensive focus on the feasibility of decision-making, while little or no attention is paid to implementation. Contrary to this, Thomas and Grindle (1990) and Tommasi (2002) have challenged the notion of irreversible policy reforms, stressing that a policy reform initiative may be altered at any stage in its life cycle.

So far, research on the political economy of policy reform has focused mainly on macroeconomic reform policy, also known as 'first-generation reforms'. Less attention was paid to the political viability of sectoral, or 'second-generation' reforms – among which pension privatisation – that amount to more complex policy and institutional changes (Graham and Naím 1998; Graham et al. 1999). It should be noted, however, that reform taxonomies are far from uniform. Today, it is becoming increasingly clear that there is a need for second-stage macroeconomic reforms in many countries.[10]

NOTES

1. While some authors perceive an emerging 'post-Washington consensus', others suggest that its policy advice still remains largely intact (Kołodko 1999; Naím 2000; Srinivasan 2000). For a recent critique see Gore (2000) and Stiglitz (2000).
2. On the notion of 'reform' see Stiglitz (2000: 551): 'The concept ... has evolved to take on "politically correct" overtones: reforms are now those changes that "we" approve of, while changes that we do not condone can be labeled with terms of censure'. For the analogous semantics of 'pension reform' see Müller (1999: 37).
3. For an overview see Rodrik (1996), Tommasi and Velasco (1996), Sturzenegger and Tommasi (1998) and Bönker (2003). See also Drazen (2000) and Frieden, Pastor and Tomz (2000).
4. See, e.g., Williamson (1994), Haggard and Kaufman (1995), Sturzenegger and Tommasi (1998), Lora (2000) and Tommasi (2002).
5. See Rodrik (1994) for a critical view of the positive impact of foreign aid and conditionality on reform.
6. For some recent contributions to the debate on conditionality see, e.g., Collier (2000), Gilbert, Powell and Vines (2000), and Hopkins et al. (2000).
7. 'It took a vehement anti-Communist such as Nixon to open diplomatic relations with the People's Republic of China ... It would have amounted to political suicide for a Democratic president to attempt such a move; exposing the party to the "soft on communism" charge – an accusation that would seem ludicrous if leveled against Nixon' (Ross 2000: 162). See also Rodrik (1994).
8. For an overview see Haggard (2000).
9. For example in Haggard and Webb (1993), Rodrik (1993), Sturzenegger and Tommasi (1998) and Lora (2000).
10. The recent crisis in Argentina has made it unusually clear that this may entail a fundamental revision of first-stage reforms.

3. Understanding pension reform

The remarkable wave of pension privatisations, embedded in a more general framework of market-oriented reforms and an anti-statist ideology in both Latin America and Eastern Europe (Grindle 2000), has triggered multidisciplinary research only recently. Although such a move has occasionally been classified as a first-generation reform, systemic pension reform is usually seen as part of a 'second-stage' package of structural reforms. Comparative studies on the politics of pension privatisation in Latin America include Brooks (1998), Busquets (2001), Coelho (2002), Huber and Stephens (2000), Hernández (2000), Kay (1998, 1999), Madrid (1999, 2002), Mesa-Lago (1999), Mesa-Lago and Müller (2002) and Mora (1999). The political economy of pension reform in the transition countries has been analysed comparatively by Müller (1999, 2000c, 2001d, 2002b), Nelson (2001), Orenstein (2000) and Horstmann and Schmähl (2002). The comparative analyses presented by Brooks (2001), Chłoń-Domińczak and Mora (2001), James (1998b), James and Brooks (2001), Madrid (1998) and Müller (2003c) aim at a broader explanatory framework.

3.1 THE TRANSMISSION OF REFORM IDEAS

In a number of Latin American and East European countries, the public–private mix in mandatory pension provision has been changed significantly over the past decade. The adoption of similar blueprints across countries and regions suggests that this is not a historical coincidence. Rather, a common international transmission mechanism of ideas may be at work (Stallings 1994). And indeed, a 'new pension orthodoxy' (Lo Vuolo 1996: 692) has been giving major impulses to radical pension reform in Latin America and Eastern Europe. The ascendancy of this new paradigm is related to the emergence of a relevant epistemic community (Merrien 2001; Müller 2003c). According to Haas (1992), an epistemic community amounts to a network of professionals in a particular domain and with a common policy enterprise, sharing faith in a set of normative and causal beliefs, having similar patterns of reasoning and using shared discursive practices. Adler and Haas (1992) find that by influencing policymakers through communicative action, epistemic communities play an important role in policy innovation and diffusion.

Conservative critics of the welfare state had long prepared the ground for a paradigm change in old-age security, as described in Hirschman (1991). It was in the wake of the end of the cold war that the terms of the prevailing discourse in old-age protection shifted, interacting with the rise of neoliberalism as the dominant paradigm in economic policymaking. This pattern is particularly obvious in developing and transition countries. While originally not contained in the 'Washington consensus', pension privatisation has become part and parcel of the neoliberal reform package by now.

In Latin America, structural pension reform concluded the era of the populist welfare state that used to hand out social benefits to interest groups in return for political support (Touraine 1989). In Eastern Europe, the paradigm shift coincided with the first post-socialist years, i.e. with the end of comprehensive social security and with a widespread move towards the market in economic policy. In the words of its most ardent advocate, pension privatisation sets up 'impenetrable barriers' against communism: 'By converting all workers into owners, the reform commits them actively to a responsible management of the economy, as well as to political stability and social peace' (Piñera 1991: 171).[1]

Radical agenda-shifting in old-age security reform has frequently been associated with World Bank involvement. In 1994, the Bank's research report on pension policy attracted global attention (World Bank 1994a). It is the best-known exemplification of what has become the new pension orthodoxy and was also its major propagating mechanism, even though a sizeable 'heterodoxy' remains.[2] Apart from the ubiquitous loans and conditionalities, channels to support pension privatisation include an expert-based knowledge transfer, thus reflecting the World Bank's twin roles as 'Conditionality Bank' and as 'Knowledge Bank' (Gilbert, Powell and Vines 2000: 54).

In recent years other IFIs and government agencies – such as the IMF, the US Agency for International Development (USAID) and the Inter-American Development Bank (IDB) – have followed suit. These global actors took part in relevant cross-conditionalities with the Bank, as well as other forms of cooperation to bring about pension privatisation. Although all of these agencies can be considered important channels of transmission, the World Bank remains the pre-eminent carrier of the new model (Nelson 2000; Madrid 2002).[3]

3.2   THE REFORM ARENA: ACTORS AND CONTEXTUAL CONSTRAINTS

While the full or partial privatisation of old-age security is clearly a major policy recommendation from abroad facing any pension reformer in Eastern Europe and Latin America, it is the domestic political process that eventually results in the adoption or rejection of radical pension reform: 'Even in the face of strong international economic pressure, politics still matter' (Brooks 1998: 31). It is therefore important to identify relevant political actors in the pension reform arena and to consider the policy context that shapes their room for manœuvre, influenced by political factors and economic conditions.

Earlier research has made it clear that in order to be adopted in the local reform arena, the new orthodox template requires not only an agent for its transmission, but also an influential domestic actor ready to adopt it – generally the Ministry of Finance (Müller 1999). Usually staffed with neoliberally trained economists, this portfolio often acted in alliance with the Ministry of Economic Affairs and the Central Bank. These important intra-government actors felt that pension privatisation perfectly matched their overall efforts to decrease the role of the state in the economy. As stated by Huber and Stephens (2000: 19), 'executives committed to neo-liberal economic restructuring put privatisation of the pension system on the agenda'. These local advocates of a globally propagated idea were supported both by relevant domestic interest groups, such as business organisations and the financial sector, and by the IFIs.

Opposition to these radical plans surfaced both within and outside government. More often than not, the Ministries of Labour, Welfare or Health, responsible for the existing old-age security schemes, were reluctant to engage in structural pension reform, thus reflecting the existing Bismarckian traditions in Eastern Europe and Latin America. In several countries, these Ministries initially objected to the radical paradigm shift, but – given the predominance of the Finance Ministry in the cabinet – proved too weak to prevent it. Typically, the Labour Ministry's influence on reform design was deliberately limited by the setting-up of small, extra-ministerial task forces. These special pension reform committees worked out the draft legislation and served to bypass the Labour Ministry's pension-related competences (Müller 1999; Nelson 2001).

Other opponents of pension privatisation included trade unions, left-wing parties, social security employees, and – last but not least – pensioners' associations and special interest groups with privileged pension schemes. Grindle (2000: 37) has pointed out that such reforms 'not only raise the specter of vulnerability and loss of protection, they also challenge deeply held beliefs and traditions about the role of government ... and its responsibility to citizens'. Clearly, the specific policy context may provide reformers or reform opponents with action resources. Mesa-Lago (1999), Mora (1999) and Mesa-Lago and Müller (2002) find that the less democratic a regime at the time of reform, the more it tends to downsize the public pension system and substitute it with a private one. In a democratic context, the executive's degree of control of the legislature amounts to a pivotal institutional variable, as do decree powers granted to some executives (Sottoli 1998). Veto points built into the political system may provide a particular group with strategic opportunities and potential political impact (Immergut 1992).

In some countries trade unions have traditional ties with the governing parties. These could be used to ease resistance, but also implied that reform opponents were in a political position that forced pension reformers to negotiate. To improve the political viability of radical pension reform, policymakers often ended up making political concessions, granting compensation and creating stakeholders. This included enabling trade unions to run their own pension funds (Graham 1998; Müller 1999; James and Brooks 2001). In addition, Pierson (1994) mentions strategies of division and obfuscation, i.e. playing off one group of beneficiaries against another and lowering the visibility of cutbacks, e.g. by increasing the complexity of reforms. Other scholars have pointed to a 'clarity-obfuscation trade-off' in pension policy (Weaver 1998: 223): the long-term sustainability of social sector reform is likely to suffer when it is pursued at the cost of transparency, accountability and public participation (Garland 2000; Fultz, Hagemejer and Ruck 2001).

Economic factors and motives appear to have had a substantial impact on the choice of the reform model. Pension privatisation has often been proposed for macroeconomic rather than social policy considerations: 'when the design of pension reform schemes has been left largely in the hands of macroeconomists in finance ministries, the costs of the scheme rather than their social objectives has been the principal concern' (Grindle 2001: 39). It was argued that a paradigm change in old-age security would lead to both a rise in saving and to efficiency improvements in financial and labour markets, thereby resulting in an increase in long-term growth (see, e.g., World Bank 1994c; Corsetti and Schmidt-Hebbel 1997; James 1998b). Madrid (1998) and James and Brooks (2001) have pointed to the increase in international capital mobility and the recent experiences of capital market crises, while suggesting that these may have prompted policymakers to try to reduce the vulnerability to capital outflows by boosting the local capital market.[4]

The role of crisis has also been a recurrent topic discussed by scholars of the political economy of pension reform. Mora (1999) argues that economic crisis translates into a pension funding crisis, while also increasing the likelihood that a package of structural reforms is adopted, which may well include pension privatisation. Fiscal crises may have an impact on the actor constellation in the pension reform arena, as they tend to turn the Minister of Finance into a potential actor. When the public pension insurance goes into the red, the resulting dependence on budgetary subsidies grants this likely advocate of the new pension orthodoxy an important stake in reforming old-age security (Müller 1999). A persistent deficit often translates into delayed or reduced benefit payments and may thus severely erode public confidence in the pension system, thereby facilitating fundamental reform (James 1998b).

Yet another economic factor had an impact on the cases of pension reform reviewed: when external debt is high and crisis looms, governments may feel inclined to stress their general commitment to market-oriented reform. In this context, the announcement of pension privatisation can be interpreted as a 'signalling' strategy (Rodrik 1998). By the mid-1990s, rating agencies had included radical pension reform as a point in favour in their country-risk assessments (James 1998a). Critical indebtedness also increases the likelihood of the IFIs' involvement in the local pension reform arena. When their recommendations are disregarded by local governments, alternative sources of market financing are often hard to obtain, as international financial markets take the IFIs' stance as a signal (Huber and Stephens 2000). Latin American policymakers were well aware that financial and/or technical support from the IFIs was only available for a pension reform that included a privatisation component (Kay 1999, 2000).

Earlier scholarship on welfare state development had stressed the importance of existing institutional arrangements for future reform paths. 'Existing policies can set the agenda for change ... by narrowing the range of feasible alternatives' (Pierson and Weaver 1993: 146). Frequently, the success of reforms depends on earlier policy choices and the policy feedback resulting from them.[5] In Bismarckian-style PAYG schemes, lock-in effects and opportunity costs are likely to result from the pension rights already earned by the insured. The size of these entitlements, also called 'implicit pension debt' (IPD), is determined by a number of factors: the percentage of the population covered and the maturity of the old system, the generosity of the entitlement conditions in the public system, the ageing of the population, the responsibilities assumed by the state during the transition, and changes in the contribution rates (Mesa-Lago 2000).[6]

When made explicit, this implicit debt may translate into very high fiscal costs. It has therefore been argued that the larger the IPD, the smaller the likelihood for radical pension reform (Orenstein 2000; Fox and Palmer 2001; James and Brooks 2001). However, estimates on the IPD should never be taken as given, as its value can be reduced by downsizing benefits and tightening eligibility in the old system before making the transition (James 1998b). It may also be reduced in size by reform design itself, e.g. by recognising only part of accrued entitlements when shifting to the new IFF tier. Palacios, Rutkowski and Yu (1999: 31) even argue that 'the government will *have to* renege on some pay-as-you-go commitments'.[7] This deliberate IPD reduction is likely to entail welfare losses to retirees and older workers (Lindeman, Rutkowski and Sluchynskyy 2000).

In the following chapters, the conceptual framework outlined above – designed to understand the political economy of pension privatisation – will be applied to eight cases of structural pension reform in Latin America and Eastern Europe: Argentina, Uruguay, Peru, Bolivia, Hungary, Poland, Croatia and Bulgaria.

NOTES

1. All foreign-language quotes have been translated by the author.
2. Mesa-Lago (1996) and Ney (2000) point to conflicting policy prescriptions by international organisations. For the early debate between the World Bank and the ILO see Beattie and McGillivray (1995) and James (1996). A recent critique of the 'new pension orthodoxy' can be found in Barr (2000), Charlton and McKinnon (2001) and Orszag and Stiglitz (2001).
3. For more recent World Bank statements on pension reform issues see Holzmann (2000) and Holzmann and Stiglitz (2001). On the request of the Bank's Chief Economist, the Social Protection Team is currently preparing a new policy document in which the multipillar approach will be recommended as a benchmark, while no longer serving as an exclusive blueprint (see, e.g., Holzmann 2002).
4. Contrary to these high hopes, the Chilean evidence suggests that pension privatisation actually had a negative impact on national saving (Mesa-Lago 1998; Uthoff 2001). On the potential impact of pension privatisation on capital markets see Walker and Lefort (2002).
5. On the concept of policy feedback see Esping-Andersen (1985) and Pierson (1993); for a recent discussion of the concept of path dependence see Pierson (2000).
6. See also James (1998b: 459): 'The implicit pension debt ... is the present value of the pension promises that are owed to current pensioners and to workers according to their years of participation in the old system'.
7. Emphasis by the author.

PART II

Privatising Old-Age Security in Latin America

4.   Regional background: old-age security in Latin America

The origins of Bismarckian-style pension schemes in Latin America can be traced back to the first decades of the 20th century. Mesa-Lago (1991b: XI) proposes to distinguish between the 'pioneer countries', an 'intermediate group' and the 'latecomer countries'. The pioneers – Brazil, Uruguay, Argentina, Cuba and Chile – set up the first pension schemes in the 1920s and 1930s. Mexico, Costa Rica, Ecuador, Panama, Colombia and Peru, forming the intermediate group, introduced their first pension programmes in the 1940s, while the latecomers – Nicaragua, Bolivia, Venezuela, Guatemala, El Salvador, Honduras and the Dominican Republic – did so in the 1950s, 1960s and 1970s (Mesa-Lago and Bertranou 1998).

The gradual expansion of coverage was based on populist-corporatist state action and the influence of pressure groups, thus reflecting the extreme stratification of Latin American society (Mesa-Lago 1978). Benefits were first accessible to powerful constituencies such as the military, public servants and unionised private sector workers, whereas weaker groups – agricultural workers, domestic servants and informal sector workers – were covered only much later, if at all.

The favourable age structure of the insured population as well as the progressive integration of new contribution groups into the pension schemes provided for a comfortable financial basis during the first decades. Yet, in a context of mounting inflation, the existing scaled premium systems[1] turned into *de facto* PAYG schemes. Pension reserves decapitalised rapidly when invested largely in public bonds, rendering negative real rates of return. At the same time, pension programmes in the pioneer countries became mature and reached the limits of coverage expansion. In the wake of the debt crisis of the 1980s, economic stabilisation and structural adjustment programmes implemented all over the subcontinent only contributed to a further decline of available resources for social policy, just when the need for compensatory state measures in the context of recession and the social costs of adjustment had become most pressing (Mesa-Lago 1997a).

Table 4.1 A comparison of Latin American pension privatisations

	Chile	Peru	Argentina	Colombia	Uruguay	Bolivia	Mexico	El Salvador	Costa Rica
Type of public mandatory tier	Phased out	Traditional PAYG; alternative to private tier	Traditional PAYG; private tier complementary	Traditional PAYG; alternative to private tier	Traditional PAYG; private tier complementary	Closed down	Closed down	Phased out	Traditional PAYG; private tier complementary
Mandatory membership in private IFF tier[a]	New entrants to labour market; others may opt to switch from public tier	Membership in either the private or the public tier is mandatory for all	All workers may redirect their contribution to the private tier	Membership in either the private or the public tier is mandatory for all	Mandatory for earners > US$800; optional for smaller earners and those aged 40+ to redirect part of their contribution to private tier	Mandatory for all workers	Mandatory for all workers	Mandatory for new entrants to labour market and insured up to age 35, optional for those aged 36–50 (women) / 36–55 (men)	Mandatory for all workers

Contribution rates to IFF tier	Individual rate: 10%	Individual rate: 8%	Individual rate: 7.14%[b]	Individual rate: 2.5%; employers' rate 7.5%	Individual rate: 12.27%	Individual rate: 10%	Individual rate: 1.125%; employers' rate: 5.2%; state subsidy: 2.2%	Individual rate: 3.25%; employers' rate: 6.75%	Individual rate: 1%; employers' rate: 3.25%
Reform type	Substitutive	Parallel	Mixed	Parallel	Mixed	Substitutive	Substitutive	Substitutive	Mixed
Starting date	1981	1993	1994	1994	1996	1997	1997	1998	2001

Notes: [a] Although the IFF tier is dominated by private pension administrators, some countries also admit publicly run pension funds.
[b] In 2001 a temporary reduction of withholdings to 5% was decreed in Argentina (this includes commissions and insurance premia).

Sources: Mesa-Lago (1998, 2000, 2001); Krishock (2001); Müller (2003b).

Apart from their financial problems, pension programmes in Latin America suffered from a number of other shortcomings. A weak contribution-benefit link coincided with generous entitlement conditions and replacement rates, even for early retirement and invalidity benefits. Consequently, contribution rates as well as state subsidies were elevated, while at the same time evasion and underreporting of income increased. Furthermore, the existing old-age security systems were highly fragmented and consisted of multiple funds, each with different legislation and management, benefits and contribution rates. This situation generated not only high costs, but also problems of equity between different groups of insured. Moreover, a substantial part of the labour force lacked formal employment and, thus, coverage (Hujo 1999).

It is well known that Chile was the first country in Latin America to privatise its pension system.[2] In 1981, in the context of an anti-statist ideology and extraordinary powers of the Pinochet regime, the existing public PAYG system was replaced by a compulsory IFF scheme run by private pension fund administrators, the so-called AFPs. The significance of the Chilean reform did not consist in developing a substantially new concept for old-age security, but in putting existing neoliberal reform proposals into practice, thereby establishing a precedent (Borzutzky 1983, 2002; Queisser 1993).

At first, it seemed to remain the bold experiment of an autocratic regime, with little attraction for democratic policymakers elsewhere. In the early 1990s, when a democratic government had taken over from the Pinochet regime, reference to the Chilean pension reform became 'politically palatable' (Mesa-Lago 1997b: 498). The Chilean precedent soon evolved as a reform paradigm for Latin America and beyond, yet without being replicated in an identical way. By now, more than half of all Latin American countries have legislated and/or implemented variations of the so-called 'Chilean model', most of them under democratic regimes (Müller 2000b; Mesa-Lago 2001, 2002; Devesa-Carpio and Vidal-Meliá 2002).

Table 4.1 shows that the substitutive model, which implies replacing the public pension scheme entirely with mandatory AFPs, is most frequent among Latin America's structural pension reforms. It was chosen in Chile (1981), Bolivia (1997), El Salvador (1997) and Mexico (1997), while Nicaragua and the Dominican Republic have recently legislated similar reforms. Peru (1993) and Colombia (1994) are the only two countries that adopted the parallel model, under which the public and private pension schemes compete for contributors. The mixed model, under which a mandatory IFF tier is added to a downsized public pension scheme, was implemented in Argentina (1994), Uruguay (1996) and Costa Rica (2001). 'Latin American countries have become the world's laboratory for pension systems based upon individual retirement savings accounts' (Kay and Kritzer 2001: 51).

Table 4.2   Latin America: some relevant pension indicators[a]

	System dependency rate[b]	Old-age dependency rate[c]	Pensioners (in % of population)	Coverage rate[d]	Replacement rate[e]	Pension spending (in % of GDP)
Argentina	64.0	27.0	13.8	53.0	46.7	4.1
Bolivia	40.0	16.2	2.0	11.7	45.3	2.5
Brazil	60.0	14.1	10.0	36.0	30.3	4.9
Chile	24.3	17.5	10.4	70.0	67.5	5.9
Colombia	11.0	16.1	1.5	33.0	63.6	1.1
Costa Rica	14.0	14.5	2.5	47.0	47.2	3.8
Ecuador	18.0	13.9	1.7	26.0	24.5	1.2
El Salvador	8.6	14.3	0.9	26.2	67.9	1.3
Guatemala	15.0	12.5	1.4	28.9	14.3	0.7
Honduras	4.0	12.0	0.4	24.0	n.a.	0.6
Mexico	12.5	12.9	1.6	30.0	66.9	0.4
Nicaragua	21.0	11.2	1.0	13.6	29.4	4.3
Panama	n.a.	14.6	3.4	50.0	50.3	4.3
Paraguay	12.5	12.0	1.5	31.0	n.a.	n.a.
Peru	31.0	14.3	2.3	20.0	22.3	1.2
Uruguay	70.0	34.5	25.8	82.0	65.0	8.7
Venezuela	5.0	13.0	0.7	23.6	n.a.	0.5

Notes: [a] Data are mostly for the mid-1990s.
       [b] Pensioners in % of contributors.
       [c] 60+ years old in % of 20–59 years old.
       [d] Contributors in % of labour force.
       [e] Average pension in % of average wage.

Sources: World Bank (2001b); ILO (2000); Mercado Lora (1994); Bernedo Alvarado (1999); Webb and Fernández Baca (2000).

While the pension reforms adopted are very similar throughout Latin America and imply the introduction of a mandatory IFF tier, the reform context is not. An intra-regional comparison of relevant pension indicators highlights substantial disparities (see Table 4.2). In all Latin American countries but Uruguay, Argentina, Brazil and Bolivia there are more than three contributors per pensioner, while the ratio is above 10:1 in Honduras, Venezuela and El Salvador. The next two columns show that most Latin American countries still have young populations, with seven or eight persons in active age for every person aged 60 or above. Only Uruguay and Argentina exhibit European levels of demographic ageing, with an active/passive ratio of around 3:1. Thus, population ageing is clearly not the main issue in Latin America.

Instead, Table 4.2 shows that the real challenge facing Latin American pension schemes is coverage. In all Latin American countries but Uruguay, Chile, Argentina and Panama, less than half of the labour force contribute to the pension scheme. As little as one-fifth of the economically active population contributes in Bolivia, Nicaragua and Peru. On the other hand, in most Latin American countries less than 3 per cent of the total population receive a retirement benefit, reflecting both low coverage and the relatively recent introduction of a mandatory pension insurance. Exceptions are Brazil, Chile, Argentina and – most notably – Uruguay, where more than a quarter of the population were drawing a pension in the mid-1990s. Compared with the OECD average of 10.5 per cent of GDP (Gillion et al. 2000), public pension expenditure is low in Latin America, exceeding 5 per cent of GDP only in Uruguay and Chile, while falling below 1 per cent in some Central American countries.[3]

Thus, a heterogeneous panorama emerges. While the Southern Cone countries and Brazil face pension-related challenges that may be considered as roughly comparable to the European ones, all other Latin American countries have young populations, favourable system dependency ratios and provide for a small number of pensioners. How could a wave of rather similar pension reforms spread throughout the subcontinent, then? The following four case studies, covering Argentina, Uruguay, Peru and Bolivia, will help to shed light on this puzzle – the political economy of pension privatisation in Latin America.

NOTES

1. Scaled premium systems amount to a variant of collective capitalisation: reserves are built up over a given period (e.g. 10 years) to cover expected pension liabilities. During this period they are invested on the capital market.
2. See Queisser (1993), Mesa-Lago and Arenas de Mesa (1997), Barrientos (1998), Edwards (1998) and Uthoff (2001).
3. Table 4.2 quotes relatively high replacement rates for many countries in the region, but in the context of sparse coverage, a large informal sector and the absence of nation-wide wage statistics in several Latin American countries, this indicator should be interpreted with caution.

5. Pension privatisation in the Southern Cone

5.1 THE CASE OF ARGENTINA

Legacy and policy context

Since the beginning of the 20th century, Argentina had seen a proliferation of pension programmes, structured along occupational lines (Mesa-Lago 1978; Alonso 2000). In 1954, collective capitalisation was replaced by PAYG financing, and in 1967 all existing funds were merged into three (Isuani and San Martino 1998). With ages 55/50 (women/men), legal retirement ages were comparatively low. Moreover, there was little connection between individual contributions and future pension levels, as only the last 10 years were taken into account in benefit calculation (Cottani and Demarco 1998). Compared with most other Latin American pension schemes, the Argentine one stood out for high coverage and a long life expectancy of the insured.[1] In 1980, when employers' contributions were eliminated, the public pension insurance started absorbing significant general tax revenues and budgetary transfers that continued after employers' contributions were reinstated in 1984. In the aftermath of the debt crisis, economic downturn and high inflation persisted (see Table 5.1), leading to a severe decline of revenues and an erosion of real benefit levels. However, several attempts to introduce parametric changes were unsuccessful.

It was not until Carlos Menem assumed the presidency in 1989 that fundamental pension reform gathered momentum. He was the first Peronist leader since 1974 to be accepted by all intra-party factions, and his political leverage enabled him to radically discontinue his party's long-standing statist orientation (Torre 1998). Contrary to his campaign promises, Menem turned out liberalising trade, privatising state-owned enterprises, altering the monetary regime and reforming the public sector. Marking the demise of neomercantilism and the corporatist state, this set of reforms amounted to the 'most dramatic turnaround in Argentine politics in this century' (Waisman 1999: 100).

25

Table 5.1   The reform context in Argentina: selected indicators

Indicators	1989	1990	1991	1992	1993
GDP change (in %)	−7.0	−1.3	10.5	10.3	6.3
Consumer prices (annual average, in %)	3,084.6	2,315.5	171.7	24.9	10.6
General gov't balance (in % of GDP)	−3.8	−1.5	−0.5	0.6	1.1
Total external debt (in % of GDP)	77.8	38.7	29.9	25.9	27.4
Public pension expenditure					
– in % of GDP	4.0	5.4	5.9	6.5	7.0
– in % of total social spending	28.6	34.8	36.6	38.5	39.6
Total social spending (in % of GDP)	14.0	15.5	16.1	16.9	17.8

Note: Only the five years up to reform adoption are considered.

Sources: IDB (1998); Lo Vuolo and Barbeito (1998).

It should be noted that at that time, the IFIs 'refused to lend to Argentina unless it committed itself to carrying out market-oriented reforms' (Madrid 2001: 194). Graham et al. (1999) have stressed the strong reform-enabling influence of economic crisis in the Argentine case. The severe crisis faced by the country in the late 1980s not only convinced people to tolerate the costs of market-oriented reforms, but also weakened traditional political actors, while trade unionists were co-opted with shares in privatised companies. In the early 1990s, the visible need for fast action facilitated a concentration of power in the executive. Menem made frequent use of emergency decrees that largely bypassed the legislature. Presidential decrees could only be vetoed by a two-third's majority in Congress, thereby raising the costs of building a veto coalition. The massive transformation towards the market was pushed through by Domingo Cavallo, the new Minister for Economic Affairs. The former director of a Córdoba-based neoliberal think-tank soon gained a reputation on international financial markets.[2]

The way towards pension privatisation

During the years of high inflation and fiscal crisis, the Argentine government had resorted to the payment of retirement benefits below the legally established replacement rates of 70 to 82 per cent. A large number of those affected filed and won lawsuits against the government. In 1986, the Alfonsín government formally declared social security in a state of emergency, thereby suspending the execution of the verdicts and temporarily halting the start of new lawsuits (Rossi 1999). Yet, this move only added to the general perception that social security was in permanent crisis (Feldman, Golbert and Isuani 1986; Golbert and Lo Vuolo 1989). In 1987, the first voluntary private pension plans were established, albeit on a small scale (Lloyd-Sherlock 1997: 91). Around the same time, more radical approaches to pension reform made themselves heard, inspired by the precedent in neighbouring Chile (see Slodky 1988; Isuani and San Martino 1993).

As early as 1987 a market-oriented research institute, FIEL, suggested to establish a two-tiered system, consisting of a minimum basic pension, financed by employers, and a private pension fund tier, financed by individual contributions. In 1990, the Association of Argentine Banks, ADEBA, presented a plan for a full transition to a mandatory system of forced savings. In the same year, Santiago de Estrada, the Secretary of Social Security, circulated a document proposing a fundamental reform of the PAYG scheme, combined with the option to redirect up to two percentage points of the contribution rate to a newly established funded tier. A 1989 World Bank report on Argentina had also proposed to replace the current retirement system with a two-tiered system, consisting of a universal basic pension and mandatory pension funds (World Bank 1996a: 50). Far-reaching pension reform seemed inevitable when the 1991 Convertibility Law transformed the Central Bank into a currency board and imposed strict limits on both monetary policy and fiscal expenditure (Hujo 2001).[3] By then, pension arrears were estimated at around US$12.5 billion, affecting almost 4 million pensioners, or 20 per cent of the electorate.[4] At the same time, public pension spending had grown to almost 40 per cent of total social spending (see Table 5.1).

In early 1991, Cavallo, the incoming Minister for Economic Affairs, appointed Walter Schulthess Secretary of Social Security. He asked him to set up a pension reform team that would be formally subordinate to the Minister of Labour. Schulthess, an expert in public finance, chose to exclude traditional social security experts and lawyers with Bismarckian leanings from his working group. Schulthess and his team, dominated by economists, were strongly inclined towards a Chilean-style reform, seeking to boost savings and to establish long-term financial instruments in Argentina (Madrid 2001).[5] The working group could draw on a series of technical studies on pension reform that had been elaborated since 1988 in the context of PRONATASS, a project run by the United Nations Development Programme (UNDP).[6]

Both PRONATASS and Schulthess' reform team were financed by the World Bank that also preferred a Chilean-style reform – 'in that sense, Bank thinking and Government thinking, whether causally related or not, were largely harmonious' (World Bank 1996a: 50). In early 1992, the Argentine government signed an Extended Fund Facility agreement with the IMF, which contained the explicitly commitment to legislate structural pension reform by 1993. Torre and Gerchunoff (1999) argue that a Chilean-style pension privatisation was intended to signal the government's reformist intentions, thereby guaranteeing access to soft loans from the IFIs, as well as offering new opportunities to the business sector. According to Brooks (1998), it was on the initiative of the Menem government that the IMF conditionality was put in place, in order to utilise it as leverage in its negotiations with Congress.

After a few months of preparatory work, the reformers started to contact political parties and social organisations, in order to put pension reform on the political agenda. The reform team generally avoided leaking concrete details of the envisaged reform to the public. Yet, on one occasion Schulthess announced that the new pension scheme would deny compensations for previous contributions to workers below age 45, raising a storm of protest (Alonso 2000). The underlying strategy has been described as 'creating the technical plan in private and informally sounding out interest groups to identify conflict points' (Graham et al. 1999: 14). Subsequently, Menem decided to negotiate pension privatisation with Congress instead of passing it by emergency decree – even though this implied trading 'immediate reform for interminable negotiation' (Alonso 2000: 98). This move had been advocated by Schulthess, who stressed the need to provide a solid legal basis for future investors in the private pensions business.

When the first draft law was presented to Congress in June 1992, Menem's reform strategy included a package deal. The president announced that pensioners would be paid full statutory benefits if the laws on pension reform and the privatisation of the state-owned oil company, YPF, were approved by Congress unaltered – 'without touching a comma' (Alonso 1998; Torre and Gerchunoff 1999). The draft law on pension reform proposed the creation of a new IFF scheme, run by private pension fund administrators, or AFJPs, and financed by individual contributions. The public tier would be downsized to a basic pension for all insured with at least 30 contributory years, to be financed by employers' contributions and tax revenues. While it was basically inspired by the Chilean precedent, the proposed scheme was more radical in that all insured under age 45 would be obliged to switch to the new system. Another difference stressed by the Argentine reformers was that the Chilean scheme had only one tier, while the pension system they had designed was two-tiered – a contentious classification, as the Chilean system includes both a minimum pension and a social assistance pension, to be paid by the state (see also Vittas 1997).

The reform proposal triggered a mixed reaction: unimpressed by Menem's bundling strategy, trade unions and pensioners' associations mobilised their members against the proposal, challenging the demise of inter-generational solidarity. Contrary to this, the local business and finance community actively advocated pension privatisation and welcomed it as a sign that market-friendly policies were to continue. When parliamentary commissions debated the draft law, it met with fierce criticism from both the opposition and parts of the governing Peronists. The most important objections included the loss of acquired rights, the exclusively private administration of the IFF scheme, its potential risks after a recent history of bank failures, and high administrative costs. Soon alternative proposals, limited to a set of parametric reforms, were circulated, most notably the one presented by the Federal Council for Social Security (COFEPRES 1992). In the light of these reactions, the government decided to withdraw and revise its reform proposal.

A modified draft law was presented to Congress in August 1992. While the idea of pension privatisation was retained, the new proposal stipulated the recognition of acquired rights by means of a compensatory pension, as well as the obligation of all insured in active age to enter the new system. These changes, which implied a steep increase in transition costs, were only the start for further political negotiations. One of the initial opponents of pension privatisation, the Peronist trade union confederation, CGT, had called a general strike against government policy in November 1992. At one point, however, they met Chilean pension fund representatives and were inspired to set up their own pension funds. Keen to balance their declining power base with the access to new resources, CGT leaders held tripartite negotiations with the government and employers. Eventually, they succeeded in having this proposal included in the law (Torre and Gerchunoff 1999; Alonso 2000). This move towards a 'mercantilisation of labour', which converted trade unions into stakeholders in market-oriented reforms, had been preceded by some unions' participation in the privatisation of state-owned enterprises (Murillo 1997, 2000).[7]

Yet, by their absence in a crucial vote in December 1992, several Peronist congresspersons made it clear that without further concessions, the government would lack the parliamentary majority required to process the pension law. An important modification that helped to win support for the reform, mainly among the advocates of the alternative proposal, was the promise to create a pension fund administered by *Banco Nación*, a state-owned bank. Contributions to this AFJP would be protected by a double state guarantee – in US$ and pesos.[8]

At the same time, dissident trade unionists and pensioners' representatives held weekly protest marches and demonstrations, demanding a pension system based on solidarity, justice and efficiency. They also collected 1.3 million signatures for a nation-wide plebiscite to be held on the reform, 'to prevent speculation and profit-seeking by big business' (ATE leaflet, undated). The UCR, the major opposition party, announced that it would obstruct the passage of reform in the legislature by denying the government the necessary quorum. Given that the ruling Peronists, together with their political ally, the small UCeDé, controlled only a narrow majority of seats in Congress, another major concession had to be made to win the support of legislators: all insured, regardless of their age, would have a choice between the public and the mixed scheme, instead of being automatically transferred to the latter. Some minor changes followed, in reaction to the 'changing market of votes and favours' (Torre and Gerchunoff 1999: 25).[9] In June 1993, the pension reform law was eventually approved by Congress, while the Senate, controlled by the Peronists, endorsed it in September 1993.

The new pension system

The Argentine pension system, in force since July 1994, combines a reformed public PAYG tier with a newly established IFF tier, consisting of competing AFJPs (Rofman 2000). The funded tier, supervised by a specialised institution, the SAFJP, is dominated by private fund managers, but trade unions, public entities, mutual funds and cooperatives are also authorised to run AFJPs. The insured can opt to redirect part of their pension contributions to one of the AFJPs, thereby participating in two mandatory, earnings-related systems of old-age security simultaneously. Alternatively, they can choose to stick to the public pension path. This choice is also open to new entrants to the labour market. However, this group is automatically moved to the mixed scheme if failing to choose.

According to the chosen option, the insured's contribution – formerly 11 per cent of gross wage, currently 5 per cent – is directed towards the public pension scheme or to an AFJP. In either case, the corresponding employers' contribution of currently 16 per cent is used to finance the public scheme, instead of being abolished, as in Chile. Another difference to the famous precedent consists in the collection of all contributions by a state entity, which channels them to ANSeS, the public social security administration, or to one of the AFJPs. Retirement age was raised to 60/65 (women/men) – maintaining a lower retirement age for women was another political concession.

Post-reform pension benefits consist of three components that differ according to the choice made by the insured. When opting for the public pension path, the insured are entitled to (1) a universal basic pension, (2) a compensatory pension, which covers their pre-reform pension entitlements, and (3) an additional pension fed by pension claims accumulated between the 1994 pension reform and retirement. If the insured choose the mixed pension path, they are entitled to the first two components, but instead of the third a so-called 'ordinary pension' will be paid by the AFJP on a strictly actuarial basis. It should be noted that any receipt of a public retirement benefit (universal basic pension, compensatory pension, additional pension) presupposes a minimum of 30 contributory years. The vesting period had already been increased from 15 to 20 years in September 1991 and is particularly difficult to meet for women, the unemployed and informal sector workers. The increase obviously provides an incentive for the mixed scheme, as there are no minimum contributory years in the IFF tier.

After a slow start, 80 per cent of all insured are now affiliated with the mixed option, even though less than 40 per cent of them contribute regularly to one of the 12 existing pension funds. With total assets amounting to over US$22 billion, Argentina's AFJPs now rank second after Mexico's IFF scheme (Müller 2003b). Since the 1993 reform, the public pension tier has been the recurrent target of fiscally motivated retrenchment, in an effort to counter the reform-induced decline of revenues (Bertranou, Grushka and Schulthess 2000; Schulthess and Demarco 2000). The mixed structure of the Argentine pension system has also been under attack. At the first conference of the Chamber of AFJPs, Menem (1997: 15) declared that the 'obsolete PAYG scheme will disappear definitively from our society'. Yet, it was his successor De la Rúa who actually attempted to phase out the state-run social security scheme in 2000. A similar proposal had been made earlier by a leading World Bank expert, albeit underestimating its political costs.[10]

In the midst of economic collapse facing the country in late 2001, both pension tiers turned out to be vulnerable. Not only were ANSeS' pension payments postponed to meet a major deadline for debt service. The government cut individual contribution rates by more than half to stimulate consumption, while also forcing the AFJPs into a massive debt restructuring and purchase of treasury bills, as a record country risk severely limited access to international capital markets. When government bonds had surpassed 80 per cent of the AFJPs' portfolio, the incoming Peronist administration suspended debt service. Moreover, shortly after the 1:1 peg with the dollar had been broken, all previously dollar-denominated government debt was converted to pesos at 1.4 pesos to US$1 (Krishock 2002a, b). Overall, these massive government interventions in the funds' portfolio are thought to have reduced the retirement savings of 8.6 million AFJP affiliates by more than 60 per cent (Hujo 2002: 250).

Conclusion

Being the first Latin American country to replicate the substitutive 'Chilean model' under a pluralistic regime, Argentina's reform aroused considerable interest. While Nobel laureate Gary S. Becker pointed to the 'social security lesson from Argentina' (1996: 9), the political economy of the Argentine reform has been studied by many domestic and foreign scholars.[11] The above account has shown that pension privatisation in Argentina is intimately linked to the market-oriented reforms pursued by a strong executive in the early 1990s, not least because it was 'promoted by neoliberal economists who came to dominate most of the key policy-making positions in the early 1990s' (Madrid 2001: 179). In the context of deep economic crisis, hyperinflation and severe indebtedness (World Bank 2001c), marketisation, pushed through by an 'unlikely' administration, was triggered by the need to boost credibility. The neoliberal agenda pursued by Menem and Cavallo can be interpreted as an exercise of signalling, aimed at attracting sufficient capital inflows to secure the viability of the (then) newly established currency board.

At the same time, substantial pension arrears and related lawsuits had severely discredited the public old-age security scheme – another ingredient for fundamental pension reform. Calls to privatise the retirement system were given additional impetus by failures of parametric reform attempts and mounting pension expenditure (see Table 5.1). The change team that was to embark on the technical preparations of the reform excluded the 'Bismarckian faction'. Its leader was appointed by the powerful Minister for Economic Affairs himself, while the Ministry of Labour played only a marginal role. Reform preparations, taking place in a highly insulated setting, could count on financial and ideational support by the World Bank. Moreover, the Argentine government committed itself to pension privatisation in an IMF accord before the respective draft law was sent to Congress.

It is interesting to note that an otherwise decretist president relied on parliamentarism and corporatism to make pension reform politically feasible, after his initial mandatist strategy had borne no result (Alonso 1998, 2000). Clearly, 15 months of bargaining left their marks on reform design, while also delaying the envisaged start of the new IFF tier. Due to ample veto opportunities enjoyed by opponents within the governing party, reformers made many concessions, such as granting stakes to Peronist trade unionists, who were transformed from staunch opponents of pension privatisation to entrepreneurs in the pension fund business.[12]

Eventually, a mixed pension system was established, thereby creating another precedent after the substitutive Chilean and the parallel Peruvian one (Arenas de Mesa and Bertranou 1997). World Bank representatives initially censured it as 'second-best' for failing to close down the public tier (Schwarz 1998: 211), yet also noted its interesting political economy. In their eyes, the 'most important lesson of the Argentine experience is that systemic and radical pension reform is feasible through a democratic process' (Vittas 1997: 38).

5.2   THE CASE OF URUGUAY

Legacy and policy context

In Uruguay, one of the pioneers in social security, the first pension schemes date back to the 19th century (Porzecanski 1978; BPS 1997). The stratified and fragmented character of Uruguayan old-age security was transformed in the context of the *Batllista* welfare approach, an important cognitive reference during much of Uruguay's 20th century history. During the first two decades of the last century, the Uruguayan state had come to take over a protective, interventionist role. During the second government of President José Batlle y Ordóñez (1911–15), the main architect of this reformist approach, social assistance, public education, housing and labour laws were established (Filgueira 1995; Nahum 1999).

By the 1950s, the near universalisation of pension coverage in Uruguay was completed.[13] Shortly afterwards, however, economic crisis and inflation triggered a shift from a scaled premium to a PAYG scheme (Papadópulos 1998). The effects of systemic maturation hit the Uruguayan PAYG scheme earlier than other Latin American pension systems, while population ageing was aggravated by a wave of youth emigration in 1963–75. Pensioners account for 25.8 per cent of the total population (see Table 4.2), turning social security into the largest public expenditure item. In 1983, it reached 52.2 per cent, almost 90 per cent of which pension expenditure (Favaro and Bensión 1993: 360).

During the military regime (1973–84), the Uruguayan retirement scheme underwent fundamental restructuring and massive retrenchment (Lacurcia 1991; Caristo and Forteza 1999). Hence, the return to democracy coincided not only with the immediate aftermath of the debt crisis, but also with a mobilisation of pensioners (Filgueira and Moraes 1999). By the mid-1980s, the PAYG scheme administered by the so-called 'Social Insurance Bank' (BPS) amounted to the main pension programme. Separate pension schemes existed for the military, police, financial sector, university professionals and notaries. Finally, there were two programmes mitigating old-age poverty among the very old and/or destitute. In the BPS scheme, old-age security was funded by employees' and employers' contributions, while the growing deficit was covered by transfers from the state budget. The retirement benefit was calculated on the average income of the last three active years only. Statutory replacement rates varied between 65 and 80 per cent, and since 1987 there was a benefit ceiling of seven minimum wages. For women and men fulfilling a vesting period of 30 years, the retirement age was 55 and 60, respectively. At retirement age, average life expectancy was still 16.7 years for men and 21.0 years for women (Gillion et al. 2000).

The way towards pension privatisation

In Uruguay, structural pension reform was preceded by almost a decade of failed reform attempts, dating from 1985 to 1994 (Papadópulos 1998). The incoming democratic government, led by *Colorado* Julio María Sanguinetti (1985–89), committed itself in an IMF accord to reduce the budget deficit by cutting pension expenditure, but was stopped by a coalition of left-wing parties and the pensioners' movement. In 1987, the government managed to win parliamentary approval for parametric pension reform, after making important concessions to the opposition. However, the newly established indexation mechanism was opposed by pensioners' associations who feared another drop in real benefit levels. The pensioners' movement started to collected signatures for a constitutional amendment stipulating full adjustment of pensions to wage increases. It managed to convinced the two traditional political parties – *Blanco* and *Colorado* – to support their referendum, that coincided with the 1989 general elections.

Both the left-wing *Frente Amplio* and the trade union confederation PIT-CNT initially opposed the pensioners' petition, criticising the indiscriminate indexing of all retirement benefits (Papadópulos 1992). In the end, however, the electoral importance of the retired prevailed over all concerns. As the referendum was approved with 82 per cent of all votes, the new indexation regime was established in the Uruguayan constitution, improving the real value of retirement benefits by 40 per cent over the next four years (Noya, Fernández Poncet and Laens 1999). At the same time, the guarantee triggered a fiscal crisis and thus only perpetuated the need for further pension reform. As an important mechanism to adjust benefit levels to fiscal needs had been abolished, more radical pension reform alternatives appeared on the political agenda. In 1989, a paper circulating among social security experts modelled the fiscal impact of Chilean-style pension privatisation for Uruguay (Roldós and Viana Martorell 1992). The proposal was taken to the political arena by Jorge Batlle. The influential *Colorado* faction leader, who would later be elected president, invited the architect of the Chilean reform, José Piñera, to Montevideo and could draw on support from employers' organisations.

After the 1989 elections a *Blanco* minority government, led by Luis Alberto Lacalle (1990–94), took over, with the *Colorado* party promising to lend support to some key projects. President Lacalle left no doubt that pension reform was a key priority for his government, while also stressing that he opposed a privatisation of old-age security. During his term in office, several attempts at pension reform were made, but all of them failed. The first reform proposal was prepared in 1990 and suggested a series of parametric reforms: an increase in retirement ages and in the vesting period, a lowering of the replacement rate and the consideration of a more significant part of the labour history in the calculation of the basic retirement benefit. The proposal clearly aimed at a reduction of pension expenditure, but could not prosper due to a lack of support from the *Colorado* party, who had a more sweeping reform in mind (Filgueira, Moraes and Moreira 1999).

Table 5.2   The reform context in Uruguay: selected indicators[a]

Indicators	1991	1992	1993	1994	1995
GDP change (in %)	3.2	7.9	3.0	6.3	−1.8
Consumer prices (annual average, in %)	102.0	68.4	54.1	44.7	42.2
General gov't balance (in % of GDP)	1.3	1.4	−0.8	−2.5	−1.1
Total external debt (in % of GDP)	41.7	38.6	35.1	31.2	29.5
Pension revenue (in % of GDP)					
– BPS	8.6	8.7	7.7	7.5	7.5
– total[b]	10.7	10.8	9.8	9.7	10.1
Pension expenditure (in % of GDP)					
– BPS	9.8	10.4	10.9	11.0	11.4
– total[b]	12.2	13.0	14.2	14.2	14.9

Notes: [a] Only the five years up to reform adoption are considered.
           [b] Includes separate pension schemes for the military, police, financial sector, university staff and notaries.

Sources: IDB (1998); Noya and Laens (2000).

In its search for consensus, the Lacalle government's next attempt at reforming old-age security followed an innovative procedure, starting in August 1991. Two multi-party pension reform commissions, a technical and a political one, were formed and included all four political parties with parliamentary representation. During eight months of work under the leadership of the BPS' president, Rodolfo Saldain, social security experts discussed four reform alternatives: (1) a parametric reform; (2) full pension privatisation; (3) a state-managed, defined contribution system of individual accounts, technically based on PAYG[14]; (4) a mixed scheme, combining a PAYG tier and an IFF scheme. According to Saldain (1999), the working group discussed the second, Chilean-style alternative at considerable length, before concluding that the resulting transition costs would be prohibitive in the Uruguayan context (see also Lacurcia 1991).

The government decided to pick the third alternative, known as the 'fictitious capitalisation', and presented a draft law to Congress in April 1992, requesting urgent consideration – a procedure that limited deliberative fora and did not pay off. The right-wing *Colorado* faction opposed the move for not going all the way towards pension privatisation, while *Frente Amplio* criticised the rupture of inter-generational solidarity (Filgueira and Moraes 1999). After this experience, the government returned to the concept of parametric reforms. In November 1992, a series of changes to the existing PAYG scheme were approved by Congress as part of the annual budget law. However, the government's bundling strategy amounted to an infringement of the Uruguayan constitution, which limits the permissible range of budget bills. Based on this formal argument, pensioners' associations and the PIT-CNT called for a plebiscite to declare the law unconstitutional. At this point, they could draw on additional action resources: since 1992, pensioners and trade unions were represented in the BPS' board of directors, alongside employers.[15] In an effort to appeal to elderly voters, leading candidates from all parties supported the plebiscite, which coincided with the 1994 elections and was approved with 74 per cent of all votes (Filgueira, Moraes and Moreira 1999).

In the meantime, two other pension reform drafts, prepared by the Lacalle government and aiming at parametric reform, had failed to prosper in Congress. While the first one was sent to the legislative in June 1993 and failed to be considered by any commission, the other one was presented in February 1994 for urgent consideration. Presented by a minority government eight months before the elections and without any preceding political negotiation, the bill was turned down by 72 to 17 votes (Filgueira, Moraes and Moreira 1999). The Lacalle government's last attempt at pension reform was started in August 1994, three months before the elections. Several different measures, from electoral reform to the composition of the BPS' board of directors, were lumped together in a plebiscite known as the '*minireforma*', which was not only rejected by the National Organisation of the Retired of Uruguay, ONAJPU, but also by 70 per cent of all voters (Kay 1998; Hernández 1999).

At the same time, the generalised recognition of the urgency of pension reform started to be reflected in opinion polls (Labadie, Canzani and Costa Bonino 1995: 42; Hernández 1999: 84–5). The fiscal effects of inaction had become ever more visible: in the mid-1990s, government subsidies to the public pension system had reached 5.3 per cent of GDP – 3.8 per cent for the BPS and 1.5 per cent for the schemes of the military and the police (Noya, Fernández Poncet and Laens 1999). This situation triggered parallel developments. In late 1993, the Minister of Economy and Finance agreed with the IDB on a major consultancy on pension reform. Under the leadership of Francisco Barreto de Oliveira, a Brazilian advocate of pension privatisation, domestic and foreign experts were to produce a series of reports on the viability of four alternative pension reform scenarios in Uruguay. These four alternatives included parametric reform, full pension privatisation, and mixed schemes with mandatory as well as optional participation in the IFF tier (for details see Barreto de Oliveira et al. 1994).[16]

In late 1994, the IDB consultancy concluded that parametric changes, however urgent, would not be sufficient to make the Uruguayan pension system financially viable, making structural pension reform 'imperative' (Barreto de Oliveira et al. 1994: 202). For financial, political and social reasons, a mixed system was recommended. The first tier would continue to supply tax-financed poverty relief, the second would consist of a reformed PAYG programme with a benefit ceiling of four minimum wages, while the third would consist of a newly created IFF tier on an optional, supplementary basis, i.e. only for the part of the salary that exceeded four minimum wages (Barreto de Oliveira et al. 1994). Neither the BPS' board of directors nor the population were informed about the studies being carried out (Papadópulos 1998).

The November 1994 elections brought a strengthening of the left, with almost 31 per cent of all votes for *Frente Amplio*. Upon this threat to their long-standing hegemony over the political system, the two traditional parties decided to join forces (Papadópulos 1998; Nahum 1999). Their bipartisan coalition endowed them with a two-third's majority in Congress and Senate, and the opportunity to introduce major political and institutional reforms. Filgueira and Moraes (1999) report that the coalition was made conditional on structural pension reform – on the request of the *Colorados*, who had reached a formal intra-party agreement on the introduction of a mixed reform in March 1994. In an attempt at broader consensus-building, Sanguinetti – the *Colorado* president-elect – created a pension reform group before his inauguration, initially formed by all four political parties with parliamentary representation. Within less than two months, the group issued a statement on the basic principles of pension reform that did not explicitly mention pension privatisation. The intention was to ensure the support of *Frente Amplio*. However, the *Frente* eventually left the group, divided over whether or not to remain involved, while the smaller *Nuevo Espacio* decided to sign the document (Comisión de Seguridad Social 1995).

In March 1995, a technical commission, staffed with pension experts from the bipartisan coalition and financed by a US$3.8 million IDB loan, started three months of work in seclusion. Drawing on the Chilean and Argentine experience, as well as on the technical knowledge accumulated over the past decade of reform attempts, they prepared a draft law for the introduction of a mixed pension system, which combined a reformed PAYG scheme with a mandatory IFF tier. A number of relevant extra-parliamentary organisations, most notably ONAJPU and PIT-CNT, were given a hearing during the discussion of the bill in Congress (Filgueira, Moraes and Moreira 1999). In spite of the opposition voiced by most of these groups, the *Blanco-Colorado* majority in Congress passed the pension reform law with few alterations in September 1995, as stipulated in their coalition agreement (CLAEH 1995).

A number of pre-emptive concessions to weaken opposition to the reform are worth mentioning. The indexation regime of 1989 remained untouched and was even extended to second-tier benefits (Caristo and Forteza 1999). Contrary to the original accord, the five privileged pension programmes – accounting for 11 per cent of all insured – were maintained, thereby avoiding the confrontation with the related pressure groups, among which the armed forces. This move amounts to a combined strategy of exclusionary compensation and division of the potential opposition. In a similar vein, the insured were split into different groups by age and income (see below for details), thereby protecting acquired rights and firmly establishing the public tier in the mixed system. Besides other roles, the BPS was obliged to set up the first fund administrator, either alone or together with three state-owned banks, in an attempt to appeal to the opponents of private old-age provision.

The new pension system

The new Uruguayan pension regime came into effect in April 1996 (Saldain 1995). It covers all insured below 40 years of age, as well as all future entrants to the labour force. Those older than age 40 at the time of the reform were free to choose between staying in the old system and joining the new system. In the mixed system, three income brackets apply (Mesa-Lago 1998; Papadópulos 1998): up to US$800, the contribution is channelled to the reformed PAYG scheme (first tier); from US$800 to US$2 400 it is sent to the newly created IFF scheme (second tier); and those parts of the income above US$2 400 can be insured by making a voluntary contribution to the IFF tier.[17] Those insured whose total income does not exceed US$800 – or 90 per cent of contributors – are free to split their contribution between the first and second tier. Those who do are rewarded by earning 1.5 pesos of pension rights in the first tier with every peso they put in the second tier. The IDB conditioned the second tranche of its first ever loan for pension privatisation upon the affiliation of 30 per cent of those in the lowest income bracket to the IFF tier, and the third tranche upon the affiliation of 70 per cent (Contrato de Préstamo 1996). Eventually, 98 per cent of potential affiliates opted to enter the IFF tier (Vera Méndez 1999: 27), thereby surprising the reformers – and increasing transition costs.

It should be noted that the calibration of parameters in the new Uruguayan pension regime allows for an implicit recognition of acquired rights, as the threshold of US$800 corresponds to the benefit ceiling in the pre-reform system (Caristo and Forteza 1999; Saldain 1999). Membership in the IFF tier therefore creates extra pension benefits instead of substituting for part of the PAYG pension. More than half of all insured have now joined the IFF tier (IMF 2001e), which consists of competing fund administrators – the so-called AFAPs, that may be public or private. *República AFAP*, owned by the BPS and two state banks, dominates the market with 56 per cent of all assets (FIAP 2001). The second tier is supervised by Uruguay's Central Bank.

The 1994 pension law also included a reform of the PAYG scheme. The retirement age for women was raised, equalising it with that for men at age 60, while the minimum vesting period was increased to 35 years. Replacement rates were lowered, and pension calculation is now based either on the average salary of the last 10 years prior to retirement, or on the average of the 20 best years in the individual labour history, up to a maximum of US$800 (Noya, Fernández Poncet and Laens 1999). Late retirement and longer vesting periods are financially rewarded. Employees' contributions were increased from 13 to 15 per cent of salaries. Employers' contributions were lowered to 12.5 per cent and are fully paid to the BPS to co-finance first-tier pension benefits – regardless of the choice or income of the insured (Saldain 1999). All contributions continue to be collected by the BPS, which also establishes a labour history for each worker. The possibility to prove contributory periods by calling witnesses was abolished.

Compared with the Argentine version of a mixed reform, structural pension reform '*a la uruguaya*' (Filgueira, Moraes and Moreira 1999: 88; Ramos Olivera 1999: 141) strikes a different balance between the public tier and the newly established IFF scheme. In Latin America, the Uruguayan system is unique in that a pension fund owned by public institutions clearly dominates the market. Moreover, in the first year all AFAPs had to invest 80 per cent of assets in treasury bonds, a minimum that is to be lowered gradually until eventually reaching 30 per cent. Such features can make partial pension privatisation palatable even to 'statists', as the interest of the Venezuelan president Hugo Chávez in the Uruguayan reform seems to suggest (La República 2000).

Pension privatisation could not be prevented or reversed by opponents of reform (see, e.g., Representación de los Trabajadores 1997) – in spite of the ample veto points embodied in the Uruguayan policy context. 'In addition to learning more about technically viable solutions, the reformers had also learned to work around powerful opposition groups' (Graham et al. 1999:

22). In 1996 and 1999, attempts to repeal the pension law by referendum and plebiscite were rejected on legal grounds, while the political support from the left started to fade away (Hernández 1999). Today, with the creation of a substantial number of reform-related stakeholders – the members and administrators of pension funds – a reversal of the Uruguayan pension reform is 'anything but likely' (Filgueira and Moraes 1999: 20).

Conclusion

The puzzle of the political feasibility of partial pension privatisation in Uruguay has triggered a number of studies.[18] In a comparative perspective, several features of the Uruguayan policy context seemed to make pension privatisation unlikely (Graham et al. 1999). When policymakers embarked on partial pension privatisation, the country faced neither economic crisis nor radical shock therapy, while veto points abounded. The historical legacy of *Batllismo* made the country stand out against the regional context for an undiminished pride in high social spending and an essentially centrist political orientation in both the population and the two traditional political parties, with neoliberal discourse holding little appeal (Favaro and Bensión 1993; Hernández 1999). Yet, in the mid-1990s, several reform-enabling developments coincided, opening a window of opportunity for a 'silent social revolution' (Ramos Olivera 1999: VII).

After the end of military rule, the country faced a challenge of multiple transitions. The first Sanguinetti government set out to cope with the authoritarian legacy, the Lacalle administration embarked on partial economic adjustment, and only the third post-authoritarian government enjoyed the political space for institutional reforms (Filgueira and Moraes 1999). The long-standing absence of strong executive authority was overcome by deliberate and unprecedented coalition-building, in reaction to the electoral success of *Frente Amplio*. Pension reform, a contentious issue on which the left had capitalised over the previous decade, featured prominently on the *Blanco-Colorado* agenda. The win-win situation for the left had hit the traditional parties by creating a permanent need for tax increases and expenditure cuts. At this point, the political cost of inaction apparently exceeded the potential blame that a more enduring reform could generate. As to the strategies of the reformers, a careful design '*a la uruguaya*' was chosen to mitigate opposition, and the bill was legislated at the very start of the electoral cycle. Strong pre-emptive agreements and a mandatist coalition implied that parliament was not the main policy forum in Uruguayan pension privatisation.

The Uruguayan case is also a tale of strong veto points and unintended effects. The power of pensioners' associations and their broad coalition with trade unions and political parties had blocked several reform attempts, in a policy context granting these well-organised opponents with special action resources, as referenda and plebiscites are common and binding in Uruguay.[19] The tools of direct democracy even enabled them to establish a generous indexation regime in the constitution. However, this move – intended to protect current and future pensioners – led to a substantial increase in pension expenditure that created significant fiscal pressure. This, in turn, increased the overall readiness for a radical change of the *status quo* in old-age security, especially given that parametric reform had been tried repeatedly and unsuccessfully (Noya, Fernández Poncet and Laens 1999).

Clearly, 'technopols' were absent (Williamson 1994), and political parties mattered more than individual actors in Uruguay. Yet, the Uruguayan case confirms the familiar pattern that underfinanced PAYG schemes, relying heavily on budgetary subsidies, tend to strengthen the role of economists over the traditional 'Bismarckian faction' in pension policy. Ariel Davrieux, the head of the influential Office for Planning and Budget (OPP) at the President's Office, took the lead over reform preparations, and fiscal pressure had induced the Minister of Economy and Finance to ask for crucial support from the IDB, which was known to be only available for full or partial privatisation.

Uruguay has a reputation for gradualism and less than intimate relations with the 'Washington twins'. However, the IFIs are no strangers to the Uruguayan policy context, as the country hovered between severe and moderate indebtedness (World Bank 2000e, 2001c). In the case of pension reform, external actors were largely involved *ex post*. The IDB – with its Uruguayan president – was the first IFI to lend international backing to the reformers, in spite of initial doubts about the *sui generis* reform design (Márquez Mosconi 1997). As noted above, the IDB financed an in-depth preparatory study. After tough negotiations, it also provided a US$150 million loan to cover transition costs.

In comparison, the World Bank initially rejected lending to the Uruguayan reformers, expressing serious reserves about the chosen reform design (Kane 1995b; World Bank 1996d), while strongly recommending to 'hasten the migration to a full capitalization system' (García-Mujica 1996: 20). The Bank endorsed the Uruguayan reform only in 1998, when it granted a US$100 million loan to cover larger than expected transition costs – a result of the extraordinarily strong response to pro-second tier incentives. '[T]he Bank did not believe the proposed new system, a home-designed reform ... , would produce beneficial results. ... Later, however, the Bank conceded that the new system – with its fully funded private pillar – is an important step toward resolving the financial problems of the social security system' (World Bank 2000e: 7).

NOTES

1. Life expectancy at retirement age was 20.0 and 28.4 years for men and women, respectively (Gillion et al. 2000). Mesa-Lago and Bertranou (1998) report a coverage rate of 79.1 per cent for 1985–88.
2. After his recent failure to halt economic collapse and the demise of the currency board arrangement he had introduced a decade ago, Cavallo lost his reputation as 'miracle worker' (Armbruster 2001).
3. In April 1991 the Argentine currency unit, the austral, was fixed at 10 000:1 to the US dollar, while being replaced by the peso at the rate of 1:1 to the dollar in January 1992. The Convertibility Law also established that the monetary base could not exceed the US$ value of international reserves.
4. In 1991–92, freely negotiable consolidation bonds, the so-called BOCONs, were issued to settle outstanding pension claims, with a six-year grace period on principal and interest (Ministerio de Trabajo 1993; Schulthess and Demarco 1993; World Bank 1993a). However, a recent report mentions almost 70 000 additional verdicts, as well as plans to launch another series of BOCONs (BID 2000).
5. See also Cavallo (1995: 69): 'We soaked up the Chilean experience in pension reform ... [T]he pension system will re-educate all Argentinians to save, which is so important for growth'.
6. For details see PRONATASS (1992).
7. Two dissident labour confederations, CTA and MTA, upheld their opposition to pension privatisation and *sindicalismo de negocios* ('business-minded trade unionism').
8. The dollar-based guarantee, strongly opposed by the banking sector who demanded a level playing-field, was eliminated in 1994. Moreover, there is a debate on the privatisation of *Banco Nación* (Hujo 1999).
9. See Isuani and San Martino (1993, 1995) and Rossi (1999) for a detailed account of the reform process in the legislature.
10. 'Within a year, it will be possible to pass a law mandating that all new employees join the private system, without causing political uproar' (Schwarz 1998: 210).
11. See Alonso (1998, 2000), Brooks (1998), Isuani and San Martino (1993, 1995), Kay (1998, 1999), Madrid (1999, 2001), Rossi (1999) and Torre and Gerchunoff (1999).
12. Trade unions had originally set up four AFJPs. As *Más Vida*, *Claridad* and *San José* were absorbed by competitors in 1997, 1998 and 1999, respectively. In 2001, the only remaining AFJP owned by trade unions was *Futura* (Alonso 2000: 130; FIAP 2001; SAFJP 2001).
13. For 1980, McGreevey (1990) reports a coverage rate of 81 per cent, while Mesa-Lago and Bertranou (1998) report a coverage rate of 73.0 per cent for 1985–88.
14. Saldain (1999) points to the parallels to the notional defined contribution approach adopted several years later in Sweden and some post-socialist countries (see Chapter 7 for details).
15. Tripartite representation was established in the 1967 constitution, but regulations were not passed until 1992. Hernández (2000) argues that this move, which met a long-standing demand of the pensioners but was also a potential tool for co-optation, contributed to a medium-term decrease in militancy.
16. A comparison with the four reform alternatives presented by the multi-party commission in 1992 reveals telling parallels and differences.
17. These thresholds are fixed in Uruguayan pesos and will be regularly adjusted (Caristo and Forteza 1999).
18. See Filgueira and Moraes (1999), Filgueira, Moraes and Moreira (1999), Hernández (1999, 2000), Jäger (2001), Kay (1998, 1999) and Papadópulos (1998). On the earlier reform attempts in Uruguay see Castiglioni (2001), Filgueira and Papadópulos (1994) and Papadópulos (1992, 1996, 2001).
19. In Uruguay, plebiscites – an instrument of direct democracy to modify the constitution – have been practised since 1918 and were established in the constitution in 1934, whereas referenda may repeal laws and were only introduced in 1967 (Lissidini 1998). See also de los Campos (1995).

6. Pension privatisation in the Andean region

6.1 THE CASE OF PERU

Legacy and policy context

The first old-age security schemes in Peru were established as early as 1850, albeit only for the military and civil servants. From the 1920s onwards, different pressure groups managed to obtain separate social security programmes. After the development of trade unions, the foundation of left-wing parties and the birth of the populist American Popular Revolutionary Alliance (APRA), repression, co-option and social concessions by successive military and civilian governments alternated for decades (McClintock 1999). Although generalised social protection was conceived by the 1930s, it was not until 1961 that pension funds for both blue- and white-collar workers were established, yet alongside the independent pension programmes that had been set up earlier. In the 1970s important steps towards the unification and standardisation of the stratified pension system were taken, although inequalities among professional groups did not cease to exist (Mesa-Lago 1973, 1978; Asesoramiento y Análisis Laborales 1997).

In 1980, a few days before the return to democratic rule, the Peruvian Social Security Institute, or IPSS, was established as the sole administrator of the general pension and health-maternity programmes. The IPSS, an autonomous agency with tripartite administration under the general control of the Ministry of Labour, proved 'too weak to overcome the fatal legacy of statistical and accounting ignorance, administrative chaos, and financial difficulties of social security' (Mesa-Lago 1989: 178). The surplus in the existing pension schemes had long subsidised health-maternity programmes, which accounted for around 60 per cent of expenditures. It is estimated that IPSS ran a total surplus until 1982, when it started to show a deficit due to evasion and payment delays in the context of mounting inflation. The lack of a registry of the insured and their employers did not help to improve contribution compliance, especially as the state proved to be the principal debtor. The IPSS pension programme used the scaled-premium method, yet the investment of reserves rendered negative rates of return (Mesa-Lago 1991a). At the same time, real benefit levels deteriorated severely, plunging by half between 1976 and 1982. Given the relatively short history of social security in Peru, Mesa-Lago (1989: 174) diagnosed a 'premature crisis'.

Social security in Peru is also marked by sparse coverage, reflecting a low percentage of salaried labour and the social exclusion of the rural and indigenous population. More than half of all men aged 65 and above are still working, and even in Lima only a quarter of the population in retirement age receives a pension (Verdera 2000). In 1988, only 38 per cent of the labour force were affiliated to IPSS. As a result, the system dependency ratio of 31 per cent was much above the old-age dependency ratio (14.3 per cent), while only 2.3 per cent of Peruvians were pensioners (see Table 4.2). '[T]he demographics are favorable for the pension system well into this century' (IMF 2001c: 61). For a full pension women and men had to fulfil a vesting period of 13 and 15 years, respectively, while the statutory retirement age was 55/60 for women/men (BID 1991). In 1987, life expectancy at birth was only 61 years in Peru, reflecting a high infant mortality (World Bank 1989). Those who reached retirement age, however, still enjoyed an average life expectancy of 16.5 years for men and 22.6 years for women (Gillion et al. 2000).

Table 6.1   The reform context in Peru: selected indicators

Indicators	1988	1989	1990	1991	1992
GDP change (in %)	−8.3	−11.7	−5.4	2.8	−1.4
Consumer prices (annual average, in %)	660.0	3,321.1	7,592.3	409.5	73.6
General gov't balance (in % of GDP)	−8.1	−8.5	−4.5	−1.5	−1.7
Total external debt (in % of GDP)	40.2	35.5	45.2	42.9	44.3
IPSS balance (in % of GDP)	−0.4	−0.1	0.0	0.2	0.0
Public pension expenditure (in % of GDP)	2.4	2.2	1.9	2.0	2.8
– IPSS	1.0	0.7	0.7	0.9	1.2
– general gov't	1.4	1.5	1.2	1.1	1.6

Note: Only the five years up to reform adoption are considered.

Sources: IDB (1998); data provided to the author by the BCRP; own calculations.

Towards the end of the heterodox experiment of Alan García's APRA government (1985–90), high inflation, economic collapse, a dramatic erosion of state capacity and politically motivated violence had plunged Peru into an all-encompassing crisis (see Table 6.1). In 1990, this unprecedented emergency prepared the ground for the election victory of a political outsider, Alberto Fujimori. It also resulted in widespread support for the radical structural reforms that he started afterwards (Crabtree and Thomas 1998; Müller 2001b). The ideational ground for the paradigm shift from a statist, inward-oriented legacy towards market-oriented reforms had been prepared by prominent representatives of neoliberalism, most notably the writer Mario Vargas Llosa, the rival candidate for the *Fredemo* party (Vargas Llosa 1989, 1992). While Fujimori had campaigned on an explicit anti-shock therapy platform, his approach to economic policy underwent fundamental change after a post-electoral trip to Washington (Gonzales de Olarte 1993). At the same time, political parties had experienced a dramatic loss of support, while trade unions and other interest groups were weakened by the severity of economic crisis, which translated into a steep reduction of their membership (Bosoer 2000; Tecco Miyano 2000). In this extraordinary context, Fujimori's leeway for an iconoclastic break with the economic model of the past was substantial (Graham 1998).

The way towards pension privatisation[1]

In 1990, under a new leadership, the IPSS went out of the red (Ausejo 1995). With 2 per cent of GDP, public pension expenditure was comparably low (see Table 6.1).[2] Meagre retirement benefits, a poor health service and low wages had made the IPSS a frequent target of popular protest during the 1980s (Cruz-Saco 1998). In the light of the IPSS' deteriorated reputation, a consensus existed about the need to reform the existing social security system (Danós O. 1994; Kiefer 1998). Yet, experts were far from unanimous about the reform path to be followed (Análisis Laboral 1990). In 1990, a first draft law, inspired by the Chilean precedent, was presented to Congress by the neoliberal *Fredemo* opposition party that had proposed the creation of 'alternative private schemes of social security' as early as 1989 (Movimiento Libertad 1989: 57). Experts in social security law, IPSS representatives and trade unions voiced their opposition to the draft law, which was eventually blocked by the APRA party. Mario Roggero, a *Fredemo* Congressman and the principal advocate of the bill, then changed sides. He helped persuade President Fujimori of the idea to offer the insured a chance to choose between the IPSS and private, Chilean-style pension administrators. According to Ortíz de Zevallos et al. (1999: 38), many bills in this early phase of the

Fujimori government were 'improvised adaptations or copies of *Fredemo* draft laws or of foreign legislation'.

In the second half of 1991, the executive was granted extraordinary legislative powers to promote investment and employment. In view of this window of opportunity, two prominent advocates of pension privatisation – the Minister of Finance, Carlos Boloña, and the Minister of Energy and Mines, Jaime Yoshiyama – proposed to include pension reform in the package of structural reforms that they were preparing. Boloña was on good terms with the IFIs and maintained close contact with Hernán Büchi and José Piñera, who had served as Ministers of Finance and Labour under Pinochet. Reportedly, radical liberalisation and privatisation met with President Fujimori's reserve at first. However, at this time Boloña and his neoliberal policy proposals carried considerable weight in Peruvian politics – not only in the context of the severe economic crisis. Peru also needed to get reinserted into the global financial markets after the García regime had partially defaulted on the country's foreign debt (Müller 1993), turning Peru into the 'pariah of the international financial community' (Fabricius 1999: 436).

Shortly before the period of extraordinary powers was coming to an end, Piñera, the architect of the Chilean pension reform, travelled to Lima to re-move Fujimori's remaining doubts (Boloña 1997; Arce 2001). In November 1991, Decree (D.L.) 724 was eventually passed by the executive, stipulating a parallel pension system. Under the new system, which was scheduled to come into force on 28 July 1992, all current and future insured would choose be-tween the public scheme and a new IFF tier. The decree was received enthu-siastically by representatives of the local finance and insurance industry, who organised seminars and conferences featuring Piñera and other prominent Chilean pension experts. However, trade unions, pensioners and IPSS repre-sentatives expressed strong opposition to pension privatisation. Opponents feared that the reform would lead to a collapse of the IPSS due to a massive diversion of contributions. Many lawyers considered the parallel model an infringement of the 1979 constitution. A formal complaint against D.L. 724 was submitted to the constitutional court in December 1991, together with 30 000 signatures that had been collected against pension privatisation.

In April 1992 such contextual constraints were removed by Fujimori's *coup d'état*. This move suspended the constitution, dissolved Congress and established authoritarian rule, while being backed by the military.[3] In the light of the international outrage caused by the coup, Boloña's role turned even more important, as Fujimori attempted to compensate for the less than democratic regime by demonstrating full compliance with the IFIs' economic agenda (Ortíz de Zevallos et al. 1999). Boloña decided to seize the chance to move the envisaged pension reform closer to the Chilean precedent, drawing on the reform team set up within his Ministry in January 1992 to prepare the enabling regulations for D.L. 724. The new Chilean-style proposal coincided with the early recommendations of the World Bank and the IDB that lent technical cooperation and financial support to the Peruvian pension reform (IDB 1992; World Bank 1992b). On the request of the president, the draft of the new law – that would have required new entrants to the labour market to join the private system – was published in mid-July 1992 (Anteproyecto 1992). Apparently, this unusual procedure was intended to poll public opinion (Ortíz de Zevallos et al. 1999).

The new reform plans were accompanied with a government campaign stressing the merits of private fund administrators. These attempts to sell the reform to the public met with strong opposition – not least from the main promoter of D.L. 724, Mario Roggero. Trade union confederations gathered under the slogan 'Save the IPSS', and worried pensioners' banners read 'Social security is a right, not a business opportunity'.[4] Apparently, this vocal opposition had an impact on Fujimori and only increased his reservations about the radical reform approach. In September 1992, he announced that the IPSS would not be closed, even though it would no longer hold a monopoly – thus implying a return to the parallel approach. Given that elections to a Constituent Assembly were due in November 1992, the president also decided to postpone the passing of the reform until shortly afterwards. In December 1992, just before the extraordinary window of opportunity was about to close, partial pension privatisation was legislated by D.L. 25 897.[5]

The new pension system

The parallel pension system that was decreed in 1992 implies that current and future workers are free to choose between the public pension insurance and a new IFF scheme. The latter started operations in June 1993, featuring competing private pension fund administrators – the so-called AFPs, the number of which dropped from eight to four in recent years. They were initially supervised by a separate state entity, the SAFP, which was later merged with the Superintendency of Banks and Insurances, as in Bolivia. In the IFF tier, individuals can retire when they reach age 65, or whenever the account balance allows for a pension of at least half of the last average earnings. As in Chile, employers' contributions are abolished when the insured switches to the AFP tier, in exchange for a one-off wage increase. Contribution collection in the IFF tier is decentralised, i.e. employers deduct individual contributions from wages and pass them on to the respective AFP. However, evasion is estimated at 49 per cent, and AFPs are involved in 120 000 lawsuits against employers who fail to transfer contributions to individual accounts (Gestión 2001a). Moreover, the level of commissions

charged raised much concern. As costs are front-loaded, they generated a
negative net return in the early years (Rojas 1998; World Bank 1999d).[6]

Although the pension reform did not touch the highly subsidised schemes
of the armed forces and civil servants, it implied a radical institutional break.
A so-called 'Office for Pension Normalisation' (ONP), placed directly under
the Ministry of Finance, took on the management of public retirement benefits
from the IPSS in 1994. Initially, the public pension insurance granted earlier
retirement than the private scheme and charged lower contribution rates.[7]
Moreover, opinion polls revealed that most Peruvians distrusted the AFPs
(APOYO 1993). Hence, two years after the start of the IFF tier, the number of
those who had left the public pension scheme amounted to less than 50 per
cent of all insured and only 13 per cent of the labour force (Cruz-Saco 1998).

Starting from 1995, a series of corrective measures were legislated, following intense lobbying by the AFP industry and critical observations by the
IFIs. With the solidarity tax and employers' contribution to the ONP scheme
abolished and individual contributions to the AFPs lowered, workers now pay
roughly the same rates to the public and private schemes. Retirement ages in
both systems were standardised at age 65, and new entrants to the labour
market are automatically enrolled in the private tier unless they request to be
affiliated with the ONP. Yet, this request must be presented in person and
within 10 days of starting employment (IMF 2001c). Another measure targeted affiliates to the civil servant pension scheme (known as D.L. 20 530),
which were also enabled to switch to the IFF tier while being offered a more
generous recognition bond than affiliates to the general public pension
scheme, known as D.L. 19 990.[8] In 2001, the D.L. 19 990 scheme covered
797 160 active workers and 366 355 pensioners, while the D.L. 20 530
scheme counted 60 247 active workers and 261 525 pensioners in 1996 (Comisión Especial 2001).[9]

Yet, two rather unfavourable features of the private system persisted for
almost a decade. Unlike the public alternative, the AFP tier did not offer a
minimum pension guarantee, and the recognition of previous contribution
payments was incomplete and restrictive, in order to reduce transition costs
(Kane 1995b).[10] Only 150 646 entitlements to recognition bonds had been
granted by mid-2001, whereas the IFF tier had 2.6 million affiliates and 1.0
million contributors (ONP 2001; FIAP 2001). Conditions for the granting of
recognition bonds were softened only in 2002, in order to induce some of the
remaining affiliates to the public schemes to switch to the IFF tier. Moreover,
a state-financed minimum pension guarantee was eventually introduced for
AFP affiliates, albeit only covering those born in 1945 or earlier who have a
minimum contribution record of 20 years in the public and/or private pension
tier.[11] The new law also introduced a temporary early retirement window for

the long-term unemployed aged 55 and above, affiliated to the IFF tier (Ley No. 27 617).[12]

Initially, Peruvian pension reformers did not opt for a linkage between pension privatisation and another, parallel structural reform – the sale of state-owned enterprises. However, in 1996–98, two pension reserve funds fed by privatisation proceeds were established, currently holding US$3.7 billion in assets: the Consolidated Pension Reserves Fund (FCR) was created to back ONP liabilities, especially the financing of recognition bonds, while the National Public Savings Fund (FONAHPU) was used to pay a biannual supplement to eligible beneficiaries of the state-run pension schemes, D.L. 19 990 and 20 530 (IMF 2001c).

When the Fujimori regime collapsed in late 2000, 75 per cent of the IPSS' former affiliates had switched to the private pension tier, while over 82 per cent of pensioners remained in the two state-run pension regimes (Gestión 2001d). The managers of the downsized public regime left no doubt about the temporary nature of their task, in spite of the ONP's official slogan 'We keep an eye on the strengthening of the state-run pension system'. Interestingly, the process of re-democratisation only intensified attacks on the parallel design of the Peruvian pension system. In early 2001, the new Finance Minister, Javier Silva Ruete, pointed out that the present value of the obligations stemming from the public pension scheme exceeded Peru's external debt (Gestión 2001b). His successor, Pedro Pablo Kuczynski, another well-known neoliberal economist, declared a few months later that the pension debt amounted to two-thirds of Peru's GDP (Gestión 2001c).

In a context of almost 17 000 lawsuits challenging the retrenchment measures enacted over the past years, a high-level commission studied the situation of the remaining state-run pension schemes (Comisión Especial 2001). In its final report, the commission stated that parametric reform had proven insufficient to ensure the financial viability of the public tier, while also admitting that its crisis had been aggravated by the creation of the private tier. The commission strongly recommended to mandate a switch of all D.L. 19 990 affiliates younger than age 55 to the IFF tier and to close the D.L. 20 530 regime for new entrants, thereby following repeated recommendations by the IFIs: 'the ONP system should be closed. This would be a more transparent policy than the cumbersome procedures used today to discourage affiliation. It would also eliminate the confusion in the system regarding the competition of ONP with the AFPs' (IMF 2001c: 67).

Conclusion

In the early 1990s, a policy context of unprecedented economic and political crisis had opened up spaces for far-reaching change in Peru. At the same

time, the country faced a breakdown of political representation, with traditional political parties and other interest groups severely weakened (McClintock 1999). Fujimori's power base in Congress was small, but he soon found
other ways to achieve a strong concentration of power in the executive that
was granted extraordinary legislative powers in 1991. Moreover, the president resorted to a self-coup and the closure of Congress shortly afterwards.
Interestingly, the Peruvian case highlights that an extraordinarily strong
executive is not the only prerequisite for a smooth introduction of radical
pension reform. In spite of the total absence of veto points after the self-coup,
pension privatisation in Peru suffered delays and was marked by poor design
and implementation. This has been interpreted as reflecting Fujimori's
wavering commitment to the iconoclastic paradigm shift (Cruz-Saco 1998),
thereby only stressing the importance of leadership in reform initiatives.

Peru was the second Latin American country after Chile to embark on pension privatisation. It adopted a parallel variant of the 'Chilean model', as the
substitutive type did not prove to be politically feasible in either 1992 or
1995, when another attempt was made to close the public scheme to new
entrants. The insured were poorly informed on the pension choices they were
facing, and although the public scheme is more attractive for low-income
workers, a number of procedures are used to discourage affiliation to the
ONP (IMF 2001c). Contrary to other country experiences, pension privatisation in Peru was not triggered by a high fiscal burden stemming from the
existing public system of old-age security. Rather, the IPSS' poor services
and deteriorated reputation, a generalised move to market-oriented reforms
and Fujimori's need to signal that he was on track economically, if not politically, were crucial enabling factors. It was in this situation that the Minister of
Finance's position was strengthened (Arce 2001). This advocate of radical
reform framed pension privatisation as a means to achieve macroeconomic
rather than social objectives (Boloña Behr 1995). The pension reform team
was established at the Finance Ministry, while the Labour Ministry was excluded from reform preparations – even though until the self-coup, the
Minister of Labour, Alfonso de los Heros, was also Prime Minister. Moreover, the redesign of public pension provision placed the newly created ONP
directly under the authority of the Finance Ministry, while the IPSS had tradi-
tionally been controlled by the Ministry of Labour.

The reform process was marked by a technocratic, decretist style and the
absence of policy dialogue with opponents. Efforts towards consensus-building were only made during the *Fredemo*'s unsuccessful attempt to find a
parliamentary majority for pension privatisation in 1990–91, but ceased
completely once Boloña adopted the reform project. Boloña and Yoshiyama
resorted to bundling when first attempting to legislate pension privatisation in
late 1991, presenting it as an integral part of market-oriented structural reform

measures. Somewhat counter-factually, it was claimed that the state pension 'system was bankrupt and becoming an unsustainable burden' (Boloña 1997: 1). By exempting powerful pressure groups – the military and civil servants – from structural pension reform, a strategy of exclusionary compensation and division was chosen. Direct compensation for those who switch to the IFF tier is much less favourable than in Chile, amounting to a fiscally driven revocation of acquired rights. Yet, reformers promised that in the AFP tier, workers would be the owners of their retirement savings. And indeed, 'a new constituency with stakes in the reform developed quickly' (Graham 1998: 114). However, Peruvians soon found that among these new stakeholders, former Finance Minister Boloña featured prominently.[13] In contrast, trade unions, among which a plan to establish their own pension fund was taking shape (Esteves O. 1994), were not permitted to run AFPs. Unlike their Bolivian counterparts, Peruvian reformers made no effort to expand the extremely low coverage and did not design a strategic linkage between pension privatisation and the sale of state-owned enterprises until well after the reform.

The IFIs had actively encouraged Fujimori to redefine the role of the state and to embark on market-oriented reforms (Fabricius 1999). Their leverage resulted not only from the country's severe indebtedness (World Bank 2001c). García's partial default had led the IMF to declare Peru ineligible, while the World Bank had put it on a non-accrual status. In order to regain access to international financial markets, the Fujimori government maintained close contact with the IFIs and needed to comply with various conditions in an interim period until lending would be resumed. The World Bank and the IDB provided technical financial assistance to the pension reform team working at the Ministry of Finance and to the superintendency (IDB 1992; World Bank 1992b). Financial sector adjustment loans were made conditional on progress towards pension privatisation, which was thought useful to 'provide better and more reliable retirement benefits, help stave off a total collapse of IPSS and supply much needed contractual savings to stimulate activity in the capital market' (World Bank 1992b: 35). A full move to a Chilean-style system has been recommended repeatedly (Kane 1995a; IMF 2001c). A decade after structural reform was decreed, pension privatisation in Peru is still an ongoing process.

6.2   THE CASE OF BOLIVIA

Legacy and policy context

While the first Bolivian pension laws date back to the beginning of the last century, a comprehensive system of old-age insurance was legislated only in

1956.[14] The Social Security Code was hailed as one of the major achievements brought about by the 1952 revolution. The original design stipulated a
single public institution that would pay retirement benefits according to uniform eligibility rules. Financed with tripartite contributions on the basic
salary, benefits amounted to 30 per cent of the last average earnings if the
insured fulfilled a vesting period of 15 years. At age 55 for men and 50 for
women, retirement age was very low.[15]

This basic system had initially been administered by the National Social
Insurance Fund (CNSS), under which pension surpluses essentially subsidised
health programmes. In 1987 the National Reserve Fund (FONARE) was put
in charge, separating pension and health finances, while in 1990 the Basic
Pension Fund (FOPEBA) took over (Mercado Lora 1998). Since the late
1960s, complementary pension funds (FONCOMs) had been established to
increase the replacement rate of retirement benefits. By the mid-1990s, a total
of 36 FONCOMs offered additional protection, increasing the total
replacement rate to 70 per cent. They had an average of 9 500 members and
charged employees only (Gersdorff 1997). The institutional fragmentation
implied not only different eligibility and benefit rules, but also high
administrative costs (Schulthess 1988). In addition, some of the FONCOMs
suffered from mismanagement and embezzlement of funds (Graham 1998).

In 1992, 81 per cent of retirees received monthly payments of less than
US$56 from FOPEBA, and the average monthly benefit from both tiers was
US$97 in 1993 (World Bank 1995b). Access to the two-tiered formal scheme
had been limited to salaried urban workers, while the large majority in the
rural and informal sector were excluded. In the 1990s, coverage dropped from
19 to 12 per cent of the economically active population (CISS 1993; Mül-
ler&Asociados 1997). A system dependency ratio of 40 per cent in FOPEBA
contrasted with an old-age dependency ratio of 16.2 per cent, and only 2 per
cent of Bolivia's population were pensioners (see Table 4.2).

The financial problems of the pension system date back to the 1980s, when
economic collapse and a dedollarisation policy led to the virtual vanishing of
the existing reserves and to a *de facto* shift to PAYG financing.[16] Several
FONCOMs were in an even worse situation. As they were branch-based, they
fully reflected the effects of massive lay-offs, not least in the mining sector.[17]
The active/passive ratio deteriorated from 5.21 in 1980 to 2.74 in 1994 (Mül-
ler&Asociados 1997).[18] In 1995, arrears by public and private employers
were estimated at US$31 million (World Bank 1995b), while supervision was
complicated by the lack of individual registries. In spite of all these problems,
the available data suggest that the pension system did not burden the general
budget in any significant way.[19] According to Morales (1995), public pension
spending amounted to a mere 0.57 per cent of GDP in 1990, and the deficits
quoted in Table 6.2 are even lower. Yet, meagre benefits and late payments

generated a perception of imminent crisis (Gray-Molina, Pérez de Rada and Yañez 1999).

After a long period of political and economic instability, Bolivia returned to democratic rule in 1982. Faced with a severe debt crisis and a dramatic hyperinflation that reached 11 750 per cent in 1985, the government of Víctor Paz Estenssoro (1985–89) embarked on a radical economic stabilisation plan, assisted by Harvard economist Jeffrey Sachs. The so-called 'New Economic Policy' had been carried out by Gonzalo Sánchez de Lozada, then Minister of Planning, and met with strong political resistance, riots and strikes (Morales 1995; Cariaga 1997). It was only a decade later, when economic crisis was long over and Sánchez de Lozada had been elected as president (1993–97), that a series of 'second-generation reforms' was launched.

It is important to note that the political party represented by Paz Estenssoro and Sánchez de Lozada – the Nationalist Revolutionary Movement (MNR) – had led the 1952 revolution, a watershed in the country's history, while it was now dismantling the state-led development model. Gray-Molina, Pérez de Rada and Yañez (1999) argue that Sánchez de Lozada had announced most of the envisaged structural reforms in his election manifesto, *Plan de Todos* ('Plan for All'), and could thus claim a popular mandate after his victory. Moreover, the MNR's coalition pacts with three smaller parties – the Tupac Katari Revolutionary Movement (MRTK), the Civic Solidarity Union (UCS) and the Free Bolivia Movement (MBL) – allowed it to control 60 per cent of all seats in the legislature. At the same time, the once powerful trade union confederation, COB, had been severely weakened by structural adjustment, not least as a consequence of the mass redundancies. Finally, both first- and second-generation reforms were endorsed by the IFIs. Given Bolivia's need for concessionary credit and debt relief to maintain its balance of payments in the light of severe indebtedness (see Table 6.2), they featured 'systematic involvement with successive governments' (World Bank 1998: i).

The way towards pension privatisation[20]

In 1990, the director of Bolivia's largest insurance company asked José Piñera and other experts from neighbouring Chile to prepare a proposal for structural pension reform. The document was presented to the Bolivian public and to the president, Jaime Paz Zamora (1989–93). Inspired by this private initiative, a USAID grant, administered by the World Bank, was made available for a pension reform team. The working group was set up in the Ministry of Finance and cooperated closely with Chilean experts. In early 1992, after 10 months in seclusion, the team had elaborated a first draft law for pension privatisation. The draft was very similar to the 'Chilean model' and faced strong opposition from two members of the cabinet: the Minister of

Health, who had been excluded from reform preparations, even though he was in charge of social security; and the Minister of Labour, representing a small Maoist party and opposing the reform proposal as 'Pinochet-style'. This intra-government controversy notwithstanding, the Minister of Finance proceeded to present the draft law to the Paris Club in October 1992, in order to mobilise the 'first allies' in the reform process (Pérez B. 2000: 3). The proximity of elections and the high transition costs led to a shelving of the proposal (Gray-Molina, Pérez de Rada and Yañez 1999). To ensure a continuation of the reform process after the change of government, however, the outgoing government passed all documents to its successor, while the World Bank put a core team of reformers on its local payroll to maintain a small pool of pension experts.

Table 6.2   The reform context in Bolivia: selected indicators[a]

Indicators	1992	1993	1994	1995	1996
GDP change (in %)	1.6	4.3	4.7	4.7	4.1
Consumer prices (annual average, in %)	12.1	8.5	7.9	10.2	12.4
General gov't balance (in % of GDP)	–4.8	–6.5	–4.0	–2.1	–2.1
Total external debt (in % of GDP)	74.8	74.9	80.9	78.1	71.5
Old pension system[b]					
– revenue (in % of GDP)	n.a.	2.20	2.28	2.26	n.a.
– expenditure (in % of GDP)	n.a.	2.35	2.50	2.49	n.a.
– deficit (in % of GDP)	n.a.	0.15	0.22	0.23	n.a.

Notes: [a] Only the five years up to reform adoption are considered.
              [b] Includes both FOPEBA and the FONCOMs.

Sources: IDB (1998); Gersdorff (1997); Gottret (1999).

The incoming Sánchez de Lozada administration decided to link the partial privatisation of the largest state-owned enterprises with structural pension reform (Ministerio de Capitalización 1997; Peirce 1997; Gottret 1999).[21] At the same time, a major conceptual and semantic effort was intended to make these iconoclastic moves politically palatable (Ramos Sánchez 1998). To start with, the transfer of state enterprises to private control, legislated in March 1994, was called 'capitalisation', in order to evade the politically sensitive term 'privatisation'. The largest state-owned enterprises were transformed into joint stock companies to allow for an injection of fresh capital, while avoiding the outright sale. Thereafter, the existing capital was doubled by a so-called 'strategic investor', selected in an international bidding process. The remaining state-owned shares were administered by newly established private pension funds. The resulting dividends were distributed to all elderly Bolivians by means of the payment of an annual pension, the *Bono Solidario*, or *Bonosol*. According to the president, this *sui generis* package would 'ensure that Bolivians benefit from their assets' (Sánchez de Lozada 1993: 3).[22] By June 1997, private investors had taken a majority stake and management control in the power, oil and gas sectors, the railroads, the national airline and telecommunications (Baldivia Urdininea 1998).[23]

During the election campaign, different versions of the *Plan de Todos* were circulating. Most of them made no mention of pension funds – let alone pension privatisation.[24] The earlier versions announced that the state-owned shares were to be administered by a Foundation for Development in Solidarity (FUNDESOL) that would finance grass-root projects at community level. Only much later would the shares be distributed free of charge among all adult Bolivians (Sánchez de Lozada and Cárdenas 1993). In a popular edition, this mass privatisation was characterised as 'a radical redistribution of wealth, only comparable to the one that was brought about by the land reform' (MNR and MRTK 1993: 20). In another summary of the plan, however, Bolivians would buy shares from FUNDESOL 'to back pension funds' (Sánchez de Lozada 1993: 4). In early 1994, following discussions with international experts, reformers decided to abandon the FUNDESOL idea, while the link with private pension funds gained importance. At first, a rather complicated model was designed: private pension funds would administer the state-owned shares and credit dividends to deferred share distribution accounts that would be opened for all adults, while all individual shares, plus capitalised dividends, were to be converted into retirement benefits when the beneficiary reached age 60 (World Bank 1995b; Mercado Lora 1998). However, pension fund administrators managing IFF accounts – the institutional channel for the transfer of resources – had yet to be created.

For a start, the government placed reform preparations in a new institutional context. The Ministry of Health was deprived of its responsibility for old-age security, and a National Pensions Office (SNP) was entrusted with both the administration of the old system and the leadership over the pension reform project. The SNP was attached to the new Ministry of Capitalisation and was financially supported by the World Bank. The new reform team started working on the draft law for pension privatisation, while drawing on the work done under the previous government. In 1994, the Capitalisation Law prescribed the obligation to create subsequent legislation for pension funds based on individual capitalisation (Ley No. 1 544). The link between capitalisation and structural pension reform was now firmly established.

A few months later, the SNP started a PR campaign to improve the acceptance of pension privatisation. While the reform was supported by the business community and the financial sector, pensioners' associations and the COB remained staunchly opposed to neoliberal economic policy in general and pension privatisation in particular. It should be noted that most of the blacklisted FONCOMs were managed by trade unionists, who would have no stakes in the Bolivian IFF system. Opponents voiced their protest to the demise of solidarity in public debates, protest marches and a 24-hour general strike.[25] By the mid-1990s, these groups had lost much clout, but the start of the controversial capitalisation programme had already put them on high alert. Their opposition was strong enough to delay the government's decision to send the pension reform laws to Congress (Morales 1995; Gamarra 1997).

However, Sánchez de Lozada was keen to complete the capitalisation programme during his administration, of which private pension funds formed an integral part. It should also be noted that one tranche of the World Bank's 'Capitalization Program Adjustment Credit' had been made conditional on the passing of structural pension reform. By 1996 it was clear that pension privatisation would have to be legislated and implemented in the run-up to general elections, and it was in this context that the government decided to redesign the link between capitalisation and pension reform. Up to now, the reform had been mainly framed in macroeconomic terms that failed to appeal to a sceptical public.[26] Contrary to this, the innovative *Bonosol* approach that was designed thereafter implied tangible, immediate benefits, once the AFPs were established. The *Bonosol* was designed to justify capitalisation and to complicate opposition to pension reform.[27] The new approach was chosen 'first, due to its simplicity; second, because a largely ignored part of the population would benefit; and third, due to the positive public image that this measure would create' (Mercado Lora 1998: 156). In mid-1996, the pension reform law was eventually sent to parliament. After a brief effort at broader consensus-building failed, the government decided to use its ample majority to pass the law in November 1996 (Gray-Molina, Pérez de Rada and Yañez 1999). It should be noted that one of the coalition partners – the small, left-wing MBL – voted against pension privatisation, in spite of the coalition pact it had signed with the MNR–MRTK in 1993. The pensioners' federation lodged a complaint at the Constitutional Court, which was rejected in 1999.

The new pension system

The Bolivian pension reform, which came into force in May 1997, is closely modelled on the Chilean prototype, while also showing important differences (Gersdorff 1997). Initially, a gradual transition to an IFF scheme had been envisaged, combined with a reform of the existing pension scheme (World

Bank 1995b). However, the final version of the law stipulated that all active insured, regardless of their age, would be moved to the private system, while FOPEBA and the FONCOMs were to be closed down immediately.[28] The current pension payments to 127 000 retirees were taken over by the Ministry of Finance. Those insured who already met the criteria for retirement under the pre-reform system, but were still active could also retire under the old system, or choose the new one. In the newly established IFF tier, the insured pay 13 per cent of their wages to one of two existing pension fund admini-strators, or AFPs, including commission and insurance premia, while also receiving a one-off wage increase to account for the discontinuation of the employers' contributions. The retirement age was raised to 65 for both men and women, implying a one-shot increase by 10 and 15 years, respectively.[29]

There is no minimum pension and no minimum rate of return guarantee.[30] Thus retirement benefits in the IFF tier will fully reflect the entire labour biography, the ups and downs of the capital market – and gender, as Bolivian legislation does not stipulate a unisex formula for benefit calculation. Those insured who were moved from the old system to the new one were promised a so-called 'compensation of contributions' (CC), a state-financed compensa-tory pension that will be added to the retirement benefit paid by the AFP. On closer examination, the formula chosen for the CC does not allow for a full recognition of acquired pension entitlements. Driven by a fiscal logic, accrual rates were reduced by as much as 40 per cent, and there is a ceiling of 20 minimum wages. Nevertheless, transition costs are high – with 4.4 per cent of GDP for 2000 alone (IMF 2001a) – and much above the pre-reform budgetary transfers to FOPEBA and the FONCOMs (Larrazábal Antezana and De La Barra Muñoz 1997).[31] They are financed with treasury bonds, of which the AFPs are contractually obliged to hold up to US$180 million annu-ally. In 2001, over 70 per cent of their portfolio was used to finance the obli-gations stemming from the old pension system (FIAP 2001).

Initially, only two AFPs were permitted in the new Bolivian IFF tier. The insured were not given a choice between fund managers, but allocated ac-cording to their domicile and date of birth. Pension reformers opted for this *sui generis* procedure in the light of the small market size (Bonadona Cossio 1998). FOPEBA had only 340 000 contributors, many of which low-wage earners. To allow for a minimum of competition, the two AFP licences were granted in a complex international bidding process (Guérard and Kelly 1997). In 1999, however, the protected duopoly turned into a *de facto* monopoly when the majority shareholders of both AFPs – the Spanish banks BBV and Argentaria – merged, forming BBVA. In April 2001, following lengthy inter-ventions by the superintendency, one of BBVA's Bolivian pension funds was sold to a competitor under an anti-monopoly ruling (Withers-Green 2001). Soon, the Bolivian market is scheduled to be opened to further competition.

As of June 2001, with 655 000 affiliates, the AFPs had managed to attract twice as many insured as FOPEBA used to have, but the number is still dwarfed by an economically active population of over 3 million (FIAP 2001; INE 2002).

As noted above, another distinctive feature of the Bolivian reform is the link between pension reform and enterprise capitalisation. The private pension funds thus administer two funds each – the individual and the collective capitalisation fund, referred to as FCI and FCC.[32] This unique reform design was meant to make the small Bolivian market attractive for international investors. To create domestic stakeholders in both enterprise capitalisation and pension privatisation (Graham 1998), the dividends generated by the FCC were distributed via the *Bonosol* – an annual payment of US$248 to all Bolivians above age 65. Future payments were to be limited to those who had attained majority on 31 December 1995. The concept needs to be understood in the context of Bolivia's high poverty, with only 1 per cent of the elderly in rural areas above the poverty line (Bauer and Bowen 1997; UDAPE 2000). The minute *Bonosol* amounted to 42 per cent of the annual minimum wage, or 27 per cent of Bolivia's per capita income (Ballivian 1997). When reformers were criticised for privileging the elderly instead of investing the dividends in Bolivia's children, they argued: 'through their efforts, the aged enabled the creation and consolidation of the capitalised state firms and that this was the reason why this benefit belonged to them' (Mercado Lora 1998: 160). The *Bonosol* was also censured for a lack of targeting, especially because the wealthy are thought to have a higher life expectancy than the poor (Ballivián 1997). Yet, it is by no means evident that efforts at explicit means testing are worth while in a context of both widespread poverty and weak administrative capacity (Larrazábal Antezana and De La Barra Muñoz 1997).

Bonosol payments started in May 1997, shortly before general elections. The programme met with an overwhelming response from the aged all over the country. Payable by the AFPs upon presentation of the identity card, the *Bonosol* conveyed substantive citizenship rights and convinced many elderly to apply for papers for the first time in their lives (Whitehead 1997). As 364 000 instead of the expected 295 000 beneficiaries presented themselves, the dividends proved insufficient to cover all *Bonosol* payments, with the AFPs resorting to loans to meet their obligations. The incoming administration of Hugo Banzer (1997–2001) stopped the *Bonosol* in January 1998, censuring it as an unsustainable manœuvre of his predecessor. Six months later, the *Bonosol* was replaced with a less generous scheme called *Bolivida*, which only started to pay out benefits in December 2000. Under the *Bolivida* scheme an annual pension of only US$60 was paid to those aged 65 and above. It was limited to those who were over 50 years old at the end of 1995. Drawing on the original concept of his political opponent, Banzer promised to distribute a large part of the FCC in the form of 'popular shares' to Bolivians between ages 21 and 50, but this programme proved to be hard to conceptualise in the given institutional framework.[33] When Sánchez de Lozada returned to power in 2002, the first major legislative initiative of his coalition government was the 'Law to Reinstate the *Bonosol*', which came into effect in December 2002 (Withers-Green 2003).[34]

Conclusion

In the 1980s, severely indebted Bolivia was perceived as one of the frontrunners in structural adjustment (Morales 1995; World Bank 2001c). However, the drastic stabilisation programme was followed by a slackening pace of change when many other countries in the region already embarked on second-generation reforms. The IFIs expressed their concern, noting that 'implementation of Washington Consensus reforms was incomplete' (World Bank 2000b: 14). It was in this context that Sánchez de Lozada launched the *Plan de Todos*, a reform programme that came to include structural pension reform, an integral part of the Washington Consensus package by 1994. After 'a decade-long policy dialogue to reduce the public sector's presence' in Bolivia (World Bank 2000b: 4), World Bank and IDB were ready to provide financial and technical support for the entire package of second-generation structural reforms, even though they disagreed with several aspects of the innovative Bolivian approach to privatisation and pension reform (Graham 1998).[35] The first pension reformers could also draw on crucial start-up financing from USAID, advice from Chilean experts and support from the local insurance sector.

Pension privatisation followed the standard pattern of policymaking in today's Bolivia, which boils down to a mandatist approach with few instances for dialogue with key affected sectors and other opponents (Gamarra 1997).[36] As noted above, ample leeway granted to the executive will not automatically lead to a smooth enactment of radical reforms, rendering political leadership crucial. Given the 'almost messianic modernising zeal' of Sánchez de Lozada and his inner circle (Bauer and Bowen 1997: 3), it is more than an irony of history that the MNR, after having led the 1952 Revolution, ended up launching its demise. Other observers have pointed to the mixture of *caudillismo* and technocracy in Sánchez de Lozada's government (Gray-Molina, Pérez de Rada and Yañez 1999). Educated in the US, technocrats maintained direct communication with the IFIs and, thus, the new pension orthodoxy. They embarked on a macroeconomic approach to pension reform, while social aspects were treated as subordinate (Cajías 1997; Pérez B. 2000). It is interesting to note that under two successive Bolivian governments, pension reform teams were set up in the Ministries of Finance and

Capitalisation, respectively, to circumvent the Bismarckian-minded Health
and Labour Ministries. At the same time, the fiscal impact of the existing
social security institutions was relatively small and, in itself, would not have
justified the closure of FOPEBA and the FONCOMs. Although contextual
factors did not point to a 'benefit of crisis', the imminent bankruptcy of the
public pension scheme featured prominently at a rhetorical level (Gamarra
1997).

The political feasibility of radical pension reform shortly before general
elections was improved by its design and packaging. The Bolivian reformers
and their foreign advisors claimed to replace 'a multi-tiered, costly system of
many retirement programs for different groups of workers with a simple,
single system covering all workers' (Guérard and Kelly 1997: 312). The
reformers also handed out financial compensation to those directly affected
by the reform, although the recognition of acquired rights by means of the
CCs is not complete. Moreover, they resorted to strategic bundling and
indirect compensation: both conceptually and institutionally, pension reform
was linked with enterprise capitalisation, thus facilitating both policy agendas.
The *Bonosol–Bolivida* scheme aimed at creating new stakeholders, most of
which had never received a pension before. Proving vulnerable to politics
from the outset, the long-term survival of this innovative programme is far
from certain. It is important to note that its funding is crucially linked to the
future of the capitalised enterprises, thereby illustrating both the merits and
constraints inherent in Sánchez de Lozada's bundling strategy. Nevertheless,
as pointed out by Whitehead (1997: 89), the *Bonosol–Bolivida* scheme stands
out as an 'unusually ambitious attempt to provide egalitarian welfare benefits
in a very poor country'.

NOTES

1. A detailed account of the political economy of pension privatisation in Peru can be found in
    Ortíz de Zevallos et al. (1999) and Arce (2001). The political feasibility of the reform is also
    discussed in Graham (1998), Graham et al. (1999), Mesa-Lago (1999) and Mesa-Lago and
    Müller (2002). One of the early pension reform actors, Mario Roggero, published his
    version of the events in a book (Roggero Villena 1993).
2. 'The argument of the IPSS' financial crisis that has been used to privatise pensions is thus
    surprising' (Verdera V. 1996: 334).
3. For an *ex post* justification of the self-coup see Fujimori (1995). Critical accounts of the
    coup and its effects can be found in Cotler (2001), Rospigliosi (2001) and Stokes (1996).
4. See also Bernedo Alvarado (1993), Delgado and Ospina (1992), Francke (1993), Neves
    Mujica (1993) and Robles (1993).
5. A detailed comparison of the decree of November 1991, the draft law of July 1992 and the
    decree of December 1992 is provided by Annex IV in Boloña Behr (1995).
6. For a critical evaluation of the performance of the new IFF tier in Peru see Asesoramiento y
    Análisis Laboral (1997), Kiefer (1998) and Cruz Saco and Ivachina Borovinskaya (1999).

7. In the private tier, individual contribution rate, commission, life insurance premium and a 1 per cent 'IPSS solidarity tax' initially added up to 15 per cent of wages, compared with 3 per cent in the public tier, where the employer paid another 6 per cent (Cruz-Saco 1998).
8. D.L. 20 530 covers selected groups of civil servants, who enjoy a more generous indexation and eligibility based on years of service only. Several attempts to close this pension scheme have been unsuccessful (World Bank 1994c).
9. It should be noted that the active–passive ratio in both schemes was worsened significantly by the post-1990 reforms (World Bank 1994c).
10. Peruvian recognition bonds earn no real interest, there is a nominal upper limit of about US$46 000 and eligibility was limited to those who had contributed to the public retirement scheme for a minimum of four years in the past decade, including the preceding six months.
11. This minimum pension was scheduled as early as 1995, but no agreement could be reached on its financing. Law 27 617 stipulates that the state will cover the difference if the individual account balance – including the recognition bond – proves insufficient to pay the minimum pension.
12. Compared with the already existing possibility to retire whenever the account balance allows for a pension of at least half of the last average earnings, the early retirement window created by Law 27 617 only requires an account balance sufficient to cover 30 per cent of the individual's earnings level over the past 60 months or, alternatively, two minimum wages.
13. Shortly after having strongly promoted the private pension fund sector as a Finance Minister, Boloña reappeared as shareholder of one AFP, creating much controversy (AFP Horizonte 1998). Though the most prominent, this does not seem to be the only case of 'collusive "revolving-door" relationships between executive and corporate posts' in the Peruvian pension privatisation process (Arce 2001: 102).
14. It is important to note that from 1924 a mandatory old-age savings plan for workers was in place that lost all reserves in a 4 000 per cent devaluation 32 years later (Müller&Asociados 1997; Albin 1999).
15. The average life expectancy at birth was only age 60 in 1994 (World Bank 1996b), thereby reflecting the high infant mortality rate. On the other hand, the remaining life expectancy of those living until age 65 was still 13 years on average (Graham 1998).
16. Officially it was still a scaled premium system (IBSS 1991; SNP and INASEP 1996).
17. The most drastic case was that of the mining company *Comibol*, where 21 000 of the 27 000 workers were dismissed in only one year (Morales and Pacheco 1999).
18. Larrazábal Antezana and De La Barra Muñoz (1997: 36) have described this as 'artificial maturity'.
19. '[F]or most of the life of the system ... the State did not pay its share of contributions, although it compensated this by making regular Treasury transfers to FOPEBA' (Ballivián 1997: 5).
20. For detailed accounts of the political economy of pension privatisation in Bolivia see Gray-Molina, Pérez de Rada and Yañez (1999) and Pérez B. (2000). The political feasibility of the reform is also discussed in Graham (1998), Graham et al. (1999), Mesa-Lago (1999), Müller (2001c) and Mesa-Lago and Müller (2002).
21. The privatisation of state-owned enterprises started during the government of Jaime Paz Zamora, but was limited to a few small firms (Morales and Pacheco 1999).
22. For parallels and differences between Bolivian capitalisation and the simultaneous East European privatisations see Brada (1997).
23. While private investors now hold 50 per cent of the capitalised enterprises, the original plan read: 'we Bolivians will hold the majority – not less than 51 per cent' (Sánchez de Lozada 1993: 3). The state now holds an average of 45.8 per cent of the capital, as employees were given the chance to buy 4.2 per cent of shares at book value (SPVS 2000). See also Bauer and Bowen (1997) and Gamarra (1997).
24. The full version of *Plan de Todos* addresses the issue of pension reform, yet proposing a parametric reform of FOPEBA and the introduction of the IFF principle to the existing complementary tier (Sánchez de Lozada and Cárdenas 1993: 80–1).

25. See Vargas del Carpio (1996) for a compilation of protest notes and newspaper articles. See also CNJRB (1995, 1996), COB (1995, 1996), Eróstegui T. (1997) and Olivares (1996a, b).
26. See e.g. Mercado Lora (1998: 180): 'pension reform will enable Bolivia to generate her own savings and, thus, allow us to be the real authors and protagonists of our own development, without having to draw permanently on grants or concessional loans from the rest of the world'.
27. The pensioners' federation found itself in an uncomfortable position: 'we argue ... that the pension reform law is unconstitutional and should be revoked – yet this law also establishes the *Bonosol*, hence we get tied up in contradictions because we defend the *Bonosol*' (CNJRB 1998: 50).
28. Available explanations for this radical choice suggest that (1) reformers had come to think that the market was so small that an IFF scheme would only be viable if made mandatory for all insured; and (2) Sánchez de Lozada expected so much resistance against parametric reforms that he thought going all the way towards pension privatisation would not make much difference in terms of political costs.
29. Workers can retire early whenever their individual fund balance allows for a monthly pension amounting to 70 per cent of the last average wage.
30. The *Bonosol* has been interpreted as an 'effective minimum pension' (Graham 1998: 159). However, its (annual) value soon dropped to a mere US$60.
31. The reformers' long-term projections suggested a lower present value for the reform costs than for the maintenance of the old system (Mercado Lora 1998). Based on their own calculations, Larrazábal Antezana and De La Barra Muñoz (1997: 70) criticised the huge fiscal impact of the reform, while also pointing out that 'the radical transition has transferred a future fiscal problem to the present'.
32. As of June 2001, the FCI – comprising all individual accounts – had accumulated US$908 million (FIAP 2001). The FCC, made up of roughly half the shares of the capitalised enterprises, was valued at US$2.6 billion at the end of 1997 (SPVS 2000).
33. One obstacle in this distributional exercise is that both the numerator and the denominator are essentially unknown: both the market value of the unlisted shares of the capitalised firms, and the size and age distribution of the Bolivian population cannot be determined with precision.
34. By now it is clear that the costs involved with the *Bonosol* scheme will exceed FCC dividends by far. Thus, the government has required the AFPs to start liquidating the shares by purchasing them as part of their FCI portfolio, meeting with fierce resistance from both AFPs (Withers-Green 2003).
35. In particular, the IFIs strongly suggested using the proceeds from capitalisation to finance the fiscal costs of pension privatisation instead of distributing them among Bolivians (Ballivián 1997).
36. The president of Bolivia's Central Bank describes the customary policy style as follows: 'In most cases the executive agrees with the IFIs to a set of reforms, without any previous consultation with Congress. Afterward, Congress is pressured to hastily approve the reforms. Dissident voices are silenced with the use of majority and strong party discipline' (Morales 1995: 26).

PART III

Privatising Old-Age Security in Eastern Europe

7.   Regional background: old-age security in the transition countries

Bismarckian-style pension insurance was established at the end of the 19th century in Central Europe, when the region was governed by the Habsburg monarchy. These early schemes were fragmented and did not protect the rural population. During the socialist era, pension provision in Eastern Europe and the Soviet Union followed similar lines. Pension schemes were unified and integrated into the state budget. Their surpluses were used to cross-subsidise other public expenditure items. Individual contributions were mostly abolished, rendering employers' contributions the only source of financing. A major achievement of the socialist years was the gradual expansion of coverage, rendering it universal by the 1960s or 1970s. Overall, the existing contribution-benefit link was weak. Pensions tended to depend on years of service rather than on contributions made on behalf of the individual. Although there was little benefit differentiation, branch privileges (a lower retirement age and higher pensions) were granted to occupations of strategic importance, marking an important departure from universalism. The insufficient adjustment of current pensions to price–wage dynamics implied that newly granted pensions were considerably higher than average retirement benefits, giving rise to problems of inter-cohort fairness and benefit adequacy (Götting 1998).

Economic transformation, starting around 1989, affected the existing PAYG systems in several ways. At the onset of market-oriented reforms, price liberalisation and the curtailment of subsidies on basic goods and services required a shift from indirect to direct transfers, resulting in rising expenditure for old-age security. Subsequently, the restructuring of the state-owned enterprises had an effect on both the revenue and the expenditure side of public pension schemes. When state-owned enterprises were privatised, downsized or closed down, part of their former workforce retired early or took out disability pensions. Designed to disguise the employment effects of structural adjustment, this policy implied that the retirement system was used as a substitute for welfare and unemployment benefits. By leading to an increased number of pensioners and a falling number of contributors to the scheme, public pension finances were destabilised.

Table 7.1   Post-socialist countries: some relevant pension indicators[a]

	System dependency rate[b]	Old-age dependency rate[c]	Pensioners (in % of population)	Coverage rate[d]	Replacement rate[e]	Pension spending (in % of GDP)
Albania	95.3	18.5	14.8	32.0	34.7	5.1
Armenia	38.0	21.7	16.2	66.6	24.0	3.1
Azerbaijan	66.0	18.5	16.4	52.0	29.0	2.5
Belarus	47.0	33.3	23.5	97.0	44.1	7.7
Bulgaria	81.0	38.5	27.5	64.0	30.0	7.3
Croatia	61.7	37.6	19.0	66.0	46.1	11.6
Czech Rep.	53.0	31.3	24.2	85.0	41.5	9.8
Estonia	60.0	33.3	25.0	76.0	31.6	7.0
Georgia	66.0	31.3	21.1	41.7	36.0	2.7
Hungary	78.1	35.7	27.5	77.0	39.1	9.7
Kazakhstan	66.0	18.9	16.0	51.0	31.0	5.0
Kyrgyzstan	64.0	18.9	11.7	44.0	45.0	6.4
Latvia	65.9	34.5	25.0	60.5	62.8	10.2
Lithuania	69.2	32.3	22.5	74.3	30.8	7.3
Macedonia	50.0	22.7	12.4	49.0	63.5	8.7
Moldova	n.a.	25.6	17.4	34.5	31.6	7.5
Poland	53.7	29.4	18.2	68.0	63.5	14.4
Romania	58.3	32.3	15.1	55.0	23.9	5.1
Russia	n.a.	30.3	25.1	n.a.	38.0	5.7
Slovakia	57.0	27.8	22.0	73.0	41.0	9.1
Slovenia	58.9	31.3	22.2	86.0	68.7	13.6
Tajikistan	n.a.	n.a.	n.a.	n.a.	27.0	3.0
Turkmenistan	n.a.	n.a.	n.a.	n.a.	26.0	2.3
Ukraine	78.0	34.5	27.1	69.8	32.0	8.6
Uzbekistan	n.a.	14.9	11.4	n.a.	42.0	5.3

Notes: [a] Data are mostly for the mid-1990s.
[b] Pensioners in % of contributors.
[c] 60+ years old in % of 20–59 years old.
[d] Contributors in % of labour force.
[e] Average pension in % of average wage.

Sources: World Bank (2000a, 2001b); Gillion et al. (2000); ILO (2000).

By the mid-1990s, system dependency ratios had deteriorated dramatically (see Table 7.1). In all post-socialist countries but Armenia, Belarus and Macedonia, there were less than two contributors per pensioner. In Albania, Bulgaria, Hungary and Ukraine system dependency rates had even risen to 95, 81 and 78 per cent, respectively. The declining revenue base and the erosion of social security are further illustrated by a dramatic drop in coverage ratios. Before 1989, with full employment and high economic activity rates of women, coverage bordered 100 per cent of the labour force. By the mid-1990s, it had plunged to 32 and 34.5 per cent in Albania and Moldova. In Georgia, the Kyrgyz Republic and Macedonia coverage rates were 42, 44 and 49 per cent, respectively. If these trends are not reversed, over half of those currently in active age may not be entitled to a retirement benefit in the future.

Life expectancy at birth in the post-socialist countries (68.4 years) has fallen below the Latin American average (69.3 years) in recent years, while the differences are even larger at retirement age.[1] Nevertheless, due to lower fertility rates, population ageing hit the CEE and the FSU more severely than Latin America (Müller 2000a). Central Asia, the Caucasus and Albania have a younger population, but demographic dependency rates in other post-socialist countries are close to EU levels. Table 7.1 indicates that there are about three persons aged 20 to 59 for everyone aged 60 and above. The ratio of pensioners to the total population is much higher than in Latin America (see Table 4.2), reflecting demography, but also the historically high coverage levels in the socialist countries. While there were 11 pensioners per 100 Uzbeks, the ratio was almost three times as high in Bulgaria, a country severely affected by the outmigration of the young.

Whereas public pension spending was on the rise in the region, only Poland and Slovenia surpassed the EU-15 average, with pension expenditure amounting to 14.4 and 13.6 per cent of GDP (Müller 2002c).[2] The lowest levels can be observed in Turkmenistan, Azerbaijan, Georgia, Tajikistan and Armenia, where replacement rates are minute. With the exception of Slovenia, Poland, Macedonia and Latvia, the entire region suffers from low benefit levels. Notably in some FSU countries, old-age benefits have fallen below subsistence (Braithwaite, Grootaert and Milanovic 2000).

Undoubtedly, the old-age security systems inherited from the socialist past were in dire need of reform. Parametric changes to the existing retirement schemes were relatively undisputed among social security experts and included the separation of pension schemes from other social insurance plans and from the state budget, the introduction of an employees' contribution, the raising of the retirement age, the abolition of branch privileges, the restriction of early retirement, the tightening of eligibility for invalidity pensions and the introduction of indexation rules to provide protection against inflation.[3]

Table 7.2 A comparison of post-socialist pension privatisations

	Kazakhstan	Hungary	Poland	Latvia	Bulgaria	Croatia	Estonia
Type of public mandatory tier	Closed down	Traditional PAYG; private tier complementary	NDC scheme; private tier complementary	NDC scheme; private tier complementary	PAYG scheme with pension points; private tier complementary	PAYG scheme, partly with pension points; private tier complementary	Traditional PAYG; private tier complementary
Mandatory membership in private IFF tier	Mandatory for all workers	Mandatory for new entrants to labour market; optional for others to redirect part of their contribution to private tier	Mandatory for those below age 30; optional for those aged 30–49 to redirect part of their contribution to private tier	Mandatory for those below age 30; optional for those aged 30–49 to redirect part of their contribution to private tier	Mandatory for those below age 42 to redirect part of their contribution to private tier	Mandatory for those below age 40; optional for those aged 40–49 to redirect part of their contribution to private tier	Mandatory for those below age 18; optional for others to redirect part of their contribution to private tier

Contribu-tion rates to IFF tier	Individual rate: 10%	Individual rate: 6%	Individual rate: 9%	Individual rate to be gradually increased to 10%	Contribution rate to be gradually increased to 5% and to be paid 50:50 by employees and employers	Individual rate: 2.5%; employer's rate: 2.5%	Individual rate: 2%; employer's rate: 4%
Reform type	Substitutive	Mixed	Mixed	Mixed	Mixed	Mixed	Mixed
Starting date	1998	1998	1999	2001	2002	2002	2002

Note: Although the IFF tier is dominated by private pension administrators, some countries also admit publicly run pension funds.

Source: Based on Müller (2002c); modified.

Several post-socialist countries opted for another potentially costly move when linking benefits closer to lifetime earnings to improve contribution incentives, e.g. by introducing German-style pension points or notional defined contribution (NDC) plans. The point system used in Germany implies a close contribution-benefit link. One earnings point is acquired for each calendar year in which individual earnings are equal to the national average. Benefit calculation is essentially based on the sum of all earnings points, thus reflecting the entire labour biography.[4] NDC schemes are also based on the entire contributions' record of the insured, while also integrating an IFF logic into the public tier. All contribution payments to the public pension insurance are recorded on individual accounts, yet capital accumulation is only virtual. Individual benefit levels essentially depend on the sum of individual contributions, while also reflecting the remaining life expectancy at retirement and the chosen retirement age. The NDC concept was developed by Swedish experts, but pioneered by Latvia in 1996 (Cichon 1999; Disney 1999).[5]

It should be noted that fierce resistance to parametric reforms, which were even blocked by constitutional courts in more than one case, often induced policymakers to compromise on the speed and scope of the required reform steps. In comparison, the first move towards a different public–private mix was much less controversial: most Central European countries, Russia, Moldova and the Baltics introduced supplementary private IFF schemes on a voluntary basis. Yet, the amount of voluntary funds collected fell short of expectations, largely reflecting income constraints. In the context of a generalised retreat of the state, a number of transition countries opted for a more radical approach, thereby stirring substantial controversy. Over the past few years, pension privatisation has been gaining considerable momentum in the post-socialist region (Rutkowski 2001; Müller 2002c). Kazakhstan is the only case of a substitutive reform so far, while being explicitly modelled on the Chilean precedent (Andrews 2001). A mixed approach was chosen by six other transition countries, among them five EU Accession Countries. Hungary, Poland, Latvia, Bulgaria, Croatia and Estonia have implemented partial pension privatisation between 1998 and 2002. Lithuania and Macedonia have recently legislated similar reforms, and several other post-socialist countries are currently preparing a partial shift to funding as well.

It is notable that the transition countries exhibit far more diversity in terms of first-tier design than the Latin American cases, where pension points and NDC schemes are virtually absent (cf. Chapter 4, Table 4.2 and Chapter 7, Table 7.2). Nevertheless, the strong inspiration from the subcontinent in terms of the underlying reform blueprint is obvious. How could Latin American-style pension reforms spread to the post-socialist region and become politically feasible there? The following four case studies, covering Hungary,

Poland, Croatia and Bulgaria, intend to shed light on this puzzle – the political economy of pension privatisation in Central and Eastern Europe.

NOTES

1. In 1985–95, remaining life expectancy at the age of 60 was 15.4 and 19.6 years for men and women in the post-socialist countries, while it was 17.9 and 20.6 years for men and women in Latin America, respectively (Gillion et al. 2000: 642–5).
2. The EU-15 average calculated by Eurostat was 12.6 per cent of GDP in 1998 (Amerini 2001).
3. For an overview on pension reforms in the transition countries see Castello Branco (1998), Palacios, Rutkowski and Yu (1999), Schwarz and Demirguc-Kunt (1999), Fultz and Ruck (2000), Lindeman, Rutkowski and Sluchynskyy (2000), Müller (2002c) and Schmähl and Horstmann (2002).
4. For a complete presentation and analysis of the German pension formula see Schmähl (1999). See also Mesa-Lago and Hohnerlein (2003) for more recent developments.
5. For more details and an example of an NDC pension formula see the Polish case in Chapter 8.

8. Pension privatisation in East-Central Europe

8.1 THE CASE OF HUNGARY[1]

Legacy and policy context

In Hungary, the first pension scheme for civil servants was introduced in 1912, while mandatory old-age provision for blue- and white-collar workers was introduced only in 1929, largely following the Bismarckian model (Ferge 1991; Czibere 1998). However, coverage amounted to a mere 31 per cent of the economically active population in the 1930s, as the pension system mainly targeted urban labour, while excluding the rural workforce. Hungary's early pension system operated on a collectively fully funded basis, but collapsed in 1944–46. Its property was largely destroyed during World War II and its aftermath.

The 1949 pension reform, passed by the incoming communist regime, involved a shift to PAYG financing (Augusztinovics 1993; Bod 1995b). The three separate schemes for workers, employees and civil servants were unified, contributions were charged exclusively from employers, and the pension scheme was integrated into the central budget. Moreover, the self-governing bodies, which had administered social insurance since its inception, were abolished. Employees' contributions were reintroduced in the mid-1950s. In 1961, the pension scheme was extended to members of agricultural cooperatives, thus increasing coverage to 82 per cent by 1970. The expansion of the Hungarian pension system was completed by Law No. II of 1975.

After 1978 the general deterioration of economic conditions in Hungary induced *ad hoc* adjustment of pensions, leading to a severe distortion of relative benefit levels. Only minimum pensions were fully adjusted to inflation, but these benefits barely sufficed to cover the subsistence level (Simonovits 1997). However, all efforts to erode benefits in real terms fell short of offsetting the maturation of the Hungarian old-age scheme, reflected in high coverage, rising system dependency ratios and soaring public pension expenditure. During the 1980s, there was a growing consensus that pension reform was inevitable: the existing pension system was thought to be 'obsolete, parsimonious, incomplete and unsustainable at the same time, full of iniquities and inconsistencies' (Ferge 1997: 2). Around one-fifth of retirees supplemented their pension by resorting to paid work (Maltby 1994; Széman 1995).

The urgency of reform was only reinforced when economic transformation aggravated the financial strain on the existing retirement scheme. Between 1989 and 1996, the number of employed Hungarians fell by 25 per cent, the number of pensioners rose by 22 per cent, and the system dependency ratio increased from 51 to 84 per cent (Müller 1999). Demographic trends did not add to the financial imbalances of the Hungarian pension system in the 1990s – the old-age dependency ratio even declined over the course of the decade (Augusztinovics et al. 2002). Early reforms introduced some changes to the organisation, financing and eligibility of the existing retirement scheme. Pension finances were separated from the state budget and from the health fund. Social insurance was granted autonomy, and self-government was reinstored. Reformers experienced resistance from trade unions and the general public when trying to increase the retirement age that had remained constant at age 60 for men and age 55 for women over several decades.[2] They succeeded in 1996, when a gradual increase to age 62 was stipulated both for men (until 2000) and for women (until 2009). The vesting period for a regular old-age pension was raised from 10 to 20 qualifying years.

Benefit calculation was still intricate, highly redistributive and only loosely linked to previous earnings, and several fiscally induced changes in the valorisation of past earnings and in the indexation of current pensions lowered retirement benefits, while only adding to the distortion of relative benefit levels (Bagdy 1995; Simonovits 1999; Augusztinovics et al. 2002). In 1997, the average monthly pension amounted to US$107 (Marsh 1997). With employment opportunities for pensioners turning increasingly unavailable, 35.7 per cent of all pensioners lived below the poverty line.[3] Although pension expenditures had started to decline in 1994, the Hungarian old-age scheme remained dependent on subsidies from the government budget (see Table 8.1). As a result, there was a permanent 'conflict between the need for fiscal restraint and pressures to improve or at least maintain current benefits' (CCET 1995: 99).

The early pension reforms in Hungary also included the creation of new old-age institutions. In 1994, voluntary private pension funds were introduced – the first move towards a diversification of Hungarian old-age provision. These financial institutions were set up as voluntary mutual benefit (VMB) funds, non-profit organisations owned by fund members themselves. The *sui generis* corporate design of the Hungarian pension funds was instrumental in making these new institutions politically palatable, as it enabled reference to 'solidarity' as one of the basic principles, alongside 'self-provision' (Ministry of Finance 1994: 9). About two-thirds of total contributions are paid by employers, and tax incentives are considerable. In 1999, there were 1 million Hungarians, or 25 per cent of the labour force, who had joined one of the voluntary funds. Initially, 270 funds were competing for customers, but their number had decreased to fewer than 110 in early 2002 (Vittas 1996; Rocha and Vittas 2001; Matits 2002).

Table 8.1 The reform context in Hungary: selected indicators

Indicators	1993	1994	1995	1996	1997
GDP change (in %)	−0.6	2.9	1.5	1.3	4.6
Consumer prices (annual average, in %)	22.5	18.8	28.2	23.6	18.3
General gov't balance (in % of GDP)	−6.6	−8.4	−6.7	−5.0	−6.6
Total external debt (in % of GDP)	63.7	68.7	70.9	61.9	53.3
Hungarian Pension Fund					
– revenues (in % of GDP)	9.2	8.8	9.0	8.2	n.a.
– expenditures (in % of GDP)	9.4	9.4	9.3	8.6	n.a.
– balance (in % of GDP)	−0.2	−0.6	−0.3	−0.4	n.a.
Public pension expenditure (in % of GDP)	11.1	11.5	10.6	9.9	n.a.

Note: Only the five years up to reform adoption are considered.

Sources: EBRD (2001); Schrooten, Smeeding and Wagner (1999).

Twenty years after the post-1968 reforms had made Hungary the spearhead of reform communism, the country's transition to democracy was negotiated in 1989. The free parliamentary elections of 1990 produced a centre-right coalition government (1990–94), led by József Antall who chose a gradual approach to economic reforms. The 1994 elections led to a victory of the post-communists, who opted for a coalition with the Free Democrats. The socialist–liberal coalition led by Gyula Horn (1994–98) controlled 72 per cent of seats in Congress. By that time, the country faced large fiscal and current account deficits, while foreign debt was on the rise (see Table 8.1). When the country suffered a sharp loss in credit standing (World Bank 1999a), there were fears that the crisis that had hit Mexico in December 1994 could spread to Hungary. In March 1995, Finance Minister Lajos Bokros reacted to this scenario by launching a drastic adjustment package (Kornai 1997). The Bokros package clashed with the post-communists' rhetoric. It proved to be extremely controversial, triggering a series of strikes, while a number of measures were stopped by the courts. After Bokros' resignation in February 1996, the new Finance Minister, Péter Medgyessy, opted for a less confrontative style. Yet, he essentially held the line, accelerating the structural reforms that had been initiated earlier – including radical pension reform (Bokros and Déthier 1998).

The way towards pension privatisation[4]

The first comprehensive pension reform proposal in post-communist Hungary dates back to 1991, when a three-tier approach was endorsed by Congress. It comprised a universal, flat-rate first tier, an earnings-related, PAYG financed second tier, and a voluntary, privately run IFF scheme as a third tier. Only the third-tier funds were turned into practical policy, however (Czúcz 1993; Augusztinovics and Martos 1996). In December 1994 the Committee for Treasury Reform, directed by the Finance Minister, reopened the quest for fundamental pension reform. The preparation of a reform proposal was delegated to the Subcommittee on Social Welfare, suggesting a thorough parametric reform of the existing public scheme in June 1995. Only a few weeks later, the Committee for Treasury Reform surprisingly presented a fundamentally different reform plan to the Hungarian government that boiled down to a privatisation of Hungarian old-age security (Ferge 1999; Czúcz and Pintér 2002). A first version of this plan – presented by Finance Minister Bokros – proposed a Chilean-style privatisation of old-age security. However, Hungarians tended to associate the 'Chilean model' with the Pinochet dictatorship, while Latin America also carried the stigma of being a less developed region (Orenstein 2000). Therefore, the Hungarian reformers soon sought to distance themselves from the Chilean precedent, while the portion of public old-age provision to be privatised was lowered to 50 per cent of contributions (Müller 1999).

Clearly, the early consensus among Hungarian pension experts and policymakers about the necessary reforms in old-age security had faded by the mid-1990s (Gál 1996; Simonovits 1997). The Ministry of Welfare and the self-government of the Pension Fund, dominated by trade union representatives, still sought to combine the Bismarckian insurance tradition with Beveridgean universalism. Thus, while the Ministry of Finance's blueprint was presented to the public as the 'single valid solution' (Ferge 1999: 237), there were three counter-proposals, presented by the Subcommittee on Social Welfare, the Pension Fund's self-government and the Welfare Ministry.

Taking up the three-tier model agreed upon in 1991, the proposals aimed at separating the provision of assistance-type benefits from social insurance functions. While the former were to be taken over by the first tier, the latter were to be assumed by an earnings-related second tier, based on a German-style point system. Mandatory private pension funds were thought to shift considerable risks towards future pensioners, whereas voluntary IFF schemes were welcomed. This group considered that 'the problems of the Hungarian Pension Reform can be solved without a forced paradigm shift' (Bod 1995a: 174).

While pension privatisation had been proposed by Finance Minister Bokros, it was Medgyessy, his successor, who carried radical pension reform through. The stalemate between the Ministries of Welfare and Finance on pension reform lasted almost two years, until the conflict was settled in April 1996. The joint reform blueprint that was subsequently presented by both Ministries strongly resembles the Ministry of Finance's earlier proposal (Ministry of Welfare and Ministry of Finance 1996). Yet, the mixed approach can be interpreted as satisfying both of the previously competing factions by a compromise. Moreover, the Ministry of Finance had agreed to lower the portion of public old-age provision to be privatised from 50 to 30 per cent of contributions. The envisaged reform would consist of two simultaneous parts (Ministry of Finance 1997). Changes in the existing public PAYG tier would include a strengthening of the link between contributions and benefits in the pension formula and a tightening of eligibility, e.g. by eliminating credits for non-contributory years and by limiting access to disability pensions. In addition, a mandatory, privately run IFF tier was to be created, designed along the lines of the already existing VMB pension funds.[5]

Soon after the inter-ministerial agreement, a pension reform committee led by István Györfi, a Commissioner to the Minister of Finance, was set up to work out the technical and legal details, thereby bypassing the exclusive competences of the Ministry of Welfare. The reform team was actively sup-ported by the World Bank's resident mission in Budapest. The Bank provided modelling capacity, invited international pension experts and channelled major financial support to the Hungarian reformers, including funds from bilateral donors (Nelson 2001). It was only towards the end of the reform process that the reform team decided to enter into a dialogue with potential opponents, most notably trade unions. These were represented both in the tripartite Interest Reconciliation Council, or ÉT, and in the self-government of the Pension Fund (Palacios and Rocha 1998). The largest Hungarian trade union confederation, MSZOSZ, was an important faction of the governing post-communist party, and parliament had made ÉT's approval of the envisaged pension reform a precondition of its own stance. Hence, the government was keen to obtain ÉT's consent and gave in to some modifications of the draft law, in exchange for a last-minute drop of the trade unions' opposition towards pension privatisation (Orenstein 2000). It is interesting to note that the Hungarian pensioners' associations were not nearly as vocal as their counterparts in other countries, even though the elderly amounted to 40 per cent of all voters. Apparently, the Hungarian government succeeded in calming current pensioners early on, by assuring them that the envisaged reform would not affect them. Moreover, pensioners were indirectly represented by the MSZOSZ, as the trade union federation counts many retirees among its membership (Müller 1999).

Concessions included the reduction in the contribution rate to the private tier from 10 to 8 per cent, thereby lessening the reduction of the PAYG tier to about one-quarter, and the elimination of the cut-off age of 47 for the partial opting-out of the public scheme.[6] Moreover, changes in the indexation rules, in the benefit formula and in the tax regime were postponed until 2013. In May 1997, a package of four pension reform laws was finally submitted to Congress, where the socialist–liberal government coalition could count on an overwhelming majority. In mid-July 1997, after only six weeks of debate, the government met its objective of winning legislative approval for structural pension reform before the 1998 elections, leaving only a few months for preparatory work and an extensive PR campaign announcing that the old pension system was about to 'retire' (for details see Ferge 1999).

The new pension system

Hungary's new pension system, in force since January 1998, is of a mixed type, combining a still dominant public PAYG scheme with a newly created funded tier, offering a choice between a purely public and a mixed pension option.[7] The first tier is PAYG and mandatory for everybody, at least as first tier, and was subject to parametric reforms. These contained a tightening of eligibility criteria, e.g. by reducing the number of non-contributory years in the vesting period; a change of annual pension adjustments from wage indexation to combined wage–price indexation by 2001; and a fundamental restructuring of the pension formula in 2009–13, including the removal of the degressive weighting of earnings and the uniformisation of accrual rates. The second tier consists of competing IFF pension funds, offering individual retirement accounts financed entirely by employees' contributions. The new mandatory pension funds reflect the cooperative-like corporate design of the VMB funds. Two layers of protection were stipulated for second-tier accounts. The first, backed by a minimum reserve in each of the pension funds, grants a relative rate of return guarantee. According to the second, backed by a Guarantee Fund, annuities would not be less than 25 per cent of the value of the individual's first pillar pension after 15 years of participation in the new system. A state guarantee behind the fund-sponsored Guarantee Fund created new contingent liabilities for the state budget (Polackova Brixi, Papp and Schick 1999).

From July 1998, all new entrants to the labour market were obliged to join the two-tiered[8] scheme, alongside the public pension tier (mixed pension path). Individuals who already had an insurance history but were not yet retired could do the same. Alternatively, they could opt to stay in the old scheme (purely public pension path). They had to decide until August 1999 whether or not they wanted to switch to the mixed pension path. Those who did redirected 6 per cent of their gross wage to one of the new private funds; an amount originally scheduled to be increased to 7 per cent in 1999 and to 8 per cent in 2000. The remaining three-quarters of the total contribution would continue to go to the existing PAYG tier. Regardless of the insured's decision for or against joining the private pension pillar, the employer's contribution of 24 per cent (currently 18 per cent) is directed to the public PAYG pillar, while the insured who opted for the mixed pension path would pay 1 per cent of their wage to the public tier (currently 2 per cent). Under the mixed pension path, employees will receive their retirement benefits from both the publicly operated PAYG scheme and the private pension fund tier. In addition to their IFF annuity, they will receive a proportionally reduced part of the 'normal' public pension after 2012. Those insured who remain in the old system will be granted an accrual rate of 1.22 per cent p.a., while those who switched to the IFF tier will be granted 1.65 per cent p.a.[9] Both the future payment of this compensatory pension and the current flow of contributions to the second tier creates transition costs, which are partly compensated by first-tier reforms and projected at less than 1 per cent of GDP until 2030, when they are expected to rise to over 2 per cent (Párniczky 2000).

The start of the second tier coincided with the crisis in Russia and a steep decline in the Budapest stock market index. Fifty-nine licences for second-tier funds had been granted in 1997–99, but the number of operative funds had dropped to 21 by 2001, which is still an extraordinarily large number for only 2.2 million affiliates. As elsewhere, almost two-thirds of the market are held by the three largest funds. Pension funds invested mainly in state securities, amounting to 78 per cent of their portfolio at the end of 2000 (Müller 2003b). Since January 2000, they were free to invest up to 10 per cent of assets in OECD securities. This threshold increased to 30 per cent in 2002. While contributions to the public tier are collected by the state tax agency, collection in the second tier was decentralised: it is the responsibility of employers' to transfer individual contributions to pension funds. The collection system functions less than smoothly (Augusztinovics et al. 2002). Currently, neither the tax authority nor the public scheme keep personal contribution records, while second-tier members receive only an annual account statement, which is not detailed enough to check the employers' transfers. No data on contribution compliance in either the first or second tier are available. The IFF tier lacks precise rules for the calculation of costs and returns that would allow for a meaningful comparison of fund performance (Rocha and Vittas 2001). Since the merger of the specialised supervisory agency for pension funds into the Hungarian Financial Supervisory Authority in April 2000, the range of published data on the second- and third-tier funds has further diminished. Moreover, the corporate governance of the Hungarian funds makes it difficult to monitor them, as their cooperative-like structure creates *de facto* – as opposed to formal – ownership structures.

Surpassing all expectations, over half of all insured persons joined the IFF tier, i.e. the mixed pension option. This promising start notwithstanding, the newly established pension system was challenged by the incoming conservative Prime Minister, Victor Orbán, and his centre-right coalition government (1998–2002). While not reversing the reform, the government introduced a number of changes that lessen the attractiveness of the IFF tier.[10] Pointing to the reform-related revenue loss, the government froze individual contributions to second-tier funds at 6 per cent, without a concomitant adjustment of the formula for compensatory pensions. The Orbán government also lowered the employers' contribution to the first tier from 24 to 18 per cent of gross wage.[11] Taken together, these measures implied that the share of the IFF tier in total contributions was lowered from 25.8 to 23.1 per cent.

Originally, switching back to the purely public pension path was possible until December 2000 only, but this deadline was later extended by two years. In April 2001, Orbán urged the insured to return massively from the private funds back to the state system (Oláh and Finczicziki 2001).[12] From January 2002, the purely public reform path was reopened to new entrants to the labour market, and the guarantee for second-tier benefits was eliminated.[13] When the Socialists returned to power in May 2002, they announced a switchback to the original rules. Hence, the permanent reform of the Hungarian pension system is set to continue in the near future (Augusztinovics et al. 2002; Ferge and Tausz 2002; Simonovits 2002).

Conclusion

The 1997 reform implies a significant reprioritisation between public and private retirement provision, even though the public tier still plays an important role in Hungarian old-age security (Charlton, McKinnon and Konopielko 1998). It is interesting to note that the first pension privatisation in the region was enacted and implemented by a government led by the post-communists. When they won Hungary's second post-1989 elections, the overall policy context was marked by a rising external debt burden, a near currency crisis and a drop in credit standing, thus forcing the centre-left coalition to demonstrate its commitment to market-oriented reforms. While the Bokros package was intended as an emergency measure, it can be argued that Hungarian policymakers opted for pension privatisation to signal their ongoing resolve to tackle outstanding structural reforms. James (1998a) points to the fact that Hungary's credit rating from Moody's improved after partial pension privatisation was adopted, in spite of the fiscal costs of the move. At the same time, the PAYG system's dependence on budgetary subsidies had granted the Ministry of Finance an important stake in the pension reform arena.

Thorough parametric reform had already proved to be hard to implement, and the public pension scheme exhibited a persistent deficit. Hence, the 'benefit of crises' hypothesis can be specified for the Hungarian case in such a way that an economic emergency and the financing needs of the public pension scheme resulted in a significant change in the actor constellation in the pension reform arena. After the principal ally of the new pension orthodoxy, the Minister of Finance, had been strengthened, he could outweigh the Welfare Minister's opposition. He also took the lead in pension reform preparations by setting up the reform team in his Ministry. Unsurprisingly, among the reformers' objectives, macroeconomic considerations featured prominently, most notably the enhancement of 'Hungary's future growth performance by promoting national savings, developing capital markets, and reducing distortions in the labor market' (World Bank 1999a: 14).

In the light of Hungary's external debt burden, which had been piling up since the 1970s and 1980s, the IFIs were important players (Lorentzen 1995).[14] Clearly, agenda-shifting in Hungarian old-age security was facilitated by the World Bank. While its early advice had been limited to reforms within the existing public PAYG scheme (World Bank 1992a), the Bank's campaign for pension privatisation in the region started at a seminar in late 1993, where most Hungarian experts rejected the plan. After the release of the Bank's 1994 report (World Bank 1994a), its pension reform recommendations to the Hungarian government turned more explicit. It advocated a 'systemic change, involving splitting the current single public scheme into two mandatory pillars – a flat citizen's pension and a ... fully funded second pillar' (World Bank 1995a: 38–40). It was argued that the existing public PAYG scheme was financially inviable and 'could explode' in the next decade (Rocha 1996: 14). At the request of the Ministry of Finance, the Bank's Budapest office became directly involved in the Hungarian pension reform around 1995 (Rocha 1996; Palacios and Rocha 1998). World Bank experts were careful not to take an active role in public discussion. They supported the reform through a Public Sector Adjustment Loan, as well as through the Pension Administration and Health Insurance Project, which had been lending technical and IT support to the public tier since 1993. Clearly, the Bank aimed at creating a precedent:

'Passage of the Hungarian pension reform by Parliament has demonstrated the political and economic feasibility of this type of reform in Central Europe' (Palacios and Rocha 1998: 213).

Pension reform was made politically palatable by a bundling strategy. Most of the politically sensitive parametric reforms were legislated simultaneously with the introduction of individual pension fund accounts. The latter amounted to a highly visible move that distracted public attention from the changes in the public tier. The IFF tier was associated with tangible property rights, while also implying a change of constituencies by the creation of new stakeholders (Graham 1997). Moreover, reformers resorted to direct financial compensation when stipulating a compensatory pension payable to those who partially opted out of the public scheme and switched to the private IFF tier. The extraordinarily quick passage of the pension reform laws in Congress was not only due to the governing coalition's strong parliamentary majority, but also to pre-legislative negotiations with relevant opponents over the pension reform draft, most notably the trade unions. In reference to corporatism, Congress had conditioned its approval of the pension laws to the ÉT's consent, turning trade unions into a veto actor. It should be noted, however, that the reformers were only willing to compromise on first-tier reforms, while their basic paradigm choice – partial pension privatisation instead of a mere parametric reform – was not put up for discussion (Müller 1999). This implied that many deficiencies of the public scheme either remained unsolved or were shelved until well into the next century (Augusztinovics et al. 2002). From hindsight, it seems that the government's strategy to opt for a mandatist approach to the legislature – instead of using Congress as a policy forum to build political consensus for the iconoclastic laws – ultimately backfired, as the subsequent government showed little commitment to the reform.

8.2   THE CASE OF POLAND[15]

Legacy and policy context

When the Polish state was re-established in 1918, it featured a diversity of retirement regimes, shaped by the late German, Austrian and Russian rulers. In 1927, a unified pension scheme for employees was established, granting earnings-related benefits, while a unified pension system for workers was set up in 1933. Both schemes were fully funded and administered by the Social Insurance Institute (ZUS). Several occupational groups were protected by separate pension schemes, whereas the rural labour force was not covered at all. Soon thereafter, the German and Soviet invasions put an end to Poland's regained independence. In 1940, the Nazi occupants deprived Poles from all social security benefits (Świątkowski 1993; Żukowski 1994).

After World War II, with the reserves of the funded schemes lost, the new communist rulers enacted a switch to PAYG financing. Other early measures comprised the financial integration of the existing social insurance funds into the state budget and the abolition of employees' contributions.[16] In the 1950s and 1960s, efforts were made to extend coverage and to unify the pension scheme. At the same time, however, all occupations were classified into work categories, reflecting their strategic importance for the development of the socialist economy. The first category was for those doing heavy, unhealthy or otherwise special work, who enjoyed higher pensions and benefited from a lower retirement age than second-category workers (Florek 1986; Czepulis-Rutkowska 1999). Subordinate to the Minister of Labour, ZUS remained in charge of social security. In 1968, the Pension Fund was separated from the state budget, whereas the Social Insurance Fund, FUS, followed only in 1986.

Retirement benefits were adjusted in an *ad hoc* fashion and lagged behind newly granted pensions, a problem known as 'old pension portfolio' (Żukowski 1997: 138) – the longer a pension was drawn, the lower its purchasing power. Benefit indexation to wages was only enacted after the emergence of the *Solidarność* movement (Flakierski 1991). However, implementation was delayed until 1986, when the backward-looking indexation scheme proved insufficient to protect pensioners against soaring inflation. Although the problem of benefit adequacy was well known to pension experts and policymakers alike, the financial difficulties of ZUS during the 1980s translated into a continuation of the low-benefit policy until the end of the communist era (Żukowski 1996). Thus, during the 1970s and 1980s about 40 per cent of the elderly continued their gainful employment, the most important source of income for three quarters of them (Czajka 1985).

The financial strain on Polish pension finances was further aggravated by economic transformation. Between 1989 and 1996, the number of employed persons fell by 14 per cent, while the number of pensioners rose by 35 per cent. Pensions were used as substitutes for unemployment benefits, providing permanent instead of temporary social benefits (Perraudin and Pujol 1994). This policy triggered an increase of the system dependency ratio from 39 per cent in 1989 to 61 per cent in 1996, when the ratio of pension expenditures to GDP had jumped to 12.2 per cent. FUS was in permanent need of subsidies from the state budget, amounting to 4.3 per cent of GDP in 1992. Demographic trends did not have a major impact on the deterioration of FUS' finances (Gomułka and Styczeń 1999).

By the mid-1990s, ZUS continued to be the largest provider of retirement pensions, alongside a separate, highly subsidised scheme for farmers (KRUS), introduced in 1991, and a special scheme for the police and the military (Golinowska, Czepulis-Rutkowska and Szczur 1997). Within ZUS, many of the old branch privileges remained in force, granting earlier retirement and higher benefits. Regular retirement age was 65 for men and 60 for women, while the vesting period was 25 and 20 years, respectively, but there were many windows for early retirement, without a concomitant benefit reduction.[17] The cost of these programmes was estimated at 12 percentage points of the 45 per cent contribution rate, paid exclusively by employers (Góra and Rutkowski 1998: 19). The long-standing problem of absolute and relative benefit levels was tackled by a new pension formula, introduced in 1990/91. It combined a universal lump-sum component with an individualised earnings-related element. All current retirement benefits were reassessed on the basis of the new formula (Żukowski 1994; Götting 1998). Moreover, automatic indexation of pensions to wage increases was introduced, raising replacement rates from 53 per cent in 1989 to 75 per cent in 1994 (Schrooten, Smeeding and Wagner 1999). The trade-off between fiscal restraint and benefit adequacy facing policymakers in transition economies had been resolved in favour of the latter.

Table 8.2   The reform context in Poland: selected indicators

Indicators	1993	1994	1995	1996	1997
GDP change (in %)	3.8	5.2	7.0	6.0	6.8
Consumer prices (annual average, in %)	35.3	32.2	27.8	19.9	14.9
General gov't balance (in % of GDP)	–2.4	–2.2	–3.1	–3.3	–3.1
Total external debt (in % of GDP)	54.9	47.1	38.0	35.3	36.6
Public pension expenditure					
– in % of GDP	12.3	12.7	12.3	12.2	11.6
– in % of social expenditure	55.4	55.5	56.4	56.2	57.4

Note: Only the five years up to reform adoption are considered.

Sources: EBRD (2001); Ministry of Labour and Social Policy (2000).

Poland's partially free elections of June 1989 had led to a sweeping victory for *Solidarność*, in the midst of an ever-worsening economic crisis, combined with hyperinflation. In cooperation with an IMF team and a group of advisors – among them Jeffrey Sachs – the Finance Minister, Leszek Balcerowicz, developed a radical reform package for which he obtained

parliamentary approval in December 1989. The country suffered from a high
level of external debt, and the chances for its reduction 'depended on
Poland's adoption of a comprehensive and radical economic programme,
which was in any case required on domestic grounds' (Balcerowicz 1995:
319). At that time, strong government, public and international support for
reform had created a window of opportunity for far-reaching reform (Landau
1997). However, the social costs of the programme proved to be larger than
expected, translating in unstable governments and a slow-down in the pace of
reform. The 1993 elections granted the post-communist SLD and the agrarian
PSL a two-third's majority in Congress. Increasingly vocal constituencies and
economic recovery complicated the continuation of reform, but did not
reverse Poland's commitment to a market-oriented course. Economic reformers were successively appointed Ministers of Finance, while also holding
the position of Deputy Prime Minister for extra leverage. In 1994, Poland was
assisted by the IFIs in settling its massive debt to private banks, thereby
restoring access to international financial markets. After the 1997 elections, a
short-lived coalition of *Solidarność*'s political wing, AWS, and the small
liberal Freedom Union, UW, held a 61 per cent majority of seats in Congress.
They set out to tackle the remaining agenda by launching a package of four
major reforms in 1999, which included structural pension reform (Szczerbiak
2001).

The way towards pension privatisation[18]

By the mid-1990s, social policy experts coincided in their analysis that the
Polish pension system needed further reform. Policymakers had experienced
formidable resistance from the 'grey lobby' when trying to introduce
parametric reforms in the early 1990s, such as a change in the pension
formula, the modification of indexation rules and the abolition of branch
privileges. Public protests against the curtailment of pension benefits were
accompanied by successful appeals to the Constitutional Tribunal (Sosenko
1995; Żukowski 1996). Apart from a minimum consensus that the pension
system had to be made uniform and more transparent, there was considerable
disagreement regarding the direction that reform should take. Since the early
1990s, a number of drafts for comprehensive reform had been presented
(Golinowska 2000).

As early as 1991, partial pension privatisation had been proposed by two
social security experts (Topiński and Wiśniewski 1991), but was considered a
too radical departure from the *status quo*.[19] In 1994, the World Bank's newly
designed pension reform concept encountered similar reservations when presented to an audience in Warsaw. The Bank's earlier recommendations to
reform Polish old-age security had also included pension privatisation (World

Bank 1993b, 1994d). In spite of its overall critical reception, pension privatisation did appeal to the Minister of Finance. Shortly after taking up office in April 1994, the Finance Minister and Deputy Prime Minister, Grzegorz Kołodko, announced his so-called 'Strategy for Poland', proposing, among other things, a transition towards pension privatisation (Kołodko 1996). The main rationale behind this move was to cut down on the budgetary subsidies to ZUS. The 'Strategy for Poland' was approved by Congress and, subsequently, was to be implemented by the respective Ministries.

When the Labour Minister, Leszek Miller, refused to operationalise the proposed move to funding, Kołodko commissioned his advisor, Marek Mazur, to prepare a blueprint for pension privatisation.[20] Mazur had studied the Latin American precedents *in situ* and designed a parallel old-age system that would give the insured a choice between a reformed, downsized ZUS and newly created private IFF pension funds. Mazur's blueprint was never formally submitted to government, but had a considerable impact (Orenstein 2000). The proposal was supported by the financial sector, and the *Solidarność* trade union also joined the ranks of the advocates of partial pension privatisation in 1995.[21] Contrary to this, reform blueprints elaborated by the Ministry of Labour in 1993 and 1995 were limited to a thorough reform of ZUS, triggering a polarised pension reform debate (Golinowska, Czepulis-Rutkowska and Szczur 1997). The advocates of pension privatisation were criticised for prioritising economic over social objectives, for contradicting the legal doctrine of social insurance and for threatening to destroy social solidarity (Kalina-Prasznic 1997; Jończyk 1997).

For a year and a half, pension reform was deadlocked by the conflict between the portfolios of Labour and Finance. In February 1996, after a cabinet reshuffle, a new Minister of Labour was appointed – Andrzej Bączkowski, an independent with a *Solidarność* background. He turned into the most important individual actor in Polish pension reform, moving his portfolio considerably closer to the Ministry of Finance's position. After having been appointed Government Plenipotentiary for Pension Reform in August 1996, Bączkowski set up a special task force for old-age reform, the so-called 'Office of the Government Plenipotentiary for Social Security Reform'. Attached to the Ministry of Labour, until September 1997 the Office was headed by a seconded World Bank economist, Michał Rutkowski. Afterwards Marek Góra, a Polish economist, took over. The outlines of the envisaged reform, published in October 1996, combined a reform of ZUS with a newly created mandatory IFF tier.

Shortly afterwards, Bączkowski died unexpectedly, and it was feared that without him the Office might lack the necessary political backing. But although the new Labour Minister, Tadeusz Zieliński, opposed radical pension reform, preparations were continued. Under Jerzy Hausner, the new Government Plenipotentiary, the Office was attached to the Prime Minister, thereby removing it institutionally from the Ministry of Labour (Hausner 2001). Hausner was firmly backed by Kołodko's successor, Marek Belka, the new Minister of Finance. In spring 1997, a detailed reform plan was presented, coining the catchy slogan 'Security through Diversity' (Biuro 1997), and a PR campaign was launched (Chłoń 2000). Bączkowski's original aim had been to pass the reform before the parliamentary elections, due in September 1997, but after the delay caused by his death, time proved to be too short for this ambitious schedule. Consequently, the original package deal of bundling up the politically difficult reforms of ZUS with the fairly popular introduction of private pension funds was abandoned. Instead, the SLD–PSL coalition resorted to deliberate sequencing. While the laws on the private pension fund tiers were enacted in summer 1997, the more intricate part – the reform of ZUS – was left to the incoming government. During the election campaign, the coalition presented itself with a nearly completed pension reform (Żukowski 1999).

In spite of the politically difficult task left to them, the new UW–AWS government decided to continue the reform started by their political opponents. The continuation of the reform course reflects a cross-party consensus about the need for systemic pension reform (Golinowska 1999; Góra 2001). The affinity of the pension reform team to the incoming government should also be noted: Bączkowski, the first Plenipotentiary for Social Security Reform, had been a member of *Solidarność*, and the Office staff had an UW background. While Balcerowicz returned to the Ministry of Finance, the UW–AWS government appointed Ewa Lewicka – *Solidarność*'s leading pension expert – Deputy Minister of Labour, as well as Government Plenipotentiary for Social Security Reform. In May 1998, the two remaining pension reform laws were submitted to Congress, triggering considerable controversy. The reformers negotiated with opponents and agreed to some modifications of the envisaged first-pillar reforms (Rymsza 1998). The equalisation of the retirement age for men and women at age 62 had to be withdrawn from the draft law, while the envisaged abolition of branch privileges also proved difficult. Trade unions were particularly keen to defend branch-specific early retirement rules. However, by 2002, the act on bridging pensions, intended as a substitute for these early retirement pensions, had not been passed yet (Chłoń-Domińczak 2002). Likewise, the reformers were unable to abolish the pensioners' right to draw a pension and earn a salary at the same time. Furthermore, reformers resorted to exclusionary compensation, as the police and military would only pay contributions when starting their service after December 1998, and a reform of the highly subsidised farmers' pension scheme, KRUS, was not even attempted.

The pension reform team was well aware of the need to build consensus, thus discussing all draft laws with social partners before sending them to Congress (Chłoń-Domińczak 2002). The formal forum for discussion was a tripartite commission set up in 1994. Having a large number of pensioners among their members, both the post-communist OPZZ, which is part of SLD, and *Solidarność*, a strong faction within AWS, fiercely opposed even modest attempts to pension reform in the early 1990s. Later, *Solidarność* even participated in the conceptual debate on systemic pension reform in Poland, supporting a partial shift to funding since 1995, and was represented in the Office by Bączkowski and Lewicka. OPZZ also ended up accepting pension privatisation and decided to set up a pension fund together with the National Chamber of Industry and Commerce, yet failing to obtain a licence. Pensioners were another relevant group, amounting to 40 per cent of Polish voters (Golinowska and Żukowski 2002). A specialised Pensioners' Party was established in May 1994 and joined the left-wing SLD. Pensioners' representatives reacted more strongly to attempts to reform the public PAYG scheme than to partial pension privatisation. Pension reformers had effectively sought to calm this constituency, indicating that the elderly would not be affected by the envisaged changes (Góra 2001).

Opposition to the reform was weakened by dividing the insured into age groups. While the acquired rights of those approaching retirement were preserved, a middle-aged group was given a choice between a purely public and a mixed reform path and the young, who had little to lose, were obliged to enter the new system. The two remaining laws were finally passed in October and December 1998. Reformers were keen to start the new pension system from 1999, together with three other major public sector reforms – health reform, education reform and decentralisation (Kolarska-Bobińska 2000; Belka 2001).

The new pension system

Poland's new mixed pension system, in force since 1999, combines a still dominant, mandatory public PAYG scheme, that underwent fundamental restructuring, with a newly created IFF tier.[22] The public tier, mandatory for all insured, is still run by ZUS. It is now based on the NDC principle, mimicking a funded scheme, while remaining PAYG financed. The new pension formula can be simplified as

$$P = C/E$$

where P = old-age pension, C = virtual retirement capital of the insured, made up of the accumulated lifetime social insurance contributions, indexed to 75 per cent of wage bill growth, and E = average life expectancy at the time of retirement. Prior to the 1999 reform, all contributions were paid by employers on a company basis, and ZUS did not collect individual contributions records. Until 2004, a hypothetical retirement value will be calculated for every insured born after 1948.[23] Post-reform contribution payments will be added subsequently to the individual 'starting capital'. From August 2002, annual statements of NDC accounts will be sent to the insured. Other first-tier reforms included changes in eligibility, a modification of ZUS' legal status and the creation of a Demographic Reserve Fund. Moreover, provision against the different risks covered by ZUS – old age, disability, sickness and accident insurance – that had previously been lumped together in the 45 per cent contribution rate, was separated within ZUS. Under the new system, 19.52 per cent of gross wage were earmarked for old-age security, paid by employers and employees in equal parts (Chłoń-Domińczak 2002).

The second tier consists of a newly created IFF pension fund system, financed entirely by employees' contributions. Pension funds are being created and managed by private pension companies, organised as joint stock companies. There are several safety regulations, e.g. a minimum return threshold and the indexation of second-tier benefits. Annuities offered in the second tier may not vary according to sex, health or region, but the specific legislation has not yet been passed by Congress. By October 2001, 18 fund administrators were operating, down from 21. With 10.8 million clients, the Polish mandatory pension fund market is second only to Mexico (Müller 2003b). It should be noted, however, that by mid-2001 22 per cent of all pension fund members did not yet have contributions registered on their accounts ('dead accounts'), which is related to substantial IT problems as well as to fraudulent practices of sales agents (Chłoń-Domińczak 2002).

By mid-2001, the three largest funds concentrated 55 per cent of all insured and 65 per cent of assets. Fifty-eight per cent of all assets were invested in government papers (Müller 2003b). In the first two years of operation, internal rates of return (net of commissions and fees) varied between –8.95 and –13.76 per cent, as costs are front-loaded and the Warsaw Stock Exchange experienced a major slump (Chłoń-Domińczak 2002). Since the start of their activities, private pension funds have suffered from a fundamental problem, putting the reform's credibility at risk (OECD 2000b). ZUS, entrusted with collection and transfer of contribution for both tiers, was not prepared to handle its new tasks. Most importantly, its new IT system, specially designed for the reform, was not ready on time. In addition, many employers could not cope with the new reporting obligations to ZUS, hence complicating the identification of payments. The relevant legislation, part of which was passed only days before the reform started, showed shortcomings. While initially as little as 5 per cent of contributions due were transferred to the private funds, the percentage subsequently increased to 70–80 per cent.

Only in August 2001, current contributions started to be processed in the new IT system, and there is still a sizeable backlog of documents and arrears from 1999 and 2000 (Chłoń-Domińczak 2002).

All Poles under 30 are obliged to join the new two-tiered[24] scheme, paying 7.3 per cent of gross wage to a private pension fund of their choice, while the remaining 12.22 per cent continue to flow to ZUS (mixed pension path). Those between 30 and 50 years of age were free to do the same – alternatively, they could stay in the reformed ZUS with the whole of the pension contribution, i.e. 19.52 per cent of gross wage (purely public pension path). This age group was granted one year to decide whether or not they wanted to switch to the mixed pension path. Those above age 50 were required to remain in the old system. Regardless of the individual's decision for or against joining the private pension fund tier, the entire employers' contribution and a part of the insured's own contribution will continue to go to ZUS. Under the mixed pension path, 62.6 per cent of the total contribution go to the first tier and 37.4 per cent to the second tier. Retirement benefits will subsequently be received from both the private and the public tier. Recent estimates show, however, that the joint replacement rate from both tiers may well be lower than in the pre-reform scheme (Chłoń-Domińczak 2002). Any difference between the combined old-age pensions from both ZUS and a private pension fund and the minimum pension will be covered by the state budget, provided the insured meets age and service requirements.

It is estimated that 60 per cent of those insured persons aged 30 to 50 decided to switch to the mixed pension path, apart from those below age 30 who were obliged to do so. The permanent drain on ZUS' revenues engenders substantial transition costs. Proceeds from the privatisation of state property were an option to finance part of these costs. The pension reform team therefore opposed the – more visible – distribution of shares, a demand raised by the *Solidarność* camp under the label of 'propertisation' (Chwila 1997).[25] As both ideas were mutually exclusive, policymakers faced difficult choices between allowing citizens to tangibly profit from privatisation and a fiscally sustainable transition to funding (Gesell-Schmidt, Müller and Süß 1999). In 1998, the government earmarked privatisation revenues worth 7 per cent of GDP for the financing of transition costs in the first post-reform years. Thereafter, the rationalisation of the public pillar and debt financing would cover the projected annual costs of 1–2 per cent of GDP (Chłoń-Domińczak 2002).

Conclusion

The partial privatisation of Polish old-age security amounts to a significant departure from local social insurance traditions. Through the introduction of a

NDC scheme, Polish first-tier reforms are also more sweeping than the ones enacted in Hungary. When this iconoclastic reform was being prepared, the severe transitional crisis was already over, although fiscal imbalances persisted (see Table 8.2). It was argued that the pension system had become 'the most important source of the budget deficit; had the pension system been balanced, Poland could have run fiscal surpluses in 1990–96' (World Bank 1997b: 72). As parametric reforms had proved politically difficult, pension privatisation came to be considered as an alternative. It should be noted that by that time Poland was severely indebted (World Bank 1996b).[26] Although important progress had been made towards a reduction of the debt burden, the country was still closely monitored by its creditors, who expressed concern about the slow-down of reforms after the Balcerowicz Plan. By the mid-1990s, pension privatisation was much recommended by the World Bank and soon turned into a key element on Poland's outstanding agenda of structural reforms (World Bank 1997b).

Pension privatisation was initiated by an 'unlikely' post-communist government, facing a special need to signal its commitment to market-oriented reforms and fiscal sustainability.[27] The macroeconomic blessings ascribed to pension reform and the fiscal impact of ZUS turned the Minister of Finance into a key actor in the pension reform arena, emerging as the winner from his conflict with the Labour Minister, Miller. Afterwards Miller's successor, Bączkowski, took a lead in the pension reform project. Contrary to their Hungarian counterparts, Polish reformers managed to build a cross-party consensus on the need for structural pension reform, allowing for a continuation of the unfinished legislative agenda in spite of the 1997 government change. The political alternatives were clearly less attractive: a continuation of the high subsidies to ZUS at the expense of other government expenditures, or drastic retrenchment in the public pension system – a politically sensitive if not impossible move, given that the Constitutional Court had effectively vetoed modifications of acquired pension entitlements (Hausner 2001).[28]

The Polish reform reflects inspiration by the recent Latvian and Swedish reforms in the first, NDC tier, while its mixed overall approach resembles the Argentine reform. Whereas the early proposals by Topiński-Wiśniewski and Mazur were clearly based on the Latin American precedents, World Bank advice amounted to another major channel of transmission. As noted above, the pension reform group was even headed by an economist on leave from the Bank, granting it a pivotal channel to support the Polish pension reform with international networking as well as technical and financial assistance (Kavalsky 1998; Nelson 2001). The World Bank and USAID sponsored trips of Polish social security experts, journalists, trade unionists and MPs to Argentina and Chile. Moreover, individual Latin American reformers passed their experiences on to Polish policymakers.[29] However, the Polish reformers resorted to 'tactical packaging', distancing themselves from the Latin American precedents (Rutkowski 1998). The reformers' strategy also included the establishment of a special task force for pension reform, in an effort to circumvent intra-government resistance. The early strategy to bundle the sensitive ZUS reforms with the introduction of the new IFF funds was soon replaced by deliberate unbundling and sequencing, thereby enabling fundamental pension reform in a pre-electoral context. The incoming government's decision to bundle pension privatisation with three other major public sector reforms, starting from 1999, has been linked to the implementation problems, as there was virtually no *vacatio legis* (Reed 2001). Pension reform was legislated by the only subsequent post-1989 governments with a large majority in Congress. Nevertheless, policymakers did not opt for mandatism, but for parliamentarism and concertation, negotiating with the opposition in the legislature and beyond, yet only compromising on first-tier reforms, not on pension privatisation.

NOTES

1. This case study draws largely on the more detailed chapter on Hungary in Müller (1999).
2. In 1994, the remaining life expectancy at retirement age was 14.7 years for men and 23.3 years for women (Gillion et al. 2000).
3. It should be noted that the well-being of pensioners compared favourably with the situation of the unemployed, temporary employees and child care receivers. Yet, their poverty incidence was clearly above the national average (Grootaert 1997).
4. For detailed accounts of the political economy of pension privatisation in Hungary see Ferge (1997, 1999), Müller (1999), Orenstein (2000) and Nelson (2001).
5. The fact that the corporate design of the mandatory pension funds mirrors that of the existing VMB funds is interpreted as a political concession to the latter (Orenstein 2000).
6. Nelson (2001) argues that the government's most important concession to trade unions was not directly related to pension reform, but amounted to a change in the formula for selecting their representatives for the self-governing bodies, who would be delegated instead of being elected.
7. For a general description of the original reform package see Ministry of Finance (1997), Palacios and Rocha (1998), Czibere (1998) and Simonovits (1999, 2000). For recent legislative changes see Rocha and Vittas (2001), Augusztinovics et al. (2002) and Simonovits (2002).
8. Strictly speaking, the new Hungarian system consists of four tiers: besides the mandatory PAYG and IFF tiers (tiers one and two), there is a 'zero' tier providing a means-tested income guarantee for the elderly and a third, voluntary savings tier run by the VMB pension funds.
9. Originally, this rate was proportional to the share of the reduced PAYG contribution in the total contribution, i.e. $23/31 \times 1.65 = 1.22$. By extending the lower accrual rates to the pre-1998 years of service, the reformers intended to make it unattractive for those born before 1957 to switch (Simonovits 2002). This strategy worked out only partially, as the new system was oversold (Rocha and Vittas 2001).

10. The Orbán government also abolished the self-governing bodies of the Pension and Health Fund that were placed under direct government supervision. Moreover, the tax advantages granted to members of third-tier funds were reduced significantly (Simonovits 2002).
11. For details on contribution rates see Augusztinovics et al. (2002: 30).
12. By then only 1.7 per cent of second-tier members had done so (Augusztinovics et al. 2002).
13. The IMF (2000c) had pointed out earlier that a 6 per cent contribution rate would deplete the Guarantee Fund, due to the effect of the move on replacement rates of future second-tier benefits (similarly OECD 2000a).
14. According to the World Bank classification (1996b), Hungary suffered from moderate indebtedness at the time of the reform.
15. This case study draws largely on the more detailed chapter on Poland in Müller (1999).
16. In 1968 employees' contributions were reintroduced, yet abolished four years later (Żukowski 1996).
17. In 1993, the remaining life expectancy at statutory retirement age was 12.5 years for men and 20.1 years for women (Gillion et al. 2000).
18. For detailed accounts of the political economy of pension privatisation in Poland see Müller (1999), Orenstein (2000), Hausner (2001), and Nelson (2001).
19. Topiński and Wiśniewski (1991) proposed a two-tiered system: a PAYG tier, mandatory for all, would insure the individual's salary up to a threshold of 120 per cent of average earnings. Individuals would be required to pay contributions on earnings above this threshold into a private IFF scheme. Wojciech Topiński was President of ZUS in 1990/91 and had acquainted himself with pension privatisation during a visit to Chile.
20. While Labour Minister Miller represented centre-left factions within the SLD, Kołodko, the Minister of Finance, was an 'outside' economic expert with market-oriented views (Orenstein 2000).
21. *Solidarność* proposed to reform ZUS and supplement it with a private IFF tier that would be mandatory, except in the case of supplementary contributions under collective labour contracts (Lewicka et al. 1996).
22. This general description of the new Polish pension system is largely based on Góra and Rutkowski (1998), Chłoń, Góra and Rutkowski (1999), Żukowski (1999) and Chłoń-Domińczak (2002).
23. The individual starting capital will be calculated on the basis of the previous pension formula, adjusted for age and reflecting pension entitlements acquired until the end of 1998.
24. By establishing two mandatory earnings-related tiers, reformers reacted to opinion polls revealing that a universal, flat-rate state pension conflicted with the prevailing notion of justice (Golinowska 1999). Besides the mandatory PAYG and IFF tiers (tiers one and two), there is a 'zero' tier providing a tax-financed minimum pension, as well as a third, voluntary savings tier including life insurance and occupational pension schemes.
25. It was argued that the state-owned enterprises were the result of the work and ideas of Poland's citizens, who, therefore, should receive propertisation vouchers. See Gesell-Schmidt, Müller and Süß (1999) for details.
26. It was only in the second half of the 1990s that Poland's status changed from 'severely indebted' to 'less indebted' (World Bank 2001c).
27. For the credit that the move earned see World Bank (1999c: 10): 'Poland can take pride in the fact that it is one of a limited number of countries which has successfully launched a complete restructuring of its social security system.'
28. There are parallels to the unintended effects in the Uruguayan case (see above), in that apparently successful moves to protect the *status quo* in old-age security can increase the likelihood of radical change.
29. A prominent example is the Polish edition (1996) of Piñera's 1991 book, with a preface entitled 'Let's learn from the Chileans!' (Wilczyński 1996). See also Schulthess and Demarco (1995) and Zabala (1995).

9. Pension privatisation in South-Eastern Europe

9.1 THE CASE OF CROATIA

Legacy and policy context

The Croatian social security system has its origin in the 19th century, when the country formed part of the Austro-Hungarian Empire. The first pension schemes covered civil servants, railway workers, miners and white-collar workers. In 1918, the Kingdom of Serbs, Croats and Slovenes was formed, later renamed Kingdom of Yugoslavia. It was only in 1937 that a universal system of old-age insurance was established in the short-lived new state. After World War II, under the new communist leadership, PAYG financing was introduced, as the pre-war assets had either been destroyed or nationalised. For a brief spell, old-age security in the Republic of Yugoslavia took on Soviet features. Labour categories were established and pension contributions abolished, while the system's finances were integrated into the state budget (Stanovnik 2002). In 1952, a Federal Insurance Institute was formed and contributory financing restored. Shortly afterwards, social insurance institutes were set up in each of the republics, with separate funds by branches of social security. However, the contribution rate was still being fixed at the federal level. After the autonomy of the republics and provinces had been increased in the 1970s, the Yugoslav Congress passed only the general guidelines, while the republics formulated the details of their own social security legislation.

In Yugoslavia, the statutory retirement was 60 for men and 55 for women after 20 insurance years. With only 15 insurance years, women could retire at age 60 and men at age 65. With 35 (40) insurance years, women (men) could retire independently of their age. While labour categories were abolished soon, dangerous and unhealthy work was compensated for by a revalorisation of individual insurance periods by up to 50 per cent, i.e. for 12 months of work a maximum of 18 months could be credited. A lower retirement age and shorter insurance periods were granted to partisans only. Pension calculation was based on the individual's best 10 years prior to retirement, yet a benefit ceiling was in place. As benefit calculation was based on individual wages, pension levels were less compressed than in other socialist countries. Moreover, old-age pensions reflected the disparities in income levels among the Yugoslav republics, with Slovene and Croat pensioners receiving the highest benefits (Pospischil 1984: 309). In 1983, when Yugoslavia was hit by a severe debt crisis, economic downturn and inflation, a federal law introduced wage-based pension indexation to halt the decrease in the standard of living of the elderly (Posrkača 1985, 1989). In Croatia, replacement rates reached more than 90 per cent of average net wages in 1988–89 (World Bank 1997a).

Table 9.1   The reform context in Croatia: selected indicators[a]

Indicators	1995	1996	1997	1998	1999
GDP change (in %)	6.8	6.0	6.5	2.5	-0.4
Consumer prices (annual average, in %)	2.0	3.5	3.6	5.7	4.2
General gov't balance (in % of GDP)	–1.4	–1.0	–1.9	–1.0	–6.5
Total external debt (in % of GDP)	20.2	26.7	37.1	44.3	49.2
Croatian Institute for Pension Insurance					
– revenues (in % of GDP)	8.8	8.8	8.8	8.8	n.a.
– expenditures (in % of GDP)	9.0	9.7	11.1	7.7	n.a.
Pension expenditure[b] (in % of GDP)	10.8	11.5	13.0	12.2	13.2

Notes: [a] Only the five years up to reform adoption are considered.
           [b] Includes Croatian Army and Croatian Defenders' funds and disability pensions.

Sources: EBRD (2001); Republika Hrvatska (2000); Ott (2000); Zrinščak (2000); own calculations.

Since the late 1980s, the troubled Yugoslav confederation was heading towards its break-up (Pavković 2000). The two most developed republics, Slovenia and Croatia, held multi-party elections in April 1990 and declared their independence in June 1991. With war on and off until the Dayton Accords of late 1995, Croatia's post-independence years were turbulent. The authoritarian streaks of the governing HDZ and its leader, the late president Franjo Tuđman, only contributed to the tarnishing of Croatia's reputation (EIU 1999). At the same time, economic crisis deepened as the country suffered from the devastating effects of the regional conflict, while Croatia's key economic sector, tourism, had all but vanished. In October 1993, the authorities implemented an economic stabilisation programme to counter hyperinflation (Valentić 1997). In the same year, Croatia also joined the World Bank, which played an important role as the country had limited access to capital markets and bilateral assistance (World Bank 1999b).[1] After assuming part of Yugoslavia's external debt, Croatia reached rescheduling agreements with the Paris Club in 1995 and the London Club in 1996, enabling it to borrow from sovereign and commercial lenders. The authorities used this option as an alternative to borrowing from the IFIs, with which strained relations prevailed from late 1997. After a rapid increase in the country's indebtedness[2] a rapprochement occurred in April 1999, with the IFIs pointing to a 'lack of progress on key structural reforms' (World Bank 1999b: 12). In January 2000, the political landscape was transformed: following the elections held after President Tuđman's death, a centre-left coalition of six parties came to power and ended Croatia's political isolation. Clearly, in the new political setting consensus-building takes more time, resulting in the rescheduling of important structural reforms.

The way towards pension privatisation

Economic transformation and the war had a severe impact on Croatian pension finances, while demographic factors were less important (World Bank 1997a). The ratio of contributors to retirees dropped from 3.0 (1990) to 1.8 in 1995 and a mere 1.4 in 1999 (Zrinščak 2000). In 1990–99, a falling number of insured (–28.6 per cent) coincided with a dramatic increase in the number of pensioners (+55.2 per cent). The employment ratio fell from 79 per cent of the population in active age in 1990 to only 62 per cent in 1995 (World Bank 1997a). In this context, early retirement was encouraged to relieve labour market strains. Under a special scheme, a purchase of up to five 'notional' years of employment was possible, thereby stimulating companies to rejuvenate their workforce.[3] Andrijašević, Kovačević and Sabolović (1997) estimate that 175 000 years of service were purchased until the mid-1990s, when this practice was halted in Croatia. The average retirement age was only age 54 and 58 in the cases of women and men, respectively.[4]

As part of the 1993 anti-inflation and fiscal adjustment package, the government decided to discontinue the wage-based indexation of retirement benefits, a move that was soon challenged at the Constitutional Court (Puljiz 1999). By 1995, replacement rates had dropped to 51 per cent of average net wage, and the majority of pensioners were threatened by poverty (Jurčević 1995; Bejaković 1998). At the same time, so-called 'merit pensions' – higher than the individual's contributory entitlements – were granted to selected groups and accounted for 16 per cent of total pension payments in 1997 (IMF

1998).[5] The Croatian Institute for Pension Insurance, or Pension Institute for short, was mainly financed through pension contributions, amounting to 25.5 per cent of total wages and split in equal parts between employees and employers in 1996 (Jurlina Alibegović 1998).[6] Budgetary transfers amounted to 2.75 per cent of GDP in 1998 (Ott et al. 2000). Table 9.1 shows that the share of public pension expenditure to GDP shot up from 7.7 per cent in 1992 to 13.2 per cent in 1999 (Zrinščak 2000).

In Croatia, pension reform had been on the agenda since the early 1990s. A reform commission established in the Pension Institute focused on parametric changes within the existing PAYG scheme. Its work was inspired by the German legislation, which had been translated into Croat and implied a break with the common Yugoslav legacy. In 1994, a draft law for pension reform proposed an increase in pensionable age and changes in the benefit formula, most notably an extension of the calculation base to the whole labour biography and the introduction of pension points (Bodiroga-Vukobrat 1994).[7] A second, funded tier based on collective capitalisation was to contribute to 'a pension system with lower contributions and higher pensions' (Jurčević 1995: 8). To this end, 14.6 per cent of the equity of the formerly socially owned enterprises were transferred to the Pension Institute, with a book value estimated at about US$2 billion (Bićanić 2001).[8] Operating as a single extra-budgetary institution, the workers' fund, the farmers' fund and the fund of the self-employed established the Croatian Pension Investment Company to manage the assets transferred to them and to provide financial support to the public pension system. Yet, in 1995, dividends from the share portfolio only came to 2.1 per cent of total pension spending. The World Bank criticised the transfer of assets to the Pension Institute from a corporate governance perspective, as it was thought to delay the restructuring of these companies (World Bank 1997a).

While the envisaged parametric changes were put off during wartime, the continuous worsening of all relevant indicators led many to believe that comprehensive pension reform was unavoidable, whatever this would entail (Rismondo 1997; Zorić 1997; Čučković 1999). At the same time, the World Bank launched its global campaign for pension privatisation, a proposal also put forward to the Croatian authorities. The former Chilean Finance Minister, Hernán Büchi, an advisor to the Croatian government, was another source of inspiration. The conceptual turning point was marked by an international pension conference held in Opatija in November 1995, organised by the Croatian government, the World Bank and the East–West Institute (Anušić, O'Keefe and Madžarević-Šujster 2003). The event was attended by high-ranking pension experts, with the architect of the 'Chilean model', José Piñera, featuring prominently (Ministarstvo Financija 1997). Other reform cases discussed in greater detail included the Hungarian, Swedish and Swiss ones, with a mandatory funded tier in place or to be introduced shortly. It was at this conference that the incoming Prime Minister, Zlatko Mateša, publicly endorsed the introduction of a mandatory IFF tier in Croatia that was to be fed by a 10 per cent contribution rate.

At first, preparative work centred largely on first-tier reforms, while the second-tier project did not proceed swiftly. The fiscal implications of pension privatisation were a matter of concern (see also IMF 1997). Consequently, envisaged second-tier contributions were lowered from 10 to 5 per cent of wages. It should also be noted that President Tuđman stood for re-election in June 1997, implying a competing use of scarce budgetary means. Moreover, the government had introduced a price indexation of retirement benefits in early 1997 (IMF 1998). It was only after the presidential elections – in September 1997 – that the first-tier law was submitted to Congress. In its first two articles, it established a three-pillar model for Croatia, while also fixing a cut-off age of 40 and a contribution rate of no less than 5 per cent to the second tier. Yet, the second and third tiers would be a matter of separate legislation. In December 1997, a World Bank report highlighted the importance of 'careful design and implementation of the transition to a multi-pillar system' (World Bank 1997a: 80). The strategies for pension privatisation presented reached from a one-shot Chilean-style privatisation to a gradual introduction of a mixed system. The Bank made it clear that a sequenced strategy would suit the Croatian context best. If first-tier reforms would be carried out first, cutting down on pension entitlements, they would allow for a lowering of the subsequent transition costs of partial pension privatisation. At the same time, the Croatian financial markets would have more time to develop if the start of the IFF tier was delayed.

In February 1998, the Croatian government eventually established a high-ranking pension reform commission. It was divided into two sub-committees: one group mainly consisted of lawyers; the other one was staffed with young economists (Anušić, O'Keefe and Madžarević-Šujster 2003). Zoran Anušic, a former deputy Minister of Finance, who had joined the World Bank, was granted leave of absence from the Bank to be appointed National Coordinator of Pension Reform in Croatia. He helped to maintain informal Bank–government communications at a time when official relations had been inter-rupted. The committee was attached to the Deputy Prime Minister, Ljerka Mintas-Hodak, instead of either the Ministry of Labour or the Ministry of Finance. However, the latter played a key role throughout the whole reform process, embodied by Borislav Škegro, a key advocate of economic reform in the HDZ. In May 1998, when the first-tier law had its second reading, the Constitutional Court ruled on the suspension of the wage-based indexation of pensions that had been decreed in 1993. Its legality had been challenged by pensioners' organisations, and the issue received much public attention. In a complex verdict, both the government decree and the 1997 price indexation were declared unlawful. Pensioners were to be compensated for the drop in replacement rates, yet no details were provided on the extent of the required compensation. The Tuđman regime claimed that it had not incurred any debt towards the pensioners – a strategy that would turn out to result in high political costs, having a negative impact on the HDZ's elderly constituency.

More immediately, however, the verdict provided a major impetus for the approval of the first-tier pension law, while also distracting the attention of the Croatian public and trade unions from the envisaged parametric changes. In July 1998, the reform of the public pension scheme was legislated with the HDZ's large majority in Congress (Ministry of Labour 1998). However, the Constitutional Court ruling endangered the reformers' fiscal calculus, as the sharp reduction in replacement rates had been seen as a window of opportunity for partial pension privatisation (Anušić, O'Keefe and Madžarević-Šujster 2003). The costs of a full compensation of pensioners for the suspension of wage-based indexation were estimated at between 5 and 22.5 per cent of projected 1998 GDP (IMF 1998). Moreover, a banking crisis hit Croatia in 1998–99, thus only heightening the population's distrust of financial institutions (IMF 2000b; Zrinščak 2000).

Eventually, the second- and third-tier legislation was passed in May 1999, stipulating that both tiers were due to start in July 2000. Yet, the political regime change occurring in early 2000 delayed the establishment of the second and third tier, not least because of the incoming government's desire to discontinue the staffing policy of the Tuđman regime (Anušić, O'Keefe and Madžarević-Šujster 2003). Moreover, the problems resulting from hasty reform implementation in Poland had come to be known in Croatia. The new centre-left government established another working group, who conducted a series of background studies on the envisaged pension privatisation in the last quarter of 2000. The new government basically endorsed the introduction of the new tiers, scheduling it first for July 2001 and then for January 2002. It also kept the previous assistant minister for pension reform issues, Snježana Plevko, thus preserving a minimum of continuity in reform implementation.

Reformers could count on strong support by the local business and financial community.[9] Yet, the context in which the ambitious reform takes place may not guarantee its success. Bićanić (2001: 162) points to Croatia's version of 'crony capitalism', which postponed restructuring and maintained a soft budget constraint. Moreover, the system of property rights and contract enforcement is still weak (World Bank 1999b). Nevertheless, only a small group of social security experts remains critical of the reform, arguing that 'it is ill-prepared and poorly adjusted to the economic situation in the country' (Puljiz 1999: 15).[10] Most trade unions also voiced opposition against pension privatisation, fearing an erosion of solidarity – except for the prosperous

Trade Union of State Employees that considered setting up a second-tier pension fund. The Croatian trade union movement is fragmented, with hundreds of registered unions and five confederations. The existence of a tripartite Economic and Social Council did not imply veto points, as it was merely used as a channel for government–union communication, while no approval of draft laws by social partners was required.

Interestingly, the Retired Persons' Trade Union agrees with the reform, considering the three-pillar model necessary in the light of the severe deterioration of the active/passive ratio, yet fearing a negative impact on first-tier benefits due to the shortfall in contributions. While the IFF tier remained unquestioned, the first-tier law has already been challenged at the Constitutional Court. At the time of writing, the issue of the indexation-related debt to pensioners, ultimately reflecting the Yugoslav legacy, was still pending. The new six-party government had campaigned on a swift and complete resolution of this issue. Yet, its law to compensate pensioners by benefit increases of up to 20 per cent did not satisfy pensioners' organisations. They demanded to return to wage-based indexation, while the difference between the retirement benefits received since 1993 and wage-indexed pensions should be paid retroactively. This maximalist position did not seem to find much backing at the Constitutional Court, however.

The new pension system

The new Croatian pension system is two-tiered[11] and came into force in a sequenced process, with first-tier reforms taking effect from January 1999, while the introduction of the IFF tier, run by private pension funds, was postponed until January 2002.[12] The 1.2 million insured are divided into three age groups: for those younger than age 40, it is mandatory to split the contribution between the reformed PAYG tier (14.5 per cent of wages) and the second, IFF tier (5 per cent of wages). They had to select one of the licensed pension funds until the end of March 2002. Those aged between 40 and 49 were given six months to choose irrevocably between the mixed and the purely public pension path. Those aged 50 and above were mandated to stay in the public tier with their entire contribution (19.5 per cent of wages). It is interesting to note that the new centre-left government decreased the total contribution rate from 21.5 to 19.5 per cent. While intended to lower labour costs, this move only exacerbated the financial difficulties of the Pension Institute (Anušić, O'Keefe and Madžarević-Šujster 2003). It also increased the share of the private tier in total pension contributions from 23.3 to 25.6 per cent.

The first tier is PAYG financed and mandatory for all insured. It is still run by the Pension Institute that ceased to be an extra-budgetary institution from July 2001. After a third of its expenditures were financed by the state budget, it was financially integrated into the latter. As before, for retirement at age 65 for men and age 60 for women only 15 insurance years are required. However, these age thresholds are now stipulated as the standard retirement age. Early retirement is possible from age 60 for men with a qualifying period of 35 years, and from age 55 for women with a qualifying period of 30 years. Yet, for every month of anticipatory retirement, benefits are reduced by 0.3 per cent. The changes in statutory retirement ages and in benefit calculation are introduced gradually and will only be fully in force from 2007 and 2009, respectively.

The new benefit formula in the PAYG tier relies largely on German-style pension points, reflecting the ratio of the worker's earnings to the average wage, with one pension point representing an average salary in each qualifying year completed after 1969. Both pension points and retirement benefits are adjusted biannually based on combined wage–price indexation. Upon retirement, the average of individual pension points is multiplied by the up-dated pension point value, as well as individual years of service. A more redistributive first-tier benefit will be paid to those below age 40. While part of their pension will be determined as explained above, reflecting their pre-2002 insurance periods, they will also receive a basic pension, consisting of two components: 0.25 per cent of the national average gross wage for every insurance year after 2001, and 25 per cent of the total actual value of the individual's post-2001 pension points. New entrants to the labour market below age 40 will only receive the basic pension. The World Bank had suggested flat-rate pensions for the first tier (Potočnjak 2000).

Inspired by the Swedish reform, a clearinghouse approach to the second tier was chosen (World Bank 2000d). The Central Registry of Insured Persons, REGOS, collects contributions and keeps records of individual accounts, while also reporting to individuals on the state of their accounts. The insured register at REGOS when choosing one of the pension funds, hence agents cannot directly recruit affiliates. This design is intended to avoid the costly operation of IFF tiers elsewhere and to ensure privacy. While REGOS exercises central record-keeping and account management functions, pension funds act as investors. The Pension Funds and Insurance Supervisory Agency, HAGENA, supervises the second and third tiers of the new pension system, as well as REGOS. 'Regulatory oversight ... is likely to be particularly crucial in Croatia, given the weakness and non-transparency of the financial sector, and broader concerns about corruption' (World Bank 2000d: 2).[13]

Initially seven fund managers were licensed for the second tier, but with the first three funds currently absorbing 89 per cent of participants, the number of funds is likely to fall in the near future (Anušić, O'Keefe and Madžarević-Šujster 2003). At least 50 per cent of the funds' portfolio have to be invested in government bonds, whereas in November 2002, no less than 83 per cent of the portfolio had actually been placed in this instrument (Anušić, O'Keefe and

Madžarević-Šujster 2003: 61). Fund managers are entitled to charge a wide spectrum of fees, thus raising concerns about operating costs in the second tier. They may charge up to 0.8 per cent of paid contributions, plus 0.8 per cent of annual net assets, a success fee of 25 per cent of annual real returns, as well as switching and exit fees. A relative rate of return guarantee is in place, with costs split between fund managers and the state budget. Upon retirement the insured will be offered price-indexed annuities, which have to be calculated on the basis of unisex tables. As distrust of financial institutions is widespread, second-tier institutions are less popular than in other countries. By April 2002, 56 per cent of all insured were registered with the second tier, among which only 23 per cent of the 'optional' cohort of those between 40 and 50 years of age. Until the end of the application period – June 2002 – the percentage had increased to 32 per cent.[14] Apart from the small size of the Croatian market, this lack of enthusiasm for private pension funds may have been one of the reasons why most insured in active age were mandated to participate in the IFF tier, whereas Hungarian and Polish reformers were more inclined towards a choice-based approach.

Conclusion

In 1994, when the World Bank published its global pension reform proposal, Croatia had not yet gained access to international capital markets and depended on the IFIs for external financing, while the war and its consequences amounted to a severe drain on the state budget. With its ascribed potential to boost the rate of domestic savings, policymakers hoped that pension privatisation would give them more financial leeway. At the same time, the move seemed useful to signal the government's commitment to market-oriented reforms at a time when the country suffered from political isolation and had fallen behind in the transition to a market economy. When the three-pillar model was eventually legislated at the end of the Tuđman era, the move earned its credit: 'Pension reform is a policy area in which Croatia joined the ranks of other reformers in Central and Eastern Europe' (World Bank 2000c: 8).

By most accounts, the World Bank served as the agenda shifter in the Croatian pension reform arena. The Bank provided not only the basic multipillar blueprint; it also co-sponsored the crucial Opatija conference and subsequent preparatory work, provided technical assistance, financed IT systems and promised a US$100 million loan to finance part of the transition costs.[15] Another source of inspiration for Croatian policymakers were the Chilean reformers, who successfully challenged the strong cognitive reference that the German model had constituted so far.[16] At a later stage the Swedish and Polish experiences also provided important lessons, which translated into design choices. Throughout the reform process, the Ministry of Finance played an important role, while the Ministry of Labour remained passive. The Pension Institute rejected the IFF tier, while actively preparing first-tier reforms. It is interesting to note the double role of the former Assistant Finance Minister, Anušic, a key domestic actor, who also channelled World Bank support after he had joined the Bank and was seconded to the Croatian pension reform team, similar to Michał Rutkowski in Poland.

The strong role of the Ministry of Finance in pension privatisation can be linked to the ever-worsening financial situation of the public pension scheme, translating into substantial budgetary transfers. The sensation of crisis intensified significantly after the Constitutional Court ruling on the indexation problem, thus facilitating the passage of substantial first-tier reforms.[17] However, the considerable delay in legislating and implementing pension privatisation in Croatia shows that there is a flip side to the economic factors and considerations that tend to push pension privatisation in most places. It was feared that the envisaged second tier would worsen the severe financial situation of the Pension Institute in the short and medium run, thus complicating compliance with budgetary targets.[18] This kind of fiscal concern may render Ministers of Finance potentially ambivalent advocates of pension privatisation (Müller 2002a).[19] Moreover, in the Croatian case poor capital market development was perceived as a constraint to the swift introduction of a mandatory IFF tier.

To ensure passage of the reform laws, the Tuđman regime relied on a mandatist policy style, without making a substantial effort to achieve consensus with opposition parties and social partners (Zrinščak 2000). Concessions made only concerned the first-tier law: the pensionable age for women and the indexation formula (Puljiz 1999). The sequencing strategy chosen by the Croatian government also deserves attention and can be linked to an economic rationale. It started with the downsizing of the public scheme and introduced the mandatory IFF tier only three years later. Yet, unbundling was only partial, as the Croatian government stipulated the multipillar approach in the first two articles of the first-tier law and legislated the remaining tiers shortly afterwards. Undoubtedly, the Tuđman era was marked by authoritarian traits, a single majority party and a powerful presidency with strong executive powers, playing an important role in decision-making. Yet, this context did not prove sufficient to guarantee an easy paradigm shift in the area of old-age security: six years elapsed between the first public announcement of pension privatisation at Opatija and its actual implementation. It is also remarkable that the iconoclastic reform project survived a major regime change.

9.2   THE CASE OF BULGARIA

Legacy and policy context

In Bulgaria, the origins of social security schemes date back to 1891 when the first law on civil servants' pensions was enacted. An important Social Insurance Law was passed in 1924, establishing a fully funded pension scheme that covered all employees in the private sector. In the early 1940s, different occupations obtained separate legislation, while coverage remained limited. The fragmented legislation was gradually unified after 1944, the year the Communist Party seized power in Bulgaria. As early as 1948, employees' contributions were abolished, and entitlements were derived from work done, not from contributions paid (Ministry of Labour 1994). The Social Insurance Law of 1949 merged all existing institutions, while also introducing contributory pensions for farmers. Only two years later, the Labour Code remodelled Bulgarian social insurance again, following the Soviet model. The entire pre-1944 legislation was repealed, while the accumulated funds were nationalised. The Pension Law of 1957 remained in force until the 1990s. In 1975, members of collective farms, which had been covered by separate legislation, were integrated into the general scheme (Jessel-Holst 1982).

Eligibility rules were linked to the system of labour categories. The first two categories covered particularly dangerous and unhealthy work, while all other occupations were lumped together in the third category. For the first category, the retirement age was 50 for men and 45 for women with a vesting period of 15 years. For the second category it was age 55 for men and age 50 for women with 20 insurance years. For the third category retirement age was 60 for men with a vesting period of 25 years, and 55 for women with 20 insurance years.[20] For women with five or more children, the armed forces and fighters against fascism and capitalism, more generous eligibility rules were in place.

A highly redistributive formula stipulated that pensions were essentially fixed as a percentage of the individual gross wage. While low-wage earners were entitled to 80 per cent of their previous earnings, only 55 per cent would be granted to those considered big earners. However, as retirement benefits were not indexed to either prices or wages until 1985, the average replacement rate amounted to only 53.4 per cent in 1980 (NSSI 2000). Moreover, reduced pensions were granted to men who had reached age 60 and fulfilled at least half of the required insurance years of the labour category that applied to them. For women, the respective age was only 55. Reduced retirement benefits amounted to 33.7 per cent of all old-age pensions in 1977 and were largely granted to farmers, whose insurance periods often turned out to be incomplete. Social pensions for the elderly and the disabled were introduced in 1973. In a context of low retirement benefits and relatively young beneficiaries, many pensioners continued their gainful employment (Jessel-Holst 1982).

Table 9.2 The reform context in Bulgaria: selected indicators[a]

Indicators	1995	1996	1997	1998	1999
GDP change (in %)	2.1	−10.9	−6.9	3.5	2.4
Consumer prices (annual average, in %)	62.0	123.0	1,082.0	22.2	0.7
General gov't balance (in % of GDP)	−5.7	−10.4	−2.1	0.9	−0.9
Total external debt (in % of GDP)	77.4	97.7	95.8	83.7	80.5
Pension expenditure (in % of GDP)	8.0	6.9	6.2	8.2	8.4
Pensioners in % of insured	78.1	69.0	69.2	71.8	83.3
Replacement rate[b]	32.9	31.6	29.2	34.5	33.9

Notes: [a] Only the five years up to reform adoption are considered.
          [b] Average monthly old-age pension to average monthly salary.

Sources: EBRD (2001); NSSI (2000).

The Bulgarian transformation started as a top-down process led by Bulgaria's Communist Party (Kassayie 1998). In November 1989, Todor Zhivkov, the long-standing Secretary-General, was overthrown by his party. In the founding elections of 1990, the renamed Bulgarian Socialist Party (BSP) won an absolute majority. Yet, the BSP government was forced to resign when an increasingly vocal opposition movement made itself heard. After a brief spell of economic liberalisation and stabilisation in 1991–92, a frozen communism/anti-communism cleavage translated in short-lived governments, with political modernisation and economic reform running markedly behind schedule (Elster et al. 1998). This period culminated in economic collapse (see Table 9.2), triggering mass demonstrations and the resignation of Zhan Videnov's BSP government (1994–96).

In the subsequent parliamentary elections, the centre-right Union of Democratic Forces (UDF) won a solid majority and formed a government led by Ivan Kostov (1997–2001). Facing a threat of default on the country's heavy external debt burden, the first government in post-1989 Bulgaria to serve its term of office was fully committed to multilateral recommendations on economic policy, relying on the support from the IMF and the World Bank. 'Bulgaria is currently heavily dependent on the multilaterals to cover its external financing requirement' (EIU 2000: 42).[21] The reform measures carried out by the Kostov government included the introduction of a currency board arrangement,[22] the privatisation of state-owned enterprises and structural pension reform.

The way towards pension privatisation

The process of economic transformation had a profound impact on the Bulgarian pension scheme (Shopov 1993). In the light of soaring unemployment, an early retirement window was opened for those made redundant, provided they had reached at least age 57 and 25 insurance years (men), or age 52 and 20 insurance years (women). Retirement benefits were reduced by 10 per cent until the beneficiaries reached the regular retirement age. In 1987–93 alone, the number of employed decreased by 28.2 per cent. The number of insured plunged by 37.0 per cent between 1989 and 1999, as many workers lost their jobs, while others left the country in search of a better future.[23] Over the same period, the number of old-age pensioners in the general scheme increased by 22.7 per cent, and the system dependency ratio jumped from 54.3 per cent in 1990 to 82.7 per cent in 1994 (NSSI 2000).

The pension scheme was in permanent need of subsidies from the state budget, amounting to 24 per cent of all revenues in 1991. The ratio of pension expenditures to GDP increased from 6.5 per cent of GDP (1980) to 10.9 per cent (1993). In reaction to the dire situation, contribution rates were raised from 30 to 35 per cent for third-category workers, while employers were charged 45 and 50 per cent for second and first-category workers (Minev 1993).[24] At the same time, average replacement rates were lowered from 41 per cent (1990) to a mere 29 per cent of average monthly salaries in 1997 (see Table 9.2). In 1999, the average monthly pension amounted to US$35 (IMF 2000a), leading to a crisis of confidence in the public scheme. 'At present in Bulgaria old age is virtually synonymous with poverty' (Ministry of Labour 1994: 77).

Social security experts had long been aware that the Pension Law of 1957 was outdated and needed to be replaced with new legislation (Jessel-Holst 1991). Under the first UDF government (1991–92), the Ministry of Labour presented a draft social security law that included the increase of the statutory retirement age to 65, the introduction of a pension formula reflecting the entire labour biography and a separation of pension finances from the state budget (ILO–CEET 1994; Götting 1998). While political pension privileges enjoyed by officials of the previous regime and so-called 'heroes of labour' had already been abolished, other merit pensions and labour categories remained essentially unchallenged.[25] Contrary to this reform concept, the Deputy

Minister of Labour, Duhomir Minev, had favoured a Chilean-style approach (Minev 1993) – an idea welcomed by World Bank representatives, but opposed by other members of government. Pension reform efforts were cut short when the government's term came to a premature end, following a vote of no confidence.

In 1993, the Ministry of Labour prepared a White Paper to set forth a strategy for social security reform. Presented in April 1994, it was more cautious than the preceding reform plans. The retirement age was only to be raised to age 63, and two alternative benefit formulae were proposed: a strictly earnings-related one and a more redistributive two-tiered one. The White Paper explicitly rejected the idea of pension privatisation: 'Any attempt to change from a pay-as-you-go financing method ... to a fully funded financing system is financially and economically impossible, given that the scheme is already mature and covers the total population' (Ministry of Labour 1994: 52).[26] The implementation of the envisaged reform programme was halted by two government changes in the second half of 1994.

Initially, the incoming BSP government was unwilling to embark on the potentially controversial parametric reforms (Götting 1998). Fully reflecting the 'new Bulgarian political system of post-communist corporatism' (Deacon and Vidinova 1992: 86), only the existing minimum consensus between the government and the social partners was turned into law in November 1995. Pension finances were separated from the budget, and an autonomous National Social Security Institute (NSSI) was created, featuring a tripartite supervisory board. The Round Table of 1990 had granted social partners an important role, stressing the government's commitment towards consensus-oriented policymaking. In 1993, a National Council for Tripartite Partnership created a more formal consultative mechanism (ILO–CEET 1994). It is interesting to note that apart from their role in the NSSI's board of directors, both trade union confederations – the post-communist KNSB and the independent *Podkrepa* – had set up supplementary private pension funds. Other participants in this newly emerging market included insurance companies. The government granted tax incentives, but did not create any regulatory framework or supervision for the existing pension funds (Georgiev 1995).[27]

Until early 1996, the Bulgarian pension insurance had been run by a special department in the Ministry of Labour and regional social insurance offices. While a computerised data base for current pensioners existed, no records were kept on the insured or on employers' payment obligations.[28] The creation of the NSSI implied building a new administrative structure, while its dire financial situation also called for an IT system to monitor and project the flow of funds. When the Bulgarian government decided to approach the World Bank in this matter, it was promised help. Over a period of four years, the Social Insurance Administration Project would hand out a US$24 million loan for hardware and software, training, study tours and consultancies (World Bank 1996c). It should be noted that in the spirit of its 1994 report, the Bank had advocated partial pension privatisation, while a full shift to funding was considered too expensive in the Bulgarian context (World Bank 1994b; Fox 1995).[29] The government's social insurance reform programme was therefore considered the 'groundwork for future reforms' (World Bank 1996c: i), i.e. only the first phase of a reform agenda that would eventually lead to a multipillar scheme, including a mandatory IFF tier.

With extremely low benefit levels and very high contribution rates, the range of options available to Bulgarian pension reformers was narrowing. Parametric reforms faced strong opposition, particularly the increase in retirement ages and the abolition of labour categories. Yet, it became increasingly clear that these sensitive reforms would have to be tackled under any reform scenario. A first step in this direction was the option to postpone retirement voluntarily by up to three years beyond statutory retirement age, which met with a strong response in the context of low retirement benefits and prepared the ground for a mandatory increase in pensionable age. Another innovative solution was developed for the problem of labour categories, following a pilot scheme for teachers. In order to streamline eligibility in the public scheme, the special rights inherent in the first and second categories were to be handled by a separate, contributory scheme. The extra contributions charged from employers for their first- and second-category workers were to be transferred to mandatory occupational pension funds, which were envisaged as second-tier institutions (World Bank 1996c).[30] Moreover, the individual savings plans offered by private pension funds were to be regulated, in order to provide a proper third tier. This phased reform plan was approved by the Videnov government a few months before its term of office came to an early end.[31]

With the country at the brink of default and in the midst of an economic emergency, a centre-right UDF government took over in April 1997 (see above). It was keen to demonstrate its full commitment to the IFIs' policy recommendations by embarking on an ambitious programme of structural reforms. While the pension reform course agreed between the previous government and the World Bank was essentially endorsed, second-tier design was moved closer to the Bank's standard recommendations: mandatory IFF funds would be established alongside the envisaged occupational funds. By enacting legislation for all three tiers, the Bulgarian government would qualify for further tranches of structural adjustment loans from the IMF and the World Bank (*Pensions International*, July and November 1999). The new Minister of Labour, Ivan Neikov, took the lead in reform preparations, arguing that 'if we do not implement a pension reform now, in three years the entire system will

collapse' (Neikov 2000: 2). A former vice president of the post-communist
KNSB trade union, he had served on the managing board of its highly successful pension fund *Doverie*.[32] In 1998, the government set up a working
group to prepare systemic pension reform, comprising representatives of the
Ministry of Labour, the NSSI and the Ministry of Finance. At a later stage, MPs,
social partners, private pension fund representatives and independent re-
searchers were also invited to discuss the draft laws. Since 1998, reform preparations, including a public awareness campaign, have been actively supported
by a USAID-sponsored team of Bulgarian and foreign experts, known as the
Bulgarian Pension Reform Project (Pension Reform Project 2000, 2001).

The Bulgarian reformers chose a sequenced approach to the legislative
process. While legislation for the first and second tier was still being prepared,
the need to regulate the existing third-tier industry implied that the respective
piece of legislation was sent to Congress ahead of the other laws – a 'back-to-
front approach to pensions reform' (*Pensions International*, March 1999). After
months of debate with the existing pension funds and the insurance lobby, the
Supplementary Voluntary Retirement Insurance Act was eventually adopted in
July 1999, including the transferability of funds between administrators, the
legal separation of pension funds and the respective management companies and
a minimum US\$1.5 million in liquid assets. Afterwards, the Mandatory Social
Insurance Code, the main legislation covering all obligatory pension tiers, was
submitted to Congress. The Commission for Labour and Social Policy invited
all organisations of beneficiaries to participate in the discussion. Most objections concerned the first-tier legislation, and on the request of trade unions reformers had to compromise on the increase in retirement age. Moreover, parliamentarians gave in to pressures from the pension fund sector to move the
envisaged start of the universal second tier forward from 2004 to 2002, while
the cut-off age was increased from age 33 to age 42, thus speeding up second-
tier development and guaranteeing a larger market.[33] The reformers' efforts at
consensus-building were crucial to make the pension reform package politically
acceptable.[34] The new Social Code was approved in December 1999, just in
time to meet the conditionality.

The pension reform laws were implemented gradually, starting with the first-
and third-tier reforms. Reformers opted to delay the start of second-tier funds
when preparations had not progressed sufficiently, keen to avoid the severe
problems facing the Polish reform, which had come to be known in Bulgaria.
Moreover, the lack of attractive investment options on the nascent Bulgarian
capital market were a matter of concern (Stanchev and Stoev 1999; Abadjiev
2000). After a pre-history of Ponzi-type schemes in the early 1990s, a regulated
capital market was opened only at the end of 1997, and actual trade is still
negligible (Stanchev 2001). So far, funds have mainly invested in government
securities or in local bank deposits. Market participants also complained about a

lack of transparency in business practices and accounting standards (Beamish-Rosenburg 2001, 2002). Weak contract enforcement, widespread corruption and high levels of state capture are problematic context factors for the new industry (Ulgenerk and Zlaoui 2000; World Bank 2001a; Hellman, Jones and Kaufmann 2000).[35]

The new pension system

The new Bulgarian pension system was phased in gradually from January 2000 to January 2002. Alongside the reformed public PAYG scheme, several funded tiers are in place. Some are mandatory and others voluntary, while all are defined contribution schemes based on IFF accounts. Private pension fund management companies can apply for licences to establish one each of the four types of funds for which provision is made in the Bulgarian reform legislation: occupational funds, universal funds, voluntary funds and privatisation voucher funds (Chiappe 2001). Currently, eight pension insurance companies are operating in Bulgaria. All of them have established occupational, universal and voluntary funds (Troev 2001).

The first tier, run by the NSSI, is still mandatory for all insured. Most importantly, an earnings-related benefit formula was introduced, inspired by the German point system. Retirement benefits are calculated by multiplying the individual insurance years with the individual coefficient and the national average monthly income. The individual coefficient is essentially defined as the ratio between the individual monthly income and the nation-wide average for the same period. For periods before 1997, transitional rules are in place. All pensions were recalculated according to the new formula (Hristoskov 2000b). Eligibility is now based on two conditions: the insured must have reached a minimum age threshold, and his/her age plus insurance period must equal or exceed a minimum number of points. After a transition period, the age threshold will be 63 for men and 60 for women, while the number of points will be 100 for men and 94 for women. This means that men will only be able to retire at age 63 if they have at least 37 insurance years, and women at age 60 solely if they have completed at least 34 insurance years. Those who fail to meet these conditions at ages 63 and 60, respectively, have to continue their working life. Yet, all insured can retire at age 65 with a vesting period of at least 15 years. Pension contributions are still high, amounting to 6.4 per cent for employees, while employers are charged 25.6 per cent, plus 3 per cent for first- and second-category workers.[36] The envisaged average replacement rate will be 40 per cent of pre-retirement income (Chiappe 2001).

The second tier consists of occupational funds and universal pension funds, both of which are mandatory for certain groups. The occupational tier started in January 2000 and is run by private pension funds. Since then, employers are mandated to contribute 12 per cent on behalf of their first-category workers and 7 per cent on behalf of their second-category workers to these newly created institutions. Reformers sharply reduced the number of occupations eligible to preferential treatment. As soon as they fulfil the post-reform eligibility criteria, the remaining first- and second-category workers can opt to take out an early retirement pension from their pension fund until they reach the regular retirement age. The benefit level will be determined by both the individual account balance and the number of years to go until the individual's regular retirement age. Alternatively, the insured can opt to continue working. In this case, they can take out their fund balance as a lump-sum payment, or add it to their universal fund account (see below). Contributions were initially placed on a special account at the NSSI, as the licensing of occupational funds started late. Those 130 000 insured who currently qualify for first- and second-tier labour categories had to choose among the licensed occupational funds until January 2001. Preliminary data suggest that 88 per cent of all affiliates had opted for the three largest funds (*Pensions International*, June 2001).

Universal second-tier funds started operations in January 2002. Participation in these new institutions is mandatory for third-category workers born after 1959, about 1.2 million persons. They must redirect part of their first-tier contributions – to be gradually increased from 2 to 5 per cent of wages – to one of the private pension fund administrators. These insured will receive their future retirement benefits simultaneously from both the public PAYG tier and the funded tier. '[C]ontributions deposited under pillar I should gradually diminish at the expense of an increase of contributions under pillar II' (Chiappe 2001: 57). Second-tier funds must invest at least half of their assets in securities issued or guaranteed by the government and may invest up to 5 per cent of assets overseas. It should be noted that the Bulgarian state provides no guarantees or commitments under the second-tier schemes (Polackova Brixi, Shatalov and Zlaoui 2000).

The existing voluntary pension funds were required to apply for third-tier licences until September 2000. Around 35 companies who failed to do so have been notified for termination of their activities (Nikolov 2000). The remaining funds counted 411 000 members. Tax incentives are granted for third-tier contributions, which can be made by the insured, his/her employer, or other persons or entities on the insured's behalf. Third-tier funds are mandated to invest at least half of their assets in securities issued or guaranteed by the government and/or bank deposits, and may invest up to 10 per cent of assets overseas (Abadjiev 2000). Against explicit World Bank advice (World Bank 1996c), the Bulgarian reformers attempted to link mass privatisation to the pension fund industry by enabling the creation of a separate type of voluntary pension funds for privatisation vouchers for up to seven years, after which the funds are to be merged with other voluntary pension funds. However, the project seems to have been unsuccessful so far, due to a distinct lack of enthusiasm among pension companies to operate voucher funds and to convert vouchers into pension payments after five years (Nikolov 2001; *Pensions International*, February 2001).[37]

Conclusion

In Bulgaria, pension reform had long been on the political agenda. In the first half of the 1990s, Bulgarian pension reformers had received conflicting advice from the IMF and the World Bank, on the one hand, and the ILO, on the other, with the latter proving more influential in the early 1990s (Minev 1993). In 1996, however, when the NSSI was set up and needed to be equipped with sophisticated IT, the World Bank proved to have a higher leverage. Its loan for the public pension scheme triggered the socialist government's commitment to a supplementary funded tier. Initially limited to those occupations that enjoyed privileged treatment, the second-tier plans were soon extended to include a universal IFF scheme, while the Bank's initial proposal to downsize the public tier to a flat-rate scheme was rejected in the light of the country's long social insurance tradition.

A fundamental conceptual change emerged when an acute economic crisis and near default resulted in the adoption of structural reforms by a centre-right government. In this context, pension privatisation was useful to signal the government's commitment to a market-oriented course. Moreover, an interaction among structural reforms can be observed: the strict fiscal discipline required under the currency board arrangement heightened the impetus for pension reform (World Bank 2001a), while reformers also thought that private pension funds could transform privatisation vouchers into tangible benefits. This account indicates that the World Bank's leverage and agenda-shifting took effect in a two-step process. Moreover, it points to a two-layered crisis shaping pension reform. In a first step, the dire state of the pension system made far-reaching reform a necessity, while the subsequent decision for partial pension privatisation was taken in the midst of a general economic emergency that granted the IFIs a powerful role, enabling them to condition structural adjustment loans to pension privatisation.

As to domestic actors in the Bulgarian reform arena, it is remarkable that the Ministry of Labour took the lead in all pension reform preparations throughout the 1990s, even after the paradigm change, whereas the Ministry of Finance played a less visible role than elsewhere. Moreover, it is interesting to note that trade unions turned out to be supportive of the envisaged multipillar model. Previously, they had been granted a role in the NSSI's tripartite board of directors and were thus aware of its financial difficulties. Moreover, trade unions had developed business interests in the pension fund industry that preceded structural pension reform. In a similar vein, Labour Minister Neikov's harmonious cooperation with the new pension orthodoxy can be related to the fact that he had been a vice president of the largest trade union confederation, while also serving a spell on the managing board of its private pension fund, *Doverie*. Other participants in the voluntary pension fund sector, such as insurance companies, were also among the stakeholders inclined towards a mandatory IFF tier, although the strict third-tier regulations affected the industry.

The Bulgarian reform process was marked by a corporatist policy style. Although trade unions were not vested with formal veto points, pension reformers made an effort to obtain their consensus prior to the legislative process. Familiar with non-Bismarckian types of pension provision and granted with stakes in the pension fund industry, they turned into important allies of the Bulgarian pension reformers, the cuts in the public scheme notwithstanding. Yet, Congress was another important forum to discuss and negotiate the envisaged reform, hence the reform process also exhibits parliamentarist features. Meanwhile, the iconoclastic reform survived its first regime change when endorsed by the newly elected government of Bulgaria's ex-monarch, Simeon Saxe-Coburg-Gotha (Tilkidjiev 2001; Troev 2001).

NOTES

1. It should be noted that from 1945 until its break-up, Yugoslavia had maintained a close relationship with the World Bank. In 1979, the country ranked among the Bank's five largest borrowers (Cullen 1979).
2. However, Croatia is still classified as 'less indebted' (World Bank 2001c).
3. The opportunity to purchase up to five years of the vesting period had been introduced by a Yugoslav law in July 1990 (Gapić 1990).
4. No data were available on life expectancy other than at birth, when it was 69.5 years for men and 85.3 years for women (UNDP 2001).
5. These groups included retired parliamentarians, war veterans, war invalids, families of war victims and refugees from other parts of former Yugoslavia (IMF 1998). See Anušić, O'Keefe and Madžarević-Šujster (2003) for the legal conflicts surrounding the funding of merit pensions.
6. The Pension Institute transferred about 5.5 per cent of the payroll to the health insurance for health care expenses of pensioners, hence the effective pension contribution was about 20 per cent. When this transfer was abolished in 1998, the pension contribution was fixed at 21.5 per cent (World Bank 1997a; IMF 1998).
7. Reportedly, a dozen versions of this Pension Insurance Law were discussed in 1992–94, contributing to basic intra-government consensus-building on the need for parametric reform.
8. Under the Law on the Transformation of Socially Owned Enterprises of 1991, the latter were commercialised and then offered to employees at a 35–40 per cent discount. Of the shares unsold after this first phase of insider privatisation, one-third was transferred to the Pension Institute, while the remaining three-thirds were allocated to the Croatian Privatisation Fund for privatisation through other methods (World Bank 1997a).

9. Personal communication by Siniša Zrinščak, May 2002. See also Croatian Chamber of Economy (2001).
10. See also Škember (2000) and Zdunić (1997).
11. Strictly speaking, the new system consists of more than two tiers: besides the mandatory PAYG and IFF tiers (tiers one and two), a third, voluntary private tier has been legislated. Moreover, those staying in the purely public scheme are entitled to a minimum pension, calculated by multiplying individual years of service with 0.825 per cent of the national average gross salary of 1998 ('zero' tier).
12. Basic information on the new system can be found in Anušić, O'Keefe and Madžarević-Šujster (2003).
13. These problems are by no means confined to Croatia. The 2001 Corruption Perception Index ranks both Croatia and Bulgaria 47th of 91 countries. Perceived corruption is thus worse than in Hungary (31), Uruguay (35), Poland (44) and Peru (44), but still less pronounced than in Argentina (57) and Bolivia (84). See Transparency International (2001).
14. See Anušić, O'Keefe and Madžarević-Šujster (2003: 35–6, 59). Apparently, computer programmes provided to the insured made it clear that most individuals in this age cohort would not be better off in the new system.
15. This loan was never realised, however (personal communication by Zoran Anušić, October 2002).
16. For a presentation and discussion of the Chilean reform in Croatia see Iglesias Palau (1997), Piñera (1997) and Bakić (2000).
17. There is an interesting parallel to the Uruguayan case in that the fight for wage-based indexation can backfire and enable a radical retrenchment of acquired rights, or even pension privatisation.
18. According to recent government estimates, the transition costs for 2002 alone will amount to 1.3–2.0 per cent of GDP (IMF 2001d). A recent World Bank study comes up with substantially lower transition costs (Anušić, O'Keefe and Madžarević-Šujster 2003: 71).
19. See also IMF (1998: 62): 'the cost due to the diversion of contributions to the second pillar does not imply a fiscal expansion ... It will, however, increase the budget deficit'.
20. In 1985–95, the remaining life expectancy at third-category retirement age was 16.0 years for men and 23.5 years for women (Gillion et al. 2000).
21. In spite of rescheduling and debt reduction, following the country's moratorium on Communist-era debt in 1990, Bulgaria continues to be classified as a severely indebted country (World Bank 2001c).
22. Since 1997, foreign exchange reserves must cover at least 100 per cent of the monetary base, and there is a ban on central bank lending to the government. Since 1999, the new Bulgarian lev is pegged to the euro (Ulgenerk and Zlaoui 2000).
23. Over the period 1989–92, Bulgaria's population of 8.9 million shrank by 500 000 persons, most of which are thought to have emigrated (Gotovska-Popova 1993; NSSI 2000). According to ILO–CEET (1994), those who left were mainly ethnic Turks, who had been subject to forced assimilation under Zhivkov.
24. Shortly afterwards, pension contributions were increased to as much as 37, 49 and 52 per cent (World Bank 1996c). In 1996, a 2 per cent individual contribution rate was added.
25. In 1993, 21 per cent of all insured were classified in the first and second labour categories (NSSI 2000).
26. 'Changing to a fully or partially funded method of financing pensions would mean that the current generation of contributors ... would have to finance the cost of pensions for the present generation of pensioners and the buildup of reserves for their own future pensions at the same time. In addition the accumulated fund would soon exceed the potential for investment in Bulgaria' (Ministry of Labour 1994: 52).
27. According to an early reform concept, voluntary retirement savings were to be deposited at a Social Security Bank, an idea opposed by World Bank experts (World Bank 1991).
28. As in other transition countries, paper records were kept by employers on behalf of employed workers, only to be forwarded to the social insurance administration upon the worker's retirement (World Bank 1996c).

29. 'A funded pension system ... cannot possibly replace a PAYG system in a country as mature as Bulgaria. This is because the existing pension debt is too large' (Fox 1995: 221).
30. A similar scheme was introduced in Slovenia, although there are conceptual differences (cf. Stanovnik 2002).
31. A comparative reading of the Bank's Staff Appraisal Report and the attached Letter of Sectoral Development Policy, signed by the Minister of Finance, the Minister of Labour and the Governor of NSSI, provides a glimpse of the remaining differences regarding the design of the second tier (see World Bank 1996c).
32. At the end of 1999, *Doverie* had nearly 82 000 clients, while the total number of affiliates to private pension funds was estimated at 450 000 (*Pensions International*, January and April 2000).
33. For the original reform concept see Bulgarian Pension Reform Strategy (1999).
34. For the extent of consensus-building see the statements by social partners in the Pension Reform Project's information booklet (Pension Reform Project 2000, 2001). However, a group of MPs challenged the mandatory private tier at the Constitutional Court (Hristoskov 2000b), albeit unsuccessfully. Moreover, a survey conducted in May 2000 found that the reform did not enjoy broad public report (UNDESA et al. 2000).
35. For an attempt to measure the high level of state capture in Bulgaria and elsewhere see Hellman, Jones and Kaufmann (2000). State capture shapes the formation of laws, rules, decrees and regulations through illicit and non-transparent private payments to public officials (Hellman and Kaufmann 2001).
36. These are the rates for the year 2000. The contribution burden will be gradually shifted from the employer to the employee, until a ratio of 1:1 is reached in 2007 (Hristoskov 2000a; Tebeyan 2000).
37. See Michailova (1997), Peev (1999) and Miller and Petranov (2000) on privatisation programmes in Bulgaria.

PART IV

Comparative Analysis and Conclusions

10. The political economy of pension privatisation

10.1 NEW ROLE MODELS BEYOND BISMARCK AND BEVERIDGE

An increasing amount of contemporary policy change is affected by the global diffusion of ideas and the translation of models into different contexts (Czarniawska and Joerges 1995; Dolowitz and Marsh 2000). In old-age security reform, it was the cognitive availability of a precedent – Chile – that turned pension privatisation from a theoretical concept into a political reality (Weyland 2001). Three of the Latin American countries analysed above are bordered by Chile – a geographical proximity that clearly facilitated the transfer of ideas. When policymakers compared their countries' economic performance to the Chilean success story, they identified pension privatisation as one of the ingredients, ascribing strong macroeconomic effects to it. The promotional activities of pension funds and social security experts from Chile contributed to the direct diffusion of the precedent all over the subcontinent. According to all accounts, José Piñera personally convinced more than one Latin American president to embark on pension privatisation.

Particularly in the first half on the 1990s, the 'Chilean model' featured prominently in Washington, and deviations from the precedent would not be encouraged. The cases of Argentina and Uruguay – where the mixed reform outcome was only seen as a 'first step' towards full pension privatisation (García-Mujica 1996; World Bank 1996d) – are telling. Reforms would be censured as 'second best' and 'home-made' (Schwarz 1998; World Bank 2000e), until eventually the realisation emerged that '[f]lexibility in the design of operations is key to benefit from government ownership of a reform program' (World Bank 2000e: 8). In this sense it can be argued that pension reformers in Eastern Europe, starting a few years later, profited from a process of policy learning inside the IFIs. Nevertheless, the recent reform trends in Latin America suggest that the 'Chilean model' is still the predominant policy advice and cognitive reference in this region.[1]

118   *Privatising old-age security*

On the other hand, it is interesting to note that 'adopters eventually become source countries themselves' (Kay 1998: 47). This is not only true for Argentina that exported its mixed model to the transition countries. Partial pension privatisation in Poland and Hungary triggered another regional contagion effect from the Baltics to the Balkans (see Table 7.2), comparable only to the impact of the 'Chilean model' in Latin America. In the Central Asian part of the post-socialist region, demonstration effects from the more radical Kazakh reform can be observed, the virtual absence of capital markets in the region notwithstanding (Müller 2003a).

10.2   PARALLELS AND DIFFERENCES IN STRUCTURAL PENSION REFORM

There are important parallels in the recent waves of pension reform in Latin America and Eastern Europe, as Chapter 4, Table 4.1 and Chapter 7, Table 7.2 indicate. In both regions, the public–private mix in the provision for old age has been changed significantly over the past decade. Before structural pension reform was implemented, most countries in both regions used to have a monolithic public pension system, as supplementary private old-age schemes were frequently non-existent. By now, policymakers have introduced private old-age provision on a mandatory basis, while at the same time downsizing or closing down the public tier. The recent move towards pension privatisation implied the adoption of a 'worker-choice model' (Lindeman, Rutkowski and Sluchynskyy 2000: 32). This system of individual retirement savings accounts, managed by competing pension funds, has also been dubbed 'mandatory, forced saving program' (Hemming 1998: 22).

While the structural pension reforms in Latin America and Eastern Europe show striking similarities in their basic design, each of these reforms is unique in its features, as their architects rightly claim, reflecting the local policy process. For example, individual accounts were originally only fed by employees' contributions in order to make people save for their own retirement and turn them into true owners of their pension fund accounts, there being no role for employers. However, in some of the more recent reforms contributions to the new mandatory private pension tiers are split between employee and employer, such as in Colombia, Costa Rica, El Salvador, Mexico, Nicaragua, Bulgaria, Croatia and Estonia, or even include a state contribution. Some countries have complemented the individually funded tier with occupational schemes.

Most importantly, however, a variety of state-market compromises can be appreciated (Brooks 1998). While fund administrators in most countries are exclusively private, in some countries public entities also play a significant role, notably in Uruguay and Kazakhstan, where they dominate the market. A cross-regional comparison suggests that the most important difference between the Latin American and East European pension privatisations concerns the size of the private IFF tier, that is, the scope of the paradigm shift. So far, structural pension reform in Latin America has predominantly implied closing down the public tier or phasing it out (five cases), while mixed and parallel reform paths were adopted less frequently (three and two cases, respectively). In the transition countries, basic reform types are more similar. There is only one post-socialist country – Kazakhstan – that replicated the 'Chilean model'. The other eight transition countries that have legislated and/or implemented pension privatisation decided to retain a downsized public pillar under a mixed reform strategy. Moreover, an overall look at both regions reveals that every second Latin American country opted for one or another variant of pension privatisation, while the majority of post-socialist transition countries still stick to PAYG-only reforms. Those East European countries that chose pension privatisation exhibit more diversity in terms of first tier design than their Latin American counterparts. Besides 'traditional' PAYG pillars, NDC schemes and pension points have been introduced in some transition countries to strengthen the contribution-benefit link in public old-age provision (see Chapter 4, Table 4.1 and Chapter 7, Table 7.2).

In both regions, public confidence in the pre-reform pension schemes had been shaken by the financial difficulties and/or the deficient management of the public PAYG schemes, resulting in delayed or reduced benefit payments. This effect was particularly pronounced in Latin America where many public schemes performed poorly, translating into an earlier move to IFF schemes, as well as a more radical privatisation of old-age security. Unlike the East European countries, Latin America featured a private financial sector in the past decades, ready to administer the accumulation of private pension capital. Capital markets, however shaky, had also been in place for a longer period of time. Moreover, the political viability of full pension privatisation is likely to have been facilitated by a lack of social cohesion and poorly spread values of social justice in most of Latin America. Argentina, Uruguay and Costa Rica, the only Latin American countries that have implemented the mixed model so far, are notable exceptions in this respect.

The predominance of the substitutive reform type in Latin America is linked to strong demonstration effects from the 'Chilean model', even though its massive diffusion had to wait for the Pinochet regime to end. Clearly, the decision to privatise pensions was shaped by the outcome of similar reform decisions made in a peer nation (Brooks 2001). When selling it to the public, however, policymakers often avoided direct reference to the model (Kay 2000) – because of a history of bilateral animosities and/or due to the political connotations of the Chilean reform. In Latin America, policymakers and interest groups became acquainted with the Chilean case long before their counterparts in Eastern Europe (Madrid 1998). On the subcontinent, autonomous policy learning by the recipient countries tended to precede systematic promotion efforts by the IFIs as agenda setters, even though virtually all reform teams were effectively financed by the latter (Nelson 2000).

Individual Latin American reformers passed their experiences on to East European policymakers, in person or via their writing.[2] Still, direct diffusion effects from Chile and other Latin American reform precedents were rather weak in the post-socialist region, with the exception of Croatia and Kazakhstan. Latin America carried the stigma of being a less developed region (Orenstein 2000), making it unsuitable as a benchmark case.[3] However, Latin American-style pension privatisation was recommended as a major reform option by the IFIs (World Bank 1994a; Vittas 1997).[4] To provide first-hand information on Latin American pension reforms, the World Bank and USAID also sponsored trips to Argentina and Chile for Polish and Bulgarian MPs, social security experts, trade unionists and journalists. Hence, it seems that in Eastern Europe, where the connotations of the 'Chilean model' were more likely to refer to the Pinochet regime than to a regional example of economic success, the IFIs played an important though mostly low-key role as agents of transmission, helping to enhance the low status of the Latin American precedents (Nelson 2000; Müller 2001a).

Otherwise, East European policymakers were more prone to look to the West than to the South in search for models, not least in the context of their aspirations at EU membership. However, there is no mainstream pension model in Western Europe. Rather, the region is characterised by a considerable heterogeneity in old-age provision. Consequently, EU accession negotiations do not entail a pension reform blueprint to be followed. Still, individual EU member states have been sending experts to the transition countries in the past decade. The Swedish reform blueprint – a multipillar system combining NDC and a small funded tier – has had an impact on some East European countries, notably those bordering the Baltic Sea. German and Italian design features – pension points and demographic factors – have been adopted by pension reformers in South-Eastern Europe.

10.3   POLITICAL ACTORS AND THE POLICY CONTEXT

The iconoclastic Latin American and East European pension reforms cannot be explained by the impact of role models alone. In order to shed light on the political feasibility of pension privatisation in both regions, this analysis discusses the findings of the eight case studies above. While drawing on some of the major hypotheses of the political economy of policy reform literature, it also includes the identification of the most important political actors in the pension reform arena. Moreover, the policy context that shaped their room for manœuvre, influenced by political factors, economic conditions and the policy legacy, is discussed comparatively (see Table 10.1).

Scholars of the political economy of policy reform have stressed the importance of leadership by committed individuals, often market-oriented economists, with an ability to communicate a coherent vision (Harberger 1993). The above case studies have shown that pension privatisation amounts to a paradigm shift that may be greatly facilitated by such policymakers. Menem and Cavallo (Argentina), Boloña (Peru), Sánchez de Lozada (Bolivia) and Bokros (Hungary) were famous for the radical, market-oriented reform packages they pushed through. In Argentina and Poland, respectively, there is unanimity that radical pension reform would have been impossible without Schulthess and Bączkowski, who set up the respective reform teams. Rutkowski and Anušić, World Bank economists on leave, played a key role in Poland and Croatia. However, a high-profile leadership by a committed neoliberal economist-turned-policymaker was clearly not a necessary condition in all of the above cases of pension privatisation. Notably in Uruguay and Bulgaria, intense efforts at consensus-building with the traditional political adversary and trade unions, respectively, substituted for seclusive technocratic teams.

In most of the above cases of pension privatisation, the most important actor in the local policy arena was the Minister of Economy and Finance. His role was especially pronounced in Argentina, Peru, Poland, Hungary and Croatia. This actor, for whom pension privatisation was a means to achieve macroeconomic rather than social objectives, was supported by local interest groups, such as business organisations and the financial sector, as well as the IFIs. In Argentina and Bolivia, local banks and insurance companies were among the first advocates of pension privatisation, elaborating detailed reform concepts and presenting it to the public. But there was also opposition to structural pension reform, both within and outside government. In all of the above country cases but Bulgaria, trade unions, social security employees and pensioners' associations held protest marches and strikes, collected signatures and wrote protest notes, claiming that social security was more than a business opportunity.

Moreover, the Ministers of Labour, Welfare or Health, responsible for the existing old-age security schemes, were usually less than enthusiastic about structural pension reform, as were most lawyers. However, given the Finance Ministry's weight in the cabinet, the opposing portfolios could not prevent the radical move. In Poland and Bulgaria, Ministers of Labour strongly opposed pension privatisation, but after a cabinet reshuffle and a government change, respectively, new Labour Ministers with an *ex ante* commitment to a mandatory funded tier were appointed to facilitate the iconoclastic move. The influence of intra-government opponents on reform design was typically limited by establishing small pension reform working groups, mostly attached to the Ministry of Finance and often excluding the 'Bismarckian faction'. This policy pattern confirms the technocratisation of decision-making in pension privatisation and the key role of 'insulated policy-making elites' in policy reform (Schamis 1999: 265). The inner circle of reformers was often educated in the US, shared the language of the IFIs and sometimes even depended on foreign aid funds for their salaries (Morales 1995).

Left-wing parties did not always join the ranks of reform opponents. As noted above, there have been many cases where market-friendly reforms have not been carried out by conservative free marketeers, but rather by left-wing governments (a 'Nixon-in-China syndrome' reversed). In this study, the Peronists in Argentina, the MNR in Bolivia and the post-socialist governments in Poland and Hungary are among the 'unlikely' administrations, formerly known for their left-wing or populist leanings, yet involved in pension privatisation. It can be argued that left-wing administrations were under a stronger pressure from international creditors to demonstrate their commitment to market-oriented reforms. Moreover, left-wing administrations were often better suited to handle opposition from trade unions. In Argentina, Hungary and Poland, the governing parties had traditional ties with the unions and used them to ease resistance. On the other side of the coin, these ties implied that pension reformers were forced to negotiate with reform opponents and to make concessions.

The specific policy context may provide reformers or reform opponents with action resources. The executive's degree of control of the legislature amounts to an important institutional variable. In Bolivia, Uruguay, Bulgaria and Hungary, the large parliamentary majority enjoyed by the governing coalition allowed for a swift passing of structural pension reform. Contrary to this, in Peru pension privatisation was not legislated by Congress, but adopted by presidential decree after President Fujimori had dissolved the legislature. While other studies have found an inverse relationship between the degree of democratisation and the degree of privateness of a pension reform (e.g. Mesa-Lago 1999), this small cross-regional sample has not confirmed this notion. Pension privatisation in Peru and Croatia – the outliers in terms of the Freedom House country rating (see Table 10.1) – was by no means faster or more radical than in the other cases. A closer look at both cases reveals a wavering commitment of the president and/or the ruling party to the iconoclastic paradigm shift. Clearly, in a context of concentrated authority, leadership in policy reform initiatives is key.

The Uruguayan case illustrates that elements of direct democracy – referenda and plebiscites – may give reform opponents a chance to reverse pension reform laws that have already been passed and to legislate on pension-related matters. However, in the cases analysed here, the use of these action resources could not prevent pension privatisation. Rather, in four cases – Uruguay, Argentina, Poland and Croatia – a successful defence of the *status quo* in old-age security ultimately backfired. In these countries, opponents won lawsuits, referenda or plebiscites against parametric reforms, but these moves resulted in high fiscal costs. By narrowing the available choice of policy alternatives, they engendered more radical reform measures than the ones that had initially been opposed. Hence, these are tales of unintended effects. Over and above the fiscal motivation, the Uruguayan and Croatian governments also looked for policy alternatives to stop the opposition from capitalising politically on their anti-retrenchment protest.

The paradigm choice in Latin American and East European old-age security appears to have been substantially influenced by economic factors and considerations. Pension privatisation has been primarily proposed for macroeconomic motives, in hope of triggering a virtuous circle leading to economic growth. Madrid (1998) and James and Brooks (2001) have pointed to the increase of international capital mobility, which may have motivated policymakers to seek to reduce the vulnerability to capital outflows by boosting domestic savings and strengthening the local capital market. Thus, investment of pension funds abroad tends to be dramatically limited by portfolio regulations. In this context, it is surprising to note that the pre-reform situation of the local capital market, however poor, was rarely perceived as a constraint to pension privatisation. The cases of Croatia and Bulgaria, where the nascent state of the capital markets amounted to one of the reasons to delay pension privatisation, are notable exceptions.

10.4   ON CRISES AND LEGACIES

Scholars of the political economy of policy reform have highlighted that a preceding crisis may induce radical change – the so-called 'benefit of crises' hypothesis (Drazen and Grilli 1993). While some scholars have suggested that crises only amount to an opportunity to introduce *ad hoc* stabilisation measures (Haggard and Webb 1993; Nelson 1994), others have shown that crises may also bring about profound institutional reforms (Wagener 1997). In all of the above case studies, pension reformers reacted to an atmosphere of crisis, but the perceived or actual emergencies clearly took different forms.

Table 10.1   *The pension reform context compared: selected indicators*

Indicators	Argentina	Uruguay	Peru	Bolivia	Hungary	Poland	Croatia	Bulgaria
Old-age dependency rate[a]	27.0	34.5	14.3	16.2	35.1	29.4	37.6	38.5
Coverage rate[b]	53.0	82.0	20.0	11.7	77.0	68.0	66.0	64.0
Estimated size of IPD[c]	305	289	45	31	213	220	350	n.a.
Public pension spending[d]	4.1	8.7	1.2	2.5	9.7	14.4	11.6	7.3
General gov't balance[e]	-1.3	-0.2	-5.7	-4.4	-6.7	-2.8	-1.3	-4.3
Total external debt[e]	43.1	36.7	41.0	77.2	66.3	43.8	32.1	88.7
Freedom House rating[f]	2.3	2.2	6.5	2.3	1.2	1.2	4.4	2.3
Reform type	mixed	mixed	parallel	substitutive	mixed	mixed	mixed	mixed

Notes: [a] 60+ years old in % of 20–59 years old; mid-1990s.
[b] Contributors in % of labour force; mid-1990s.
[c] Implicit pension debt in % of GDP.
[d] In % of GDP; mid-1990s.
[e] In % of GDP; four-year average prior to reform adoption.
[f] Numbers ranging from 1 to 7; the lower the number, the higher the freedom rating for the year of reform adoption.

Sources: Chapter 4, Table 4.2 and Chapter 7, Table 7.1.; Madrid (2001); EBRD (2001); IDB (1998); Freedom House (2000).

While a rising deficit in the public pension scheme may be a straightforward motive for change, in a number of countries the state of pension accounting did not allow policymakers to tell whether the old-age scheme was in deficit. However, it is usually possible to determine the percentage of public pension spending to GDP and the old-age dependency ratio, which may also be on the increase. As noted above, successful action of reform opponents may block retrenchment and, thus, future cost-containment options. Moreover, public pension expenditure may be considered too high in a context of general fiscal imbalances. In addition, some of the above countries witnessed economic collapse shortly before pension privatisation occurred. In a context of high external indebtedness, this kind of emergency triggered a series of measures suitable to signal good behaviour to the IFIs and rating agencies, including pension privatisation. The country cases analysed here indicate that under all three scenarios – a crisis of the pension system, a fiscal emergency, and economic crisis *cum* high external debt – policymakers tended to warn against the imminent collapse of the PAYG scheme, even if the available data indicated otherwise. Therefore, in the following paragraphs an effort is made to identify the facts behind this common discourse.[5]

Table 10.2 presents a comparative view of the different patterns of emergency observed in the above country cases.[6] Almost all countries experienced a sizeable fiscal deficit and/or high pension expenditure prior to reform. In Uruguay the state budget was almost balanced and acute economic crisis had long passed, but the old-age and system dependency ratios, as well as pension spending in per cent of GDP, were by far the highest in Latin America, clearly alarming policymakers (see Chapter 4, Table 4.2). Contrary to this, Peru and Bolivia still have a young population and spend a very low share of their GDP on old-age security, whereas the Peruvian pension system was not even in the red before the reform. However, both countries suffered from high fiscal imbalances and severe external indebtedness. Conversely, Croatia's external debt burden and fiscal deficits were low, but public pension spending and system dependency ratios soared. Argentina, Peru, Hungary and Bulgaria witnessed a grave economic crisis shortly before embarking on pension privatisation. In Argentina and Bulgaria, the need for fiscal restraint was heightened by the adoption of a currency board shortly before preparations for pension reform began.

Crises may enable policy reform because they can change the relevant constellation of actors. In the pension reform arena, they are likely to reinforce the 'privatisation faction'. Fiscal crises turn the Ministry of Finance into a potential actor in the pension reform arena. More specifically, when pension finances display a deficit, the resulting dependence on budgetary subsidies grants this likely advocate of the new pension orthodoxy an important stake in old-age security reform (Müller 1999).

Table 10.2 A typology of crises

Reform context	Argentina	Uruguay	Peru	Bolivia	Hungary	Poland	Croatia	Bulgaria
Deficit in PAYG scheme	n.a.	yes	no	yes	yes	n.a.	yes	yes
Public pension spending	moderate; rising	high; rising	low; constant	very low	high; falling	high; constant	high; rising	high; constant
Fiscal imbalances	low; falling	low; rising	high; falling	high; falling	high; constant	high; constant	low; rising	high; falling
Economic crisis	yes	no	yes	no	yes	no	no	yes
External indebtedness[a]	severe	moderate	severe	severe	moderate	severe	low	severe
Other critical context factors	currency board; lawsuits against retrenchment	wage-based pension indexation in constitution	default on foreign debt; int'l outrage over self-coup	none	first post-communist gov't after 1989	first post-communist gov't after 1989; legal action against retrenchment	war; int'l isolation; legal action against retrenchment	currency board

Note: [a] World Bank classification at the time of reform.

Sources: Chapter 5, Tables 5.1, 5.2; Chapter 6, Tables 6.1, 6.2; Chapter 8, Tables 8.1, 8.2; Chapter 9, Tables 9.1, 9.2; country studies above.

However, pension privatisation engenders transition costs that are likely to have a considerable fiscal impact. Hence, there is a flip side to the economic factors and considerations that tend to push pension privatisation in the first place (Müller 2002a). In this context, it is interesting to note that the IFIs have recently softened their stance on fiscal deficits stemming from a shift to funding. In the Hungarian case the World Bank (1999a: 44) argued that 'the transitional deficit is not a fiscal deficit in the usual sense', while the IMF (1998: 62) followed a similar line of reasoning with regard to Croatia.

As noted above, governments often stress their general commitment to market-oriented reform when external debt is high and economic crisis looms. The announcement of pension privatisation can be interpreted as a 'signalling' strategy (Rodrik 1998), as rating agencies include radical pension reform as a point in favour in their country-risk assessments, in spite of its fiscal impact. In Argentina, Peru, Bolivia and Bulgaria, pension privatisation was firmly embedded in a package of 'Washington consensus' reforms. Critical indebtedness also makes it more likely that the IFIs get involved in the local pension reform arena (Brooks 1998, 2001). The World Bank, with its prominent stance in international old-age security reform, amounts to a powerful external actor in a number of highly indebted Latin American and East European countries. Together with other IFIs and government agencies, it exerted its influence first and foremost as an agenda shifter in the local debate, engaging in an expert-based knowledge transfer. Moreover, lending activities and conditionalities were a central instrument to support pension privatisation in Latin America and Eastern Europe (Holzmann 2000).

Five of the countries analysed above were classified as severely indebted at the time of pension privatisation (Argentina, Peru, Bolivia, Poland and Bulgaria). Hungary and Uruguay were characterised by moderate indebtedness, while Croatia's indebtedness was low (World Bank 1996b; 2001c). However, Croatia's political isolation under Tuđman still rendered the IFIs important international allies. Whereas in Hungary, the World Bank's important involvement was kept low-key, in other countries (e.g. in Argentina) local policymakers explicitly asked to include pension privatisation in an IMF accord as a form of 'blame avoidance' (Weaver 1986). In Poland and Croatia, the special task force for pension reform was headed by a World Bank economist on leave, granting this prominent external actor extra leverage. In recent years other IFIs and government agencies – such as the IMF, USAID and the IDB – have also supported pension privatisation. Although they took part in cross-conditionalities as well as other forms of cooperation, overall they played a less outstanding role than the Bank. Yet, there are exceptions: in Uruguay reformers could initially only count on IDB support, as the World Bank disapproved of the mixed reform design. In Bulgaria, USAID provided key technical support in the implementation phase – after the crucial conditionalities had been worked out and negotiated by the World Bank.

As to legacies, it is remarkable that in all of the above country cases, funded schemes were in place in the first half of the 20th century. Throughout, reserves were lost due to war, hyperinflation, mismanagement or expropriation. However, this experience – that reflects the fact that funded schemes are by no means immune to political and economic risks – was in no way reflected as a lesson or caution in the reform process. Contrary to this, existing institutional arrangements did play a role in terms of policy feedback or path dependence. The Peruvian case shows that legal constraints can influence pension reform outcomes. The constitution established social security as a responsibility of the state, and private pension provision was only permitted on a supplementary basis. This was one of the reasons why policymakers opted for a parallel pension reform path (Mesa-Lago 1999).

Moreover, in Bismarckian-style PAYG schemes, the entitlements already earned by the insured may pose constraints to radical reform. The size of the so-called implicit pension debt (IPD), which translates into high fiscal costs when made explicit, is largely determined by the percentage of the population covered, the generosity and the maturity of the public scheme. These three factors differ substantially with regard to Latin America and Eastern Europe, as shown in Chapter 4, Table 4.2 and Chapter 7, Table 7.1. It has been argued that the larger the IPD, the smaller the likelihood for radical pension privatisation (James and Brooks 2001). The fact that most East European countries – a region where coverage approached 100 per cent in the recent past – have opted for the mixed reform path supports this hypothesis. In the Latin American context, the IPD hypothesis seems helpful to explain the cases of Argentina and Uruguay, where pre-reform coverage was high and reformers opted for a mixed scheme. Contrary to this, Bolivian reformers faced a much smaller implicit debt and a considerably younger population, hence they considered that radical pension privatisation was economically feasible (see Table 10.1). However, when Peruvian reformers were heading for a substitutive reform in a similar context, they faced political and legal obstacles. This indicates that the IPD is but one explanatory variable.

Moreover, IPD estimates should be interpreted with considerable caution, not least because they may be reduced in size by reform design. 'The ability of governments to change the rules breaks the equivalence between implicit and explicit liabilities' (Barr 2000: 15). Somewhat counter-intuitively, it was under the Pinochet dictatorship that recognition of pre-reform pension claims was most comprehensive (Mesa-Lago 2000). Contrary to this precedent, second-generation reformers rarely recognised existing pension claims to the full, in order to allow for a reduction of the fiscal costs of the shift to funding. Among the above case studies, Peru is a particularly striking case, where a fiscally driven revocation of acquired rights occurred through exclusionary conditions attached to recognition bonds. A closer look at the Chilean precedent reveals, however, that the Pinochet regime only recognised those pension entitlements that remained in place after the substantial retrenchment measures of the 1970s. Hence, it can be concluded that strategies to reduce the IPD have included the revocation of pension entitlements before, during or after pension privatisation. The timing of these retrenchment measures has strategic implications, to be discussed below.

10.5   POLICY STYLES AND REFORM DESIGN

Following the classification of policy styles by Bresser Pereira, Maravall and Przeworski (1993) mentioned in Chapter 2, it is notable that in a significant number of the above case studies – and in all but one of the Latin American cases – pension privatisation was pushed through by decretism (Peru) or mandatism (Uruguay, Bolivia, Croatia). In Hungary, corporatism was combined with mandatism. In comparison, a parliamentarist and/or corporatist policy style was chosen in Argentina, Bulgaria and Poland. Exclusionary policy styles, such as decretism and mandatism, are widely observed phenomena in policy reform, and pension privatisation is no exception. However, some of the case studies – notably Bolivia and Hungary – highlight that insufficient consensus-building on pension privatisation may backfire, as it can lead to severe alterations in reform design by subsequent governments that may ultimately threaten the sustainability of the reform. Contrary to this, it is interesting to note that Argentine pension reformers convinced an otherwise decretist president of the need to provide a solid legal basis for future investors by legislating pension privatisation through Congress.

In several of the above country cases, reformers attached great importance to reform design, with a view of lowering the political resistance to pension reform. The relevance of tactical sequencing, strategic bundling, packaging and compensation has been stressed by scholars of the political economy of policy reform (Haggard and Webb 1993; Rodrik 1993; Sturzenegger and Tommasi 1998). The Hungarian and Polish reformers resorted to tactical packaging when distancing themselves from the Latin American models and stressing the originality of local reform efforts (e.g. Rutkowski 1998).[7] In spite of the obvious conceptual parallels that indicate a *de facto* inclination to the Latin American models, policymakers decided to avoid all reference to these precedents, as soon as they found out about the inconvenient connotations among the Central European public (Müller 1999; Orenstein 2000).

In order to mitigate potential resistance to pension privatisation, reformers resorted to direct compensation by granting recognition bonds or compensatory pensions to those who switched to the newly established IFF tier – even though for fiscal reasons acquired pension entitlements were rarely recognised completely (see above). With the exception of Bolivia, Hungary and Croatia, where the new pension system is truly universal, reformers opted for a strategy of exclusionary compensation and division of potential opponents by exempting powerful pressure groups – most notably the military, but also some privileged professions – from structural pension reform. Moreover, in Uruguay, Poland, Croatia and Bulgaria opposition to pension privatisation was weakened by dividing the insured into age groups with regard to their participation in the new funded tier.

The Bolivian case is an example of strategic bundling and indirect compensation. In an effort to facilitate both policy agendas, pension reform was linked with enterprise capitalisation. At the same time, the modest *Bonosol–Bolivida* scheme was aimed at creating new stakeholders, most of which had never received a pension before – a high-impact strategy in a context of extremely low coverage. It is interesting to note that this strategy was chosen against the explicit advice by the IFIs, which had strongly suggested using the proceeds from capitalisation to finance the fiscal costs of pension privatisation.

Policymakers in Poland, Peru and Bulgaria also intended to link the privatisation of state-owned enterprises with structural pension reform. For different reasons, they failed to exploit the linkage's strategic potential, however. Polish policymakers decided to use privatisation proceeds to cover transition costs by supplying them to the state budget. While helping to solve the fiscal consequences of a partial shift to funding, this use of privatisation proceeds completely lacked visibility (Gesell-Schmidt, Müller and Süß 1999). In Peru, it was only in the aftermath of the unpopular pension reform that the government decided to link it with the privatisation of state-owned enterprises. In an attempt to ensure both fiscal benefits and visibility, two pension reserve funds fed by privatisation proceeds were established, one of which was to finance recognition bonds, while the other was used to pay a biannual supplement to beneficiaries of the state-run pension schemes. In Bulgaria, reformers thought that private pension funds could transform privatisation vouchers into tangible benefits, but met with a lack of enthusiasm among private pension fund administrators to convert vouchers into retirement benefits.

Full or partial pension privatisation enables policymakers to hand out potentially attractive stakes to potential opponents, thus creating constituencies (Graham 1997). 'Shifting to a funded scheme ... allows for arguments that all can win, thus abandoning intractable zero-sum games' (Holzmann 1997: 3).

Most notably in Argentina, reformers granted trade unions the right to run their own pension funds, thus converting them into stakeholders of pension privatisation. In Bulgaria, the trade unions' business interests in the private pension industry even preceded plans to establish a mandatory funded tier, thus facilitating a broad consensus on pension privatisation. Contrary to this, Peruvian trade unions, among which a plan to establish their own pension fund was taking shape, were banned from running AFPs.

As stressed by Pierson (1994), the political costs of reform can be lowered by increasing its complexity. In several Latin American and East European countries, the reformers' strategy amounted to bundling up some unavoidable, yet politically sensitive reforms of the public PAYG tier with the more visible introduction of individual pension fund accounts (Holzmann 2000). This 'obfuscation strategy' in Pierson's terms (1994: 21) entails the potential to lower the visibility of the envisaged cutbacks and to draw public attention to the granting of individualised ownership claims. The introduction of the individual pension fund accounts tended to be perceived as the creation of a monitorable track record of individual property rights over time, which the political system would be less likely to take away (Müller 1999).[8] However, the prospect of new privately run pension funds was received less enthusiastically in Croatia and Bulgaria, where memories of fraudulent pyramid schemes and failing banks were fresh.

In contrast to the unfavourable public perception of parametric reforms, the drawbacks related to pension privatisation are easier to conceal (Müller 1999). In most Latin American and East European countries, the scope and financing of transition costs – a major fiscal and distributional issue when it comes to a shift from PAYG to funded schemes – were successfully shielded from public debate. In most of the above country cases, the public perception of the strengths and weaknesses of pension privatisation was biased towards its advantages, while the concomitant fiscal burdens were ignored. This asymmetry of perception may explain the observable fact that policymakers have legislated structural pension reform in pre-electoral periods (see, e.g., Bolivia, Peru, Hungary, Poland). This timing is contrary to the conventional notion that retrenchment and radical reforms are unlikely when the hazards of accountability are high, thus suggesting that the perceived attractiveness of pension privatisation may outweigh its blame-generating potential. In this respect, the strategic potentials of pension privatisation and of parametric reforms differ markedly.

However, the above country cases suggest that not all pension reformers resorted to the simultaneous introduction of parametric and systemic reforms. In both Croatia and Bulgaria, a fiscally motivated sequencing strategy was chosen that started with a downsizing of the public scheme and introduced an IFF tier only three years later. However, as the different components of pension reform were legislated almost simultaneously, an underlying bundling strategy can still be observed (Anušić, O'Keefe and Madžarević-Šujster 2003). Contrary to this, Polish policymakers resorted to deliberate unbundling in the legislative process, mainly driven by the political business cycle. Pension privatisation was legislated before the elections, while the restructuring of the public tier was left to the new government.

Yet in the Polish case, the implementation of the entire pension reform package was bundled up with three other structural reforms, which were to come into force simultaneously. The latter turned out to be a very costly strategy. Pension reform preparations, most notably the IT system, were not ready on time, but the reform 'had to' start anyway, resulting in substantial implementation problems that persist until the present day. This example highlights that the reformers' desire to exploit a political window of opportunity to pass pension privatisation may clash with optimal reform preparations and existing state capacities. Similar lessons can also be drawn from the Hungarian and Peruvian cases, which required a substantial amount of *ex post* corrective legislation.

NOTES

1. Yet, according to Weyland (2001: 37), the 'Chilean model ... was "over-sold", based on theoretical speculation and little evidence'.
2. See, e.g., Piñera (1996, 1997, 2000, 2001) for appeals to Poles, Croats, Russians and Romanians.
3. See also Nowotny (1997), Lessenich (2000) and Müller (2002e).
4. For similar recommendations see also Holzmann (1994) and Fougerolles (1996).
5. In their study of the US, Canada, Britain, Germany and Sweden, Pierson and Weaver (1993) found that although the affordability of current pension spending levels clearly was an issue in the local political debates, the size of budget deficits and the timing of loss impositions were in no way connected. Thus, economic pressures, measured in terms of general fiscal imbalances or as the share of pension expenditures in particular, were insufficient to explain pension reform outcomes. Hence, more complex patterns of crisis are considered here.
6. For statistical and contextual details see the case studies above.
7. But cf. Müller (1998).
8. The recent Argentine experience shows that this may not necessarily be the case (see Chapter 5, Section 5.1).

11. Conclusions

Since Huntington's 'third wave' hypothesis, comparisons between East European and Latin American transformations have lost their exotic touch.[1] Obvious differences regarding the scope and sequence of transformations need not be passed over to allow for a fruitful comparison between both transitional regions. While the interdependence between economic and political change attracted much interest, there has been little comparative research on the political economy of individual policy areas, which were often reformed along similar lines.

This study has shown that pension reform is a particularly suitable case for this kind of cross-regional analysis. In spite of being geographically and culturally distant, both regions witnessed the almost simultaneous introduction of systems of individual retirement savings accounts, managed by predominantly private pension funds, which either compete with, substitute or complement the public PAYG scheme. It has been shown here that this parallel development is no coincidence, but a result of a *sui generis* institutional transfer from the South to the East, facilitated by a generalised retreat of the state in both regions. The most important differences between the pension privatisations in both regions concern the scope of the paradigm shift and the diversity in terms of first-tier design. Overall, the state retains a greater role in post-socialist old-age security than in Latin America and continues to fulfil its first-tier functions in increasingly diverse ways.

Unlike most other contemporary pensions-related research, this study did not discuss the desirability of a shift to funding. Neither did it attempt to draw early lessons from pension privatisation in both regions – much to the chagrin of local policymakers.[2] Instead, it sought to explain how pension privatisation came to be adopted in eight Latin American and East European countries. In order to shed light on this puzzle, the observable pension reform choices of individual and collective actors were analysed in the context of the existing economic, political and institutional constraints. While strongly encouraged by the IFIs, the radical paradigm change in old-age security was mainly advocated by the Ministry of Finance, staffed with neoliberally trained economists. Pension privatisation perfectly matched their overall efforts to decrease the role of the state in both regions. These important allies of the new pension orthodoxy often faced intra-government opposition from the Ministry of Labour, usually committed to the Bismarckian traditions in both regions. Interestingly, trade unions played a variety of roles: while staunchly defending the PAYG scheme in some countries, they turned into stakeholders of pension privatisation elsewhere. In several of the countries analysed above, an initially successful defence of the *status quo* in old-age security by the retired and their political allies backfired, leading to a shift to funding as the alternative reform path, based on parametric changes, was effectively blocked.

Insights from the literature on the political economy of policy reform have proved useful to explain the radical paradigm shift in old-age security, although they needed to be qualified. While the 'benefit of crises' hypothesis could be confirmed in all of the above case studies, the perceived or actual emergencies clearly took different forms: a crisis of the pension system, a fiscal emergency, and economic crisis *cum* high external debt. These contextual factors had an impact on pensions-related decision-making, as they tended to strengthen the leverage of the local and external allies of the new pension orthodoxy. As regards other hypotheses from the political economy of policy reform literature, a high-profile leadership by committed neoliberal economists-turned-policymakers played an important role in several of the above case studies. More often than not, this set of reform-minded actors translated into exclusionary policy styles. While useful to speed up the passing of pension privatisation, they failed to generate the necessary long-term support for this radical move. In comparison, in two of the above cases intense efforts at consensus-building substituted for seclusive technocratic teams, while a careful reform design contributed to the political acceptance of this far-reaching reform effort.

The above case studies present pension privatisation as a multi-faceted process. On the one hand, they show that a painstaking analysis and thorough understanding of the domestic policy process is needed to explain the political feasibility of the iconoclastic move in a specific country. On the other, they also point to the strong impact of the international policy context on domestic policymaking. By identifying the new pension orthodoxy and its influence in each of the eight country cases, the relevance of a prominent policy transfer mechanism in pension reform was highlighted, whereas it was also argued that peer nations played an important role in both Latin America and Eastern Europe.

This study has thus pointed to the conditions under which a radical paradigm shift in the area of old-age security can be politically feasible. More comparative research will be needed to account for the emerging diversity of patterns in the political economy of pension privatisation – the political economy of reform has not yet been examined in many of the recent cases of full or partial pension privatisation, and it is likely that second- and third-generation reforms will follow different patterns than the regional precedents.

Moreover, the existing literature on the political economy of pension reform exhibits an extensive focus on the feasibility of political decision-making, while little or no attention is paid to the implementation of the new schemes, that has proved to be complicated in more than one case. Barr (2000: 48) has convincingly argued that private pensions will *not* 'get government out of the pensions business'. Public sector capacity and decision-making matters even after pension privatisation. Only recently, the Argentine crisis has challenged the notion of irreversible policy reforms, making it clear that 'poster childs' can quickly turn into 'basket cases' (Pastor and Wise 2001). It is becoming increasingly clear that some of the factors driving radical change and the political tactics used to bring it about may not facilitate the consolidation of reforms. Moreover, crises do not necessarily seem to be the best conditions for the enactment of good policy choices (Tommasi 2002). As the dynamics of these 'second-stage' processes will ultimately determine whether the bold promises of the advocates of pension privatisation will hold, they clearly deserve more attention by scholars of the political economy of policy reform.

NOTES

1. Classical cross-regional contributions on transition and consolidation include Karl and Schmitter (1991), Przeworski (1991), Przeworski et al. (1995) and Linz and Stepan (1996).
2. For an evaluation of the recent pension reforms in Latin America and Eastern Europe see, e.g., Müller (2000b, 2002c, 2003b).

References

Abadjiev, Nikola (2000), 'Supplementary Voluntary Pension Insurance – General Overview, Players', in Pension Reform Project (ed.), *The Bulgarian Pension Model*, Sofia: USAID, pp. 21–3.

Adler, Emanuel and Peter M. Haas (1992), 'Conclusion: epistemic communities, world order, and the creation of a reflective research program', *International Organization*, **46** (1), 367–90.

AFP Horizonte (1998), *5 Años del Sistema Privado de Pensiones: Perú 1993–1998*, Lima: AFP Horizonte.

Albin, Alexandra Inés (1999), *Rentenreform und 'Kapitalisierung': Der bolivianische Sonderweg der Alterssicherung*, Degree Dissertation, Humboldt University Berlin, mimeo.

Alonso, Guillermo V. (1998), 'Democracia y reformas: Las tensiones entre decretismo y deliberación. El caso de la reforma previsional argentina', *Desarrollo Económico*, **38** (150), 595–626.

Alonso, Guillermo V. (2000), *Política y seguridad social en la Argentina de los '90*, Madrid and Buenos Aires: Miño y Dávila Editores and FLACSO.

Amerini, Giuliano (2001), 'Social protection: expenditure on pensions', *Statistics in focus*, Population and Living Conditions, Theme 3 (9), 1–7.

Análisis Laboral (1990), 'La Seguridad Social y el IPSS en la Transición hasta un Nuevo Marco Político', *Análisis Laboral*, **XIV** (153), 3–5.

Andrews, Emily S. (2001), 'Kazakhstan: An Ambitious Pension Reform', World Bank, SP Discussion Paper No. 0104, Washington DC.

Andrijašević, Sanja, Branko Kovačević and Duško Sabolović (1997), 'A Model for Pension Insurance in Croatia', in Nada Stropnik (ed.), *Social and Economic Aspects of Ageing Societies: An Important Social Development Issue*, Ljubljana: Institute for Economic Research, pp. 235–49.

'Anteproyecto de la Ley sobre el Sistema Privado de Administración de Pensiones (SPP) y su reglamento', *El Peruano*, 16 July 1992, 3–24.

Anušić, Zoran, Philip O'Keefe and Sanja Madžarević-Šujster (2003), 'Pension Reform in Croatia', World Bank, Pension Reform Primer, Washington DC.

APOYO S.A. (1993), *Monitor de AFP*, 15 December, Lima, mimeo.

Arce, Moisés (2001), 'The Politics of Pension Reform in Peru', *Studies in Comparative International Development*, **36** (3), 88–113.

Arenas de Mesa, Alberto and Fabio Bertranou (1997), 'Learning from Social Security Reforms: Two Different Cases, Chile and Argentina', *World Development*, **25** (3), 329–48.

Armbruster, Stefan (2001), 'Argentina's failed "miracle worker"', *BBC News*, 11 December: http://news.bbc.co.uk.

Asesoramiento y Análisis Laborales (1997), *Propuesta de un sistema previsional integral. Proyecto de Análisis, Planeamiento y Ejecución de Políticas (PAPI)*, Convenio USAID–Gobierno Peruano, Lima, mimeo.

ATE leaflet (undated), *Un millón de firmas por los jubilados de hoy y mañana*, Asociación Trabajadores del Estado, Centro Nacional de Jubilados y Pensionados, Buenos Aires, mimeo.

Augusztinovics, Mária (1993), 'The Social Security Crisis in Hungary', in István P. Székely and David M.G. Newbery (eds), *Hungary: An Economy in Transition*, Cambridge: Cambridge University Press, pp. 296–320.

Augusztinovics, Mária and Béla Martos (1996), 'Pension Reform: Calculations and Conclusions', *Acta Oeconomica*, **48** (1–2), 119–60.

Augusztinovics, Mária, Róbert I. Gál, Ágnes Matits, Levente Máté, András Simonovits and János Stahl (2002), 'The Hungarian Pension System Before and After the 1998 Reform', in Elaine Fultz (ed.), *Pension Reform in Central and Eastern Europe*, vol. 1: Restructuring with Privatization: Case Studies of Hungary and Poland, Budapest: ILO–CEET, pp. 25–93.

Ausejo, Flavio (1995), 'La reforma del Instituto Peruano de Seguridad Social', in Augusto Alvarez Rodrich and Gabriel Ortíz de Zevallos (eds), *Implementación de Políticas Públicas en el Perú*, Lima: Editorial Apoyo, pp. 133–44.

Baer, Werner and Joseph L. Love (eds) (2000), *Liberalization and its Consequences: A Comparative Perspective on Latin America and Eastern Europe*, Cheltenham and Northampton MA: Edward Elgar.

Bagdy, Gábor (1995), 'The Social Protection System of Hungary', in Michael Cichon (ed.), *Social Protection in the Visegrád Countries: Four Country Profiles*, ILO–CEET Report 13, Budapest: ILO–CEET, pp. 39–56.

Bakić, Nenad (2000), 'Mogu li se čileanska iskustva primijeniti u hrvatskoj mirovinskoj reformi?', *Financijska teorija i praksa*, **XXIV** (3), 321–8.

Balcerowicz, Leszek (1995), *Socialism, Capitalism, Transformation*, Budapest: CEU Press.

Baldivia Urdininea, José (1998), 'La capitalización. Apuntes para una evaluación', in Juan Carlos Chávez Corrales (ed.), *Las reformas estructurales en Bolivia*, La Paz: Fundación Milenio, pp. 53–123.

Ballivián, Amparo (1997), *Pension Reform in Bolivia: Fiscal and Social Impacts*. Washington DC, mimeo.

Barr, Nicholas (2000), 'Reforming Pensions: Myths, Truths, and Policy Choices', IMF, Working Paper WP/007139, Washington DC.

Barreto de Oliveira, Francisco E. et al. (1994), *Viabilidad de la Seguridad Social. Diagnóstico y Perspectivas de la Seguridad Social en el Uruguay*, Programa de Cooperación Técnica BID 704/OC-UR, mimeo.

Barrientos, Armando (1998), *Pension Reform in Latin America*, Aldershot and Brookfield: Ashgate.

Bauer, Richard and Sally Bowen (1997), *The Bolivian Formula: From State Capitalism to Capitalisation*, Santiago de Chile: McGraw–Hill and Interamericana de Chile.

Beamish-Rosenburg, Sylvia (2001), 'Over a million now signed up with Bulgaria's mandatory universal funds', *Pensions International* (35), 5.

Beamish-Rosenburg, Sylvia (2002), 'Foreign community calls for progress', *Pensions International* (36), 8–9.

Beattie, Roger and Warren McGillivray (1995), 'A Risky Strategy: Reflections on the World Bank Report "Averting the Old Age Crisis"', *International Social Security Review*, **48** (3–4), 5–22.

Becker, Gary S. (1996), 'A Social Security Lesson from Argentina', *Business Week*, 21 October, 9.

Bejaković, Predrag (1998), *Welfare Policy and Social Transfers in the Republic of Croatia*, Zagreb, mimeo.

Belka, Marek (2001), 'Lessons from the Polish transition', in George Blazyca and Ryszard Rapacki (eds), *Poland into the New Millennium*, Cheltenham and Northampton MA: Edward Elgar, pp. 13–32.

Bernedo Alvarado, Jorge (1993), 'El inmortal seguro', *Cuadernos Laborales*, **XIII** (87), 4–6.

Bernedo Alvarado, Jorge (1999), 'El Incierto Destino de los Pensionistas', *Análisis Laboral*, **XXIII** (April), 16–18.

Bertranou, Fabio, Carlos Grushka and Walter Schulthess (2000), 'Proyección de responsabilidades fiscales asociadas a la reforma previsional en Argentina', CEPAL, Serie Financiamiento del Desarrollo No. 94, Santiago de Chile.

Bery, Suman K. (1990), 'Economic Policy Reform in Developing Countries: The Role and Management of Political Factors', *World Development*, **18** (8), 1123–31.

Bićanić, Ivo (2001), 'Croatia', in Thanos Veremis and Daniel Daianu (eds), *Balkan Reconstruction*, London and Portland: Frank Cass, pp. 158–73.

BID (1991), *Progreso Económico y Social en América Latina: Informe 1991*, Washington DC: BID.

BID (2000), *Argentina. El sistema previsional: Situación actual y perspectivas – Estudio técnico*, Washington DC: BID.

Biuro Pełnomocnika Rządu do Spraw Reformy Zabezpieczenia Społecznego (1997), *Bezpieczeństwo dzięki różnorodności*, Warsaw, mimeo.

Bod, Péter (1995a), 'For the Pension System and Reform', in Éva Ehrlich and Gábor Révész (eds), *Human Resources and Social Stability During Transition in Hungary*, San Francisco: International Center for Growth, pp. 173–4.

Bod, Péter (1995b), 'Formation of the Hungarian Social Insurance Based Pension System', in Éva Ehrlich and Gábor Révész (eds), *Human Resources and Social Stability During Transition in Hungary*, San Francisco: International Center for Growth, pp. 175–83.

Bodiroga-Vukobrat, Nada (1994), 'Überblick über das System der sozialen Sicherung in Kroatien', *Zeitschrift für ausländisches und internationales Arbeits- und Sozialrecht*, **8** (2), 326–38.

Bokros, Lajos and Jean-Jacques Déthier (eds) (1998), *Public Finance Reform during the Transition: The Experience of Hungary*, Washington DC: World Bank.

Boloña Behr, Carlos (1995), *¿Dueño de tu jubilación?*, Lima: Instituto de Economía del Libre Mercado.

Boloña, Carlos (1997), *Testimony: Pension Reform in Peru*, International Center for Pension Reform: http://www.pensionreform.org/articles/carlos_bolona.html.

Bonadona Cossio, Alberto (1998), *Marco regulador, privatización y reforma de pensiones*, La Paz: Ediciones ABC.

Bönker, Frank (1995), 'The Dog That Did Not Bark? Politische Restriktionen und ökonomische Reformen in den Visegrád-Ländern', in Hellmut Wollmann, Helmut Wiesenthal and Frank Bönker (eds), *Transformation sozialistischer Gesellschaften: Am Ende des Anfangs*, Opladen: Westdeutscher Verlag, pp. 180–206.

Bönker, Frank (2003), *The Political Economy of Fiscal Reform in Eastern Europe*, Cheltenham and Northampton MA: Edward Elgar, forthcoming.

Börsch-Supan, Axel (1998), 'Germany: A Social Security System on the Verge of Collapse', in Horst Siebert (ed.), *Redesigning Social Security*, Tübingen: Mohr, pp. 129–59.

Borzutzky, Silvia (1983), *Chilean Politics and Social Security Policies*, PhD Dissertation, University of Pittsburgh, mimeo.

Borzutzky, Silvia (2002), *Vital Connections: Politics, Social Security, and Inequality in Chile*, Notre Dame: University of Notre Dame Press.

Bosoer, Fabián (2000), 'Democracias andinas, ¿sin partidos y sin Estado?', *Ciencias sociales* (42), 2–4.

BPS (1997), *Seguridad Social en el Uruguay*, Montevideo: BPS.

Brada, Josef (1997), 'Bolivian Capitalization and East European Privatization: Parallels and Differences', in Margaret Hollis Peirce (ed.), *Capitalization: A Bolivian Model of Social and Economic Reform*, Miami: North South Center, pp. 259–89.

Braithwaite, Jeanine, Christiaan Grootaert and Branko Milanovic (2000), *Poverty and Social Assistance in Transition Countries*, New York: St. Martin's Press.

Bresser Pereira, Luiz Carlos, José María Maravall and Adam Przeworski (1993), *Economic Reforms in New Democracies: A Social-democratic Approach*, Cambridge: Cambridge University Press.

Brooks, Sarah (1998), *Social Protection in a Global Economy: The Case of Pension Reform in Latin America*, Duke University, mimeo.

Brooks, Sarah (2001), *The diffusion of pension privatization over time and space*, paper prepared for the 2001 Annual Meeting of the American Political Science Association, San Francisco, 30 August–2 September, mimeo.

Bulgarian Pension Reform Strategy of 19 July 1999, presented as Room Document No. 5 at the OECD Forum on Private Pensions, Prague, 3–7 April 2000, mimeo.

Busquets, José Miguel (2001), *Análisis comparado de 8 casos de reforma estructural de la Seguridad Social en América Latina (1981–1995)*, paper prepared for the 2001 Meeting of the Latin American Studies Association, Washington DC, 6–8 September, mimeo.

Cajías, Huáscar J. (1997), 'La reforma de seguro de pensiones en Bolivia: una aproximación crítica', in Comisión de Política Social de la Cámara de Diputados (ed.), *Ley de Pensiones: Aportes a un Debate*, La Paz: Fondo Editorial de Diputados, pp. 85–101.

Cariaga, Juan L. (1997), *Estabilización y Desarrollo: Importantes lecciones del Programa Económico de Bolivia*, Mexiko and La Paz: Fondo de Cultura Económica and Los Amigos del Libro.

Caristo, Anna M. and Alvaro Forteza (1999), 'Introducción', in Alvaro Forteza (ed.), *La reforma de la seguridad social en Uruguay: efectos macroeconómicos y mercados de capitales*, Montevideo: Universidad de la República, pp. 13–33.

Castello Branco, Marta de (1998), 'Pension Reform in the Baltics, Russia, and other Countries of the Former Soviet Union (BRO)', IMF, European II Department WP/98/11, Washington DC.

Castiglioni, Rossana (2001), *Changes and Continuities: The Politics of Pension and Health Care Reform under Military Rule in Uruguay, 1973–1985*, paper prepared for the 2001 Meeting of the Latin American Studies Association, Washington DC, 6–8 September, mimeo.

Cavallo, Domingo F. (1995), 'Discurso del Ministro de Economía y Obras y Servicios Públicos de la Nación', in IDEA (ed.), *Empleo – Responsabilidad de todos*, XXI Coloquio Anual, Buenos Aires: Instituto para el Desarrollo Empresarial de la Argentina, pp. 68–81.

CCET (1995), *Social and Labour Market Policies in Hungary*, Paris: OECD.

Charlton, Roger and Roddy McKinnon (2001), *Pensions in Development*, Aldershot et al.: Ashgate.

Charlton, Roger, Roddy McKinnon and Łukasz Konopielko (1998), 'Pensions Reform, Privatisation and Restructuring in the Transition: Unfinished Business or Inappropriate Agendas?', *Europe-Asia Studies*, **50** (8), 1413–46.

Chávez Corrales, Juan Carlos (ed.) (1998), *Las reformas estructurales en Bolivia*, La Paz: Fundación Milenio.

Chiappe, Rosa (2001), 'Pension Reform in Bulgaria', in OECD (ed.), *OECD Private Pensions Conference 2000*, Private Pensions Series No. 3, Paris: OECD, pp. 43–63.

Chłoń, Agnieszka (2000), *Pension Reform and Public Information in Poland*, World Bank, SP Discussion Paper No. 0019, Washington DC.

Chłoń, Agnieszka, Marek Góra and Michał Rutkowski (1999), *Shaping Pension Reform in Poland: Security Through Diversity*, World Bank, SP Discussion Paper No. 9923, Washington DC.

Chłoń-Domińczak, Agnieszka (2002), 'The Polish Pension Reform of 1999', in Elaine Fultz (ed.), *Pension Reform in Central and Eastern Europe*, vol. 1: Restructuring with Privatization: Case Studies of Hungary and Poland, Budapest: ILO–CEET, pp. 95–205.

Chłoń-Domińczak, Agnieszka and Marek Mora (2001), *Commitment and Consensus in Pension Reforms*, paper prepared for the IIASA World Bank Workshop 'The Political Economy of Pension Reform', Laxenburg, 5 April, mimeo.

Chwila, Krystyna (1997), 'Uwłaszczenie: Marzenie milionów – Tabliczka dzielenia', *POLITYKA*, 22 November 1997, 83–4.

Cichon, Michael (1999), 'Notional defined-contribution schemes: Old wine in new bottles?' *International Social Security Review*, **52** (4), 87–105.

CISS (1993), *La Seguridad Social a Largo Plazo: Diagnóstico y una Alternativa de Solución*, La Paz: Centro de Investigaciones de la Seguridad Social.

CLAEH (ed.) (1995), 'Ágora parlamentaria: Trámite legislativo de la Ley de Seguridad Social', *Cuadernos del CLAEH*, **20** (2–3), 7–41.

CNJRB (1995), *Cuestionamiento Técnico al Proyecto de la Ley del Sistema de Fondo de Pensiones*, La Paz: Confederación Nacional de Jubilados y Rentistas de Bolivia.

CNJRB (1996), *Defensa de la Seguridad Social Boliviana*, La Paz: Confederación Nacional de Jubilados y Rentistas de Bolivia.

CNJRB (1998), *Memoria del III Congreso Nacional*, La Paz: Confederación Nacional de Jubilados y Rentistas de Bolivia.

COB (1995), *Pliego Unico Nacional de la Central Obrera Boliviana*, La Paz, 21 December, mimeo.

COB (1996), *Pliego Nacional de la Central Obrera Boliviana*, La Paz, 19 December, mimeo.

Coelho, Vera Schattan P. (2002), 'El poder ejecutivo y la reforma de la seguridad social: los casos de la Argentina, Brasil y Uruguay', *Desarrollo Económico*, **42** (165), 45–62.

COFEPRES (1992), *Reforma Previsional: Proyectos Legislativos, Estudios de Factibilidad Económica*, Buenos Aires: Consejo Federal de Previsión Social.

Collier, Paul (2000), 'Conditionality, dependence and coordination: three current debates in aid policy', in Christopher L. Gilbert and David Vines (eds), *The World Bank – Structure and Policies*, Cambridge: Cambridge University Press, pp. 299–324.

Comisión de Seguridad Social (1995), *Acuerdo de base*, Montevideo, 24 February, mimeo.

Comisión Especial (2001), *Informe de la Comisión especial encargada de estudiar la situación de los regímenes pensionarios de los Decretos Leyes No. 19 990 y No. 20 530 y otros a cargo del Estado*, Lima, 15 July, mimeo.

Contrato de Préstamo No. 921/OC-UR entre la República Oriental del Uruguay y el Banco Interamericano de Desarrollo, Programa Sectorial de Reforma de la Seguridad Social, Montevideo and Washington DC, 18 March 1996, mimeo.

Corbo, Vittorio (2000), 'Economic Policy Reform in Latin America', in Anne O. Krueger (ed.), *Economic Policy Reform: The Second Stage*, Chicago and London: The University of Chicago Press, pp. 61–95.

Corsetti, Giancarlo and Klaus Schmidt-Hebbel (1997), 'Pension Reform and Growth', in Salvador Valdés-Prieto (ed.), *The Economics of Pensions: Principles, Policies, and International Experience*, Cambridge: Cambridge University Press, pp. 127–59.

Cotler, Julio (2001), 'Regierbarkeit in Peru: zwischen Autoritarismus und Demokratie', in Rafael Sevilla and David Sobrevilla (eds), *Peru – Land des Versprechens?*, Bad Honnef: Horlemann, pp. 20–47.

Cottani, Joaquín and Gustavo Demarco (1998), 'The Shift to a Funded Social Security System: The Case of Argentina', in Martin Feldstein (ed.), *Privatizing Social Security*, Chicago and London: The University of Chicago Press, pp. 177–206.

Crabtree, John and Jim Thomas (eds) (1998), *Fujimori's Peru: The Political Economy*, London: Institute of Latin American Studies.

Croatian Chamber of Economy (2001), *Pension Reform in the Republic of Croatia*, Zagreb: Croatian Chamber of Economy.

Cruz Saco, María Amparo and Victoria Ivachina Borovinskaya (1999), '¿Capitalización para quién? La Industria de las AFPs', *Apuntes* (45), 37–63.

Cruz-Saco Oyague, María Amparo (1998), 'The Pension System Reform in Peru: Economic Rationale Versus Political Will', in María Amparo Cruz-Saco Oyague and Carmelo Mesa-Lago (eds), *Do Options Exist? The Reform of Pension and Health Care Systems in Latin America*, Pittsburgh: University of Pittsburgh Press, pp. 165–85.

Čučković, Nevenka (1999), *The Pension Reform in Croatia: Some Key Issues*, paper prepared for the ICEG Conference, Budapest, 16–18 April, mimeo.

Cukierman, Alex and Mariano Tommasi (1998a), 'Credibility of Policymakers and of Economic Reforms', in Federico Sturzenegger and Mariano Tommasi (eds), *The Political Economy of Reform*, Cambridge MA and London: MIT Press, pp. 329–47.

Cukierman, Alex and Mariano Tommasi (1998b), 'When Does It Take a Nixon to Go to China?', *American Economic Review*, **88** (1), 180–97.

Cullen, Tim (1979), *Yugoslavia and the World Bank*, World Bank, Report No. 13358, Washington DC.

Czajka, Stanisław (1985), *Renten und Pensionen in Polen*, Dresden: Zentrales Forschungsinstitut für Arbeit.

Czarniawska, Barbara and Bernward Joerges (1995), *Travels of Ideas – Organizational Change as Translation*, WZB, FS II 95–501, Berlin.

Czepulis-Rutkowska, Zofia (1999), 'The Polish Pension System and Its Problems', in Katharina Müller, Andreas Ryll and Hans-Jürgen Wagener (eds), *Transformation of Social Security: Pensions in Central-Eastern Europe*, Heidelberg: Physica, pp. 143–58.

Czibere, Károly (1998), 'Pension System and Pension Reform', in Martin Brusis (ed.), *Central and Eastern Europe on the Way into the European Union: Welfare State Reforms in the Czech Republic, Hungary, Poland and Slovakia*, Munich: Centre for Applied Policy Research, pp. 29–35.

Czúcz, Ottó (1993), 'Das Rentensystem in Ungarn – Leistungsarten, Voraussetzungen ihrer Liquidierung und Hauptgründe der notwendigen Umgestaltung des Systems', *Deutsche Rentenversicherung* (11), 737–50.

Czúcz, Ottó and Mária Pintér (2002), 'Transformation of Old-age Security in Hungary', in Winfried Schmähl and Sabine Horstmann (eds), *Transformation of Pension Systems in Central and Eastern Europe*, Cheltenham and Northampton MA: Edward Elgar, pp. 277–304.

Danós O., José (1994), 'El Instituto Peruano de Seguridad Social y el Sistema Privado de Pensiones', in CEDAL (ed.), *Sistema Privado de Pensiones: Desafíos y respuestas*, Lima: CEDAL, pp. 11–30.

De los Campos, Hugo (1995), *El Plebiscito de la Seguridad Social: Orígenes, antecedentes y reflexiones críticas*, Montevideo: Fundación de Cultura Universitaria.

Deacon, Bob and Anna Vidinova (1992), 'Social Policy in Bulgaria', in Bob Deacon et al. (eds), *The New Eastern Europe: Social policy past, present and future*, London: Sage, pp. 67–90.

'Decreto Legislativo No. 724', *El Peruano*, 11 November 1991, 101613–8.

'Decreto Ley No. 25 897', *El Peruano*, 6 December 1992, 110939–52.

Delgado, Eva and Estela Ospina (1992), 'Privatización de la Seguridad Social', ISAT, Cuaderno Salud y Trabajo No. 8, Lima.

Devesa-Carpio, José E. and Carlos Vidal-Meliá (2002), 'The Reformed Pension Systems in Latin America', World Bank, SP Discussion Paper No. 0209, Washington DC.

Disney, Richard (1999), 'Notional Accounts as a Pension Reform Strategy: An Evaluation', World Bank, SP Discussion Paper No. 9928, Washington DC.

Dolowitz, David P. and David Marsh (2000), 'Learning from Abroad: The Role of Policy Transfer in Contemporary Policy-making', *Governance: An International Journal of Policy and Administration*, **13** (1), 5–24.

Drazen, Allan (2000), *Political Economy in Macroeconomics*, Princeton: Princeton University Press.

Drazen, Allan and Vittorio Grilli (1993), 'The Benefit of Crises for Economic Reforms', *American Economic Review*, **83** (3), 598–607.

EBRD (2001), *Transition Report 2001: Energy in Transition*, London: European Bank for Reconstruction and Development.

Edwards, Sebastian (1998), 'The Chilean Pension Reform: A Pioneering Program', in Martin Feldstein (ed.), *Privatizing Social Security*, Chicago and London: The University of Chicago Press, pp. 33–57.

EIU (1999), *Croatia Country Profile 1999–2000*, London: The Economist Intelligence Unit.

EIU (2000), *Bulgaria Country Profile 2000*, London: The Economist Intelligence Unit.

Elster, Jon, Claus Offe and Ulrich K. Preuss with Frank Bönker, Ulrike Götting and Friedbert W. Rüb (1998), *Institutional Design in Post-communist Societies: Rebuilding the Ship at Sea*, Cambridge: Cambridge University Press.

Eróstegui T., Rodolfo (1997), 'El debate en Bolivia sobre la reforma de la Seguridad Social. Los actores en movimiento', in Jaime Ensignia and Rolando Díaz (eds), *La seguridad social en América Latina ¿reforma o liquidación?*, Caracas: Editorial Nueva Sociedad, pp. 137–48.

Esping-Andersen, Gøsta (1985), *Politics Against Markets: The Social Democratic Road to Power*, Princeton: Princeton University Press.

Esteves O., Carlos (1994), 'A.F.P. de los trabajadores: Una opción posible', in CEDAL (ed.), *Sistema Privado de Pensiones: Desafíos y respuestas*, Lima: CEDAL, pp. 205–36.

Fabricius, Michael (1999), *Merry Sisterhood or Guarded Watchfulness? The Cooperation between the IMF and the World Bank*, PhD Dissertation, Princeton University, mimeo.

Favaro, Edgardo and Alberto Bensión (1993), 'Uruguay', in Simon Rottenberg (ed.), *Costa Rica and Uruguay. A World Bank Comparative Study*, Oxford: Oxford University Press, pp. 185–362.

Feldman, Jorge, Laura Golbert and Ernesto A. Isuani (1986), 'Maduración y crisis del sistema previsional argentino', *Boletín Informativo Techint* (240), 57–92.

Ferge, Zsuzsa (1991), 'Recent Trends in Social Policy in Hungary', in Jan Adam (ed.), *Economic Reforms and Welfare Systems in the USSR, Poland and Hungary: Social Contract in Transformation*, London: Macmillan, pp. 132–55.

Ferge, Zsuzsa (1997), *The Actors of the Hungarian Pension Reform*, Vienna, mimeo.

Ferge, Zsuzsa (1999), 'The Politics of the Hungarian Pension Reform', in Katharina Müller, Andreas Ryll and Hans-Jürgen Wagener (eds), *Transformation of Social Security: Pensions in Central-Eastern Europe*, Heidelberg: Physica, pp. 231–46.

Ferge, Zsuzsa and Katalin Tausz (2002), 'Social Security in Hungary: A Balance Sheet after Twelve Years', *Social Policy and Administration*, **36** (2), 176–99.

FIAP (2001), 'Información Estadística al 30 de Junio de 2001', FIAP, Boletín No. 10, Santiago de Chile: http://www.fiap.cl.

Filgueira, Fernando (1995), 'A Century of Social Welfare in Uruguay: Growth to the Limit of the Batllista Social State', Kellogg Institute, Democracy and Social Policy Series, Working Paper No. 5, Notre Dame.

Filgueira, Fernando and Juan Andrés Moraes (1999), 'Political environments, sector specific configurations, and strategic devices: understanding institutional reform in Uruguay', IDB, Documento de Trabajo R-351, Washington DC.

Filgueira, Fernando, Juan Andrés Moraes and Constanza Moreira (1999), 'Efectos políticos de la reforma', in Nelson Noya (ed.), *La reforma de la seguridad social en Uruguay*, Montevideo: CINVE, pp. 57–115.

Filgueira, Fernando and Jorge Papadópulos (1994), *La Reforma del Sistema de Seguridad Social en Uruguay. Voluntad Política y Bloqueos Decisionales*, paper prepared for the 1994 Meeting of the Latin American Studies Association, Atlanta, 10–12 March, mimeo.

Flakierski, Henryk (1991), 'Social Policies in the 1980s in Poland: A Discussion of New Approaches', in Jan Adam (ed.), *Economic Reforms and Welfare Systems in the USSR, Poland and Hungary: Social Contract in Transformation*, London: Macmillan, pp. 85–109.

Florek, Ludwik (1986), 'Einführung zum Gesetz über die Rentenversorgung der Arbeitnehmer und ihrer Familien', *Jahrbuch für Ostrecht*, **XXVII** (2), 396–408.

Fougerolles, Jean de (1996), 'Pension Privatization in Latin America – Lessons for Central and Eastern Europe', *Russian and East-European Finance and Trade*, **32** (3), 86–104.

Fox, Louise (1995), 'Social Insurance and Social Assistance', in Željko Bogetić and Arye L. Hillman (eds), *Financing Government in the Transition: Bulgaria. The Political Economy of Tax Policies. Tax Bases, and Tax Evasion*, Washington DC: World Bank, pp. 203–23.

Fox, Louise and Edward Palmer (2001), 'New Approaches to Multi-Pillar Pension Systems: What in the World is Going On?', in Robert Holzmann and Joseph E. Stiglitz (eds), *New Ideas about Old Age Security. Toward Sustainable Pension Systems in the 21st Century*, Washington DC: World Bank, pp. 90–132.

Francke, Pedro (1993), 'Realidades y dudas sobre las AFPs', *Actualidad Económica*, **XV** (140), 14–16.

Freedom House (2000), *Annual Survey of Freedom Country Ratings 1972–73 to 1999–00*: http://www.freedomhouse.org/ratings/ratings.pdf.

Frieden, Jeffrey, Manuel Pastor Jr. and Michael Tomz (eds) (2000), *Modern Political Economy and Latin America: Theory and Policy*, Boulder and Oxford: Westview Press.

Fujimori, Alberto (1995), 'A Momentous Decision', in Orin Starn, Carlos Iván Degregori and Robin Kirk (eds), *The Peru Reader: History, Culture, Politics*, Durham and London: Duke University Press, pp. 438–45.

Fultz, Elaine, Krzysztof Hagemejer and Markus Ruck (2001), *The Political Economy of Pension Reform in Central and Eastern Europe*, paper prepared for a conference organised by the Czech Ministry of Labour and Social Affairs and the World Bank, Prague, 5–6 November, mimeo.

Fultz, Elaine and Markus Ruck (2000), 'Pension Reform in Central and Eastern Europe: An Update on the Restructuring of National Pension Schemes in Selected Countries', ILO–CEET, Report No. 25, Budapest.

Gál, Róbert I. (1996), *The Hungarian Pension Reform: Trends and Issues*, Budapest, mimeo.

Gamarra, Eduardo A. (1997), 'Neoliberalism Reconsidered: The Politics of Privatization and Capitalization in Bolivia', in Margaret Hollis Peirce (ed.), *Capitalization: A Bolivian Model of Social and Economic Reform*, Miami: North South Center, pp. 97–126.

Gapić, Marija (1990), 'Changes in the Pension and Disability Insurance System', *Yugoslav Survey*, **31** (4), 117–26.

García-Mujica, Jorge (1996), 'Fiscal Impact of Switching from a Pay as You Go to a Capitalization System: The Case of Uruguay's Largest Pension System, BPS', World Bank, Country Dept. I, Latin America Region, Economic Notes No. 11, Washington DC.

Garland, Allison M. (2000), 'The Politics and Administration of Social Development in Latin America', in Joseph S. Tulchin and Allison M. Garland (eds), *Social Development in Latin America: The Politics of Reform*, Boulder and London: Lynne Rienner, pp. 1–14.

Georgiev, Stoyan (1995), 'Building of Pension Funds in Bulgaria in Recent Years', *Institute for Market Economics – Newsletter*, **1** (10–11), 12–13.

Gersdorff, Hermann von (1997), 'Pension Reform in Bolivia: Innovative Solutions to Common Problems', World Bank, Policy Research Working Paper No. 1832, Washington DC.

Gesell-Schmidt, Rainer, Katharina Müller and Dirck Süß (1999), 'Social Security Reform and Privatisation in Poland: Parallel Projects or Integrated Agenda?', *Osteuropa-Wirtschaft*, **44** (4), 428–50.

Gestión (2001a), 'AFPs tienen 120,000 juicios con empresas que no cumplen con pago de aportes', *Diario Gestión*, 5 September: http://www.gestion.com.pe/archivo/2001/set/05/5fina.htm.

Gestión (2001b), 'MEF: Deuda a pensionistas supera al nivel de la deuda externa', *Diario Gestión*, 15 February: http://www.gestion.com.pe/archivo/2001/feb/15\1ECON.HTM.

Gestión (2001c), 'MEF solicita a BCR que trate con urgencia reducción de tasas de interés', *Diario Gestión*, 28 September: http://www.gestion.com.pe/archivo/2001/set/28/1fina.htm.

Gestión (2001d), 'Rentabilidad de recursos del Sistema Nacional de Pensiones fue del 7.22% anual', *Diario Gestión*, 15 May: http://www.gestion.com.pe/archivo/2001/may/15/5fina.htm.

Gilbert, Christopher L., Andrew Powell and David Vines (2000), 'Positioning the World Bank', in Christopher L. Gilbert and David Vines (eds), *The World Bank – Structure and Policies*, Cambridge: Cambridge University Press, pp. 39–86.

Gillion, Colin, John Turner, Clive Bailey and Denis Latulippe (eds) (2000), *Social Security Pensions: Development and Reform*, Geneva: ILO.

Golbert, Laura and Rubén Lo Vuolo (1989), 'El sistema previsional en discusión', in Ernesto Isuani and Emilio Tenti (eds), *Estado Democrático y Política Social*, Buenos Aires: Editorial Universitaria, pp. 125–69.

Golinowska, Stanisława (1999), 'Political Actors and Reform Paradigms in Old-age Security in Poland', in Katharina Müller, Andreas Ryll and Hans-Jürgen Wagener (eds), *Transformation of Social Security: Pensions in Central-Eastern Europe*, Heidelberg: Physica, pp. 173–99.

Golinowska, Stanisława (2000), 'Zaniedbywane fazy w procesie reformowania – o reformie systemu emerytalnego', in Jerzy Kubin and Jerzy Kwaśniewski (eds), *Socjotechnika. Kontrowersje, Rozwój, Perspektywy*, Warszawa: Uniwersitet Warszawski, pp. 187–208.

Golinowska, Stanisława, Zofia Czepulis-Rutkowska and Maria Szczur (1997), 'The Case of Poland', in Mária Augusztinovics et al., *Pension Systems and Reforms – Britain, Hungary, Italy, Poland, Sweden*, Phare ACE Research Project P95-2139-R, Final Report, Budapest, mimeo, pp. 107–31.

Golinowska, Stanisława and Maciej Żukowski (2002), 'Transformation of Old-age Security in Poland', in Winfried Schmähl and Sabine Horstmann (eds), *Transformation of Pension Systems in Central and Eastern Europe*, Cheltenham and Northampton MA: Edward Elgar, pp. 185–221.

Gomułka, Stanisław and Marek Styczeń (1999), 'Estimating the Impact of the 1999 Pension Reform in Poland, 2000–2050', CASE–CEU, Working Paper Series No. 27, Warsaw.

Gonzales de Olarte, Efraín (1993), 'Economic Stabilization and Structural Adjustment Under Fujimori', *Journal of Interamerican Studies and World Affairs*, 35 (2), 51–80.

Góra, Marek (2001), 'Going beyond transition: pension reform in Poland', in George Blazyca and Ryszard Rapacki (eds), *Poland into the New Millennium*, Cheltenham and Northampton MA: Edward Elgar, pp. 188–203.

Góra, Marek and Michał Rutkowski (1998), *The Quest for Pension Reform: Poland's Security through Diversity*, Warsaw: Office of the Government Plenipotentiary for Social Security Reform.

Gore, Charles (2000), 'The Rise and Fall of the Washington Consensus as a Paradigm for Developing Countries', *World Development*, 28 (5), 789–804.

Gotovska-Popova, Teodoritchka (1993), 'Bulgaria's Troubled Social Security System', *RFE/RL Research Report*, **2** (26), 43–7.

Götting, Ulrike (1998), *Transformation der Wohlfahrtsstaaten in Mittel- und Osteuropa. Eine Zwischenbilanz*, Opladen: Leske+Budrich.

Gottret, Pablo (1999), *Bolivia: Capitalisation, Pension Reform and their Impact on Capital Markets*, paper presented at the Thirteenth Plenary Session of the OECD Advisory Group on Privatisation, Paris, 21–22 September, mimeo.

Graham, Carol (1997), 'From Safety Nets to Social Policy: Lessons for the Transition Economies from the Developing Countries', in Joan Nelson, Charles Tilly and Lee Walker (eds), *Transforming Post-communist Political Economies*, Washington DC: National Academies Press, pp. 385–99.

Graham, Carol (1998), *Private Markets for Public Goods: Raising the Stakes in Economic Reform*, Brookings Institution Press: Washington DC.

Graham, Carol, Merilee Grindle, Eduardo Lora and Jessica Seddon (1999), *Improving the Odds: Political Strategies for Institutional Reform in Latin America*, Washington DC: IDB.

Graham, Carol and Moisés Naím (1998), 'The Political Economy of Institutional Reform in Latin America', in Nancy Birdsall, Carol Graham and Richard H. Sabot (eds), *Beyond Tradeoffs: Market Reform and Equitable Growth in Latin America*, Washington DC: IDB and Brookings Institution Press, pp. 321–62.

Gray-Molina, George, Ernesto Pérez de Rada and Ernesto Yañez (1999), 'La economía política de reformas institucionales en Bolivia', IDB, Documento de Trabajo R-350, Washington DC.

Grindle, Merilee S. (2000), 'The Social Agenda and the Politics of Reform in Latin America', in Joseph S. Tulchin and Allison M. Garland (eds), *Social Development in Latin America: The Politics of Reform*, Boulder and London: Lynne Rienner, pp. 17–52.

Grindle, Merilee S. (2001), 'In Quest of the Political: The Political Economy of Development Policymaking', in Gerald M. Meier and Joseph E. Stiglitz (eds), *Frontiers of Development Economics: The Future in Perspective*, New York: Oxford University Press and World Bank, pp. 345–80.

Grootaert, Christiaan (1997), 'Poverty and Social Transfers in Hungary', World Bank, Policy Research Working Paper No. 1770, Washington DC.

Guérard, Yves and Martha Kelly (1997), 'The Republic of Bolivia Pension Reform: Decisions in Designing the Structure of the System', in Margaret Hollis Peirce (ed.), *Capitalization: A Bolivian Model of Social and Economic Reform*, Miami: North South Center, pp. 311–54.

Haas, Peter M. (1992), 'Introduction: epistemic communities and international policy coordination', *International Organization*, **46** (1), 1–35.

Haggard, Stephan (2000), 'Interests, Institutions, and Policy Reform', in Anne O. Krueger (ed.), *Economic Policy Reform: The Second Stage*, Chicago and London: The University of Chicago Press, pp. 21–57.

Haggard, Stephan and Robert R. Kaufman (1995), *The Political Economy of Democratic Transitions*, Princeton: Princeton University Press.

Haggard, Stephan and Steven B. Webb (1993), 'What Do We Know about the Political Economy of Economic Policy Reform?', *The World Bank Research Observer*, **8** (2), 143–68.

Harberger, Arnold C. (1993), 'Secrets of Success: A Handful of Heroes', *American Economic Review – Papers and Proceedings*, **83** (2), 342–50.

Hausner, Jerzy (2001), 'Security through Diversity: Conditions for Successful Reform of the Pension System in Poland', in János Kornai, Stephen Haggard and Robert R. Kaufman (eds), *Reforming the State: Fiscal and Welfare Reform in Post-socialist Countries*, Cambridge: Cambridge University Press, pp. 210–34.

Havrylyshyn, Oleh and Saleh M. Nsouli (eds) (2001), *A Decade of Transition: Achievements and Challenges*, Washington DC: IMF.

Hellman, Joel S., Geraint Jones and Daniel Kaufmann (2000), '"Seize the State, Seize the Day": State Capture, Corruption, and Influence in Transition', World Bank, Policy Research Working Paper No. 2444, Washington DC.

Hellman, Joel S. and Daniel Kaufmann (2001), 'Confronting the Challenges of State Capture in Transition Economies', *Finance and Development*, **38** (3): http://www.imf.org/external/pubs/ft/fandd/.

Hemming, Richard (1998), 'Should Public Pensions be Funded?', IMF, Fiscal Affairs Department WP/98/35, Washington DC.

Hernández, Diego (1999), *Reforma de la Seguridad Social: desembarco, conquista y retirada de un actor no reformista*, Montevideo, mimeo.

Hernández, Diego (2000), *Acerca del aprendizaje democrático: Seguridad social en el Uruguay, una perspectiva comparada*, Informe Final CLACSO, Montevideo, mimeo.

Hirschman, Albert O. (1991), *The Rhetoric of Reaction: Perversity, Futility, Jeopardy*, Cambridge MA: Harvard University Press.

Holzmann, Robert (1994), 'Funded and Private Pensions for Eastern European Countries in Transition?', *Revista de Análisis Económico*, **9** (1), 183–210.

Holzmann, Robert (1997), 'On Economic Benefits and Fiscal Requirements of Moving from Unfunded to Funded Pensions', University of Saarland, Forschungsbericht 9702, Saarbrücken.

Holzmann, Robert (2000), The World Bank approach to pension reform, *International Social Security Review*, **53** (1), 11–34.

Holzmann, Robert (2002), *The World Bank's Position on Pension Reform: Rationale, Issues and Open Questions*, presentation at the OECD Seminar 'Practical Lessons in Pension Reform: Sharing the Experiences of Transition and OECD Countries', Warsaw, 27–28 May, mimeo.

Holzmann, Robert and Joseph E. Stiglitz (eds) (2001), *New Ideas about Old Age Security: Toward Sustainable Pension Systems in the 21st Century*, Washington DC: World Bank.

Hopkins, Raul, Andrew Powell, Amlan Roy and Christopher L. Gilbert (2000), 'The World Bank, conditionality and the Comprehensive Development Framework', in Christopher L. Gilbert and David Vines (eds), *The World Bank – Structure and Policies*, Cambridge: Cambridge University Press, pp. 282–98.

Horstmann, Sabine and Winfried Schmähl (2002), 'Explaining Reforms', in Winfried Schmähl and Sabine Horstmann (eds), *Transformation of Pension Systems in Central and Eastern Europe*, Cheltenham and Northampton MA: Edward Elgar, pp. 63–85.

Hristoskov, Jordan (2000a), 'Mandatory Social Insurance – Changes, Nature and Content of the Mandatory Social Insurance Code', in Pension Reform Project (ed.), *The Bulgarian Pension Model*, Sofia: USAID, pp. 10–16.

Hristoskov, Jordan (2000b), 'The reform works at the NSSI', *BASPIC Newsletter* (2), 4–5.

Huber, Evelyne and John D. Stephens (2000), 'The Political Economy of Pension Reform: Latin America in Comparative Perspective', UNRISD, Occasional Paper No. 7, Geneva.

Hujo, Katja (1999), 'Paradigmatic Change in Old Age Security: Latin American Cases', in Katharina Müller, Andreas Ryll and Hans-Jürgen Wagener (eds), *Transformation of Social Security: Pensions in Central-Eastern Europe*, Heidelberg: Physica, pp. 121–39.

Hujo, Katja (2001), *Privatising Pensions in the Context of Stabilisation and Structural Adjustment: The Case of Argentina*, paper prepared for the 2001 Meeting of the Latin American Studies Association, Washington DC, 6–8 September, mimeo.

Hujo, Katja (2002), *Soziale Sicherung im Kontext von Stabilisierung und Strukturanpassung: Die Reform der Rentenversicherung in Argentinien*, Doctoral Dissertation, Free University Berlin, mimeo.

Huntington, Samuel (1991), *The Third Wave: Democratization in the Late Twentieth Century*, Norman: University of Oklahoma.

IBSS (1991), *Estudio Matemático Actuarial. Régimen Básico de Pensiones 1991–1995*, La Paz: Instituto Boliviano de Seguridad Social.

IDB (1992), *Peru – Financial Sector Loan (PE-0033)*, Washington DC: IDB.

IDB (1998), *Facing Up to Inequality in Latin America: Economic and Social Progress in Latin America, 1998–99 Report*, Washington DC: IDB.

Iglesias Palau, Augusto (1997), 'Pension Reform: The Chilean Case', in Nevenka Čučković (ed.), *Pension System Reform in Croatia*, Zagreb: IMO, Friedrich-Ebert-Stiftung and ICEG, pp. 21–34.

ILO (2000), *World Labour Report 2000*, Geneva: ILO.

ILO–CEET (1994), *The Bulgarian Challenge: Reforming Labour Market and Social Policy*, Budapest: ILO–CEET.

IMF (1997), 'Croatia – Selected Issues and Statistical Appendix', IMF, Staff Country Report No. 97/35, Washington DC.

IMF (1998), 'Republic of Croatia: Selected Issues and Statistical Appendix', IMF, Staff Country Report No. 98/90, Washington DC.

IMF (2000a), 'Bulgaria: Selected Issues and Statistical Appendix', IMF, Staff Country Report No. 00/54, Washington DC.

IMF (2000b), 'Republic of Croatia: Selected Issues and Statistical Appendix', IMF, Staff Country Report No. 00/22, Washington DC.

IMF (2000c), 'Hungary: Selected Issues and Statistical Appendix', IMF, Staff Country Report No. 00/59, Washington DC.

IMF (2001a), 'Bolivia: 2001 Article IV Consultation and Request for Third Annual Arrangement Under the Poverty Reduction and Growth Facility', IMF, Country Report No. 01/92, Washington DC.

IMF (2001b), *Conditionality in Fund-supported Programs – Overview*, Washington DC: http://www.imf.org.

IMF (2001c), 'Peru: Selected Issues', IMF, Country Report No. 01/51, Washington DC.

IMF (2001d), 'Republic of Croatia: First Review of the Stand-by Arrangement – Staff Report', IMF, Country Report No. 01/209, Washington DC.

IMF (2001e), 'Uruguay: Recent Economic Developments', IMF, Country Report No. 01/47, Washington DC.

Immergut, Ellen M. (1992), *Health Politics – Interests and Institutions in Western Europe*, Cambridge: Cambridge University Press.

INE (2002), *Información Estadística*, Instituto Nacional de Estadística, La Paz: http://www.ine.gov.bo.

Isuani, Ernesto Aldo and Jorge A. San Martino (1993), *La Reforma Previsional Argentina: Opciones y riesgos*, Buenos Aires: Miño y Dávila Editores.

Isuani, Ernesto Aldo and Jorge A. San Martino (1995), 'El nuevo sistema previsional argentino ¿Punto final a una larga crisis?' Primera parte, *Boletín Informativo Techint* (281), 41–56; Segunda parte, *Boletín Informativo Techint* (282), 43–67.

Isuani, Ernesto Aldo and Jorge A. San Martino (1998), 'The New Argentine Social Security System: A Mixed Model', in María Amparo Cruz-Saco Oyague and Carmelo Mesa-Lago (eds), *Do Options Exist? The Reform of Pension and Health Care Systems in Latin America*, Pittsburgh: University of Pittsburgh Press, pp. 130–49.

Jäger, Johannes (2001), 'Politische Ökonomie der Sozialpolitik: Uruguay und Chile im lateinamerikanischen Kontext', in Johannes Jäger, Gerhard Melinz and Susan Zimmermann (eds), *Sozialpolitik in der Peripherie. Entwicklungsmuster und Wandel in Lateinamerika, Afrika, Asien und Osteuropa*, Frankfurt/Main and Vienna: Brandes&Apsel and Südwind, pp. 37–56.

James, Estelle (1996), 'Protecting the Old and Promoting Growth: A Defense of "Averting the Old Age Crisis"', World Bank, Policy Research Working Paper No. 1570, Washington DC.

James, Estelle (1998a), 'New Models for Old Age Security: Experiments, Evidence, and Unanswered Questions', *The World Bank Research Observer*, **13** (2), 271–301.

James, Estelle (1998b), 'The Political Economy of Social Security Reform: A Cross-Country Review', *Annals of Public and Cooperative Economics*, **69** (4), 451–82.

James, Estelle and Sarah Brooks (2001), 'The Political Economy of Structural Pension Reform', in Robert Holzmann and Joseph E. Stiglitz (eds), *New Ideas about Old Age Security: Toward Sustainable Pension Systems in the 21ˢᵗ Century*, Washington DC: World Bank, pp. 133–70.

Jessel-Holst, Christa (1982), 'Das Sozialversicherungs- und Versorgungsrecht Bulgariens', *Jahrbuch für Ostrecht*, **23**, 201–43.

Jessel-Holst, Christa (1991), 'Das bulgarische Sozialrecht', *Zeitschrift für ausländisches und internationales Arbeits- und Sozialrecht* (5), 352–72.

Jończyk, Jan (1997), 'Reforma emerytur: Kosztowna prywatyzacja ryzyka starości', *Rzeczpospolita*, 23 April, 17.

Jurčević, Živko (1995), 'Social Security Policy of the Republic of Croatia', IRMO, Reform Round Table Working Paper No. 15, Zagreb.

Jurlina Alibegovic, Dubravka (1998), 'Pension Systems in CEECs: Croatia', *The Vienna Institute Monthly Report* (1), 2–5.

Kalina-Prasznic, Urszula (1997), 'Uwagi o reformowaniu systemu emerytalnego', *Praca i Zabezpieczenie Społeczne* (9), 2–6.

Kane, Cheikh T. (1995a), 'Peru: Reforming the Pension System', World Bank, ESP Discussion Paper Series No. 69, Washington DC

Kane, Cheikh T. (1995b), 'Uruguay: Options for Pension Reform', World Bank, ESP Discussion Paper Series No. 68, Washington DC.

Karl, Terry Lynn and Philippe C. Schmitter (1991), 'Modes of transition in Latin America, Southern and Eastern Europe', *International Social Science Journal*, 128, 268–84.

Kassayie, Berhanu (1998), 'The Evolution of Social Democracy in Reforming Bulgaria', *Journal of Communist Studies and Transition Politics*, 14 (3), 109–25.

Kavalsky, Basil G. (1998), 'System emerytalno-rentowy – Reforma jest po prostu niezbędna', *Rzeczpospolita*, 27 October: http://www.rzeczpospolita.pl.

Kay, Stephen J. (1998), *Politics and Social Security Reform in the Southern Cone and Brazil*, PhD Dissertation, University of California at Los Angeles, mimeo.

Kay, Stephen J. (1999), 'Unexpected Privatizations. Politics and Social Security Reforms in the Southern Cone', *Comparative Politics*, 31 (4), 403–22.

Kay, Stephen J. (2000), 'Recent changes in Latin American welfare states: is there social dumping?', *Journal of European Social Policy*, 10 (2), 185–203.

Kay, Stephen J. and Barbara E. Kritzer (2001), 'Social Security in Latin America: Recent Reforms and Challenges', *Economic Review* (First Quarter 2001), 41–52.

Kester, Eddy (2001), 'Hungarian PM puts the skids under private plans', *Pensions International* (30), 8.

Kiefer, Manfred (1998), *Die Rentenreform in Peru: Auswirkungen auf soziale Sicherung, Finanzmärkte und Staatsfinanzen*, Frankfurt/Main et al.: Peter Lang.

Klimentová, Jana (1997), 'Důchodové systémy zemí Střední a Východní Evropy v období transformace', *Sociální Politika* (10), 2–3.

Kolarska-Bobińska, Lena (ed.) (2000), *Cztery reformy. Od koncepcij do realizacji*, Warsaw: Instytut Spraw Publicznych.

Kołodko, Grzegorz (1996), 'Continuity and Change in the Polish Transformation 1993–2000', *EMERGO*, 3 (2), 58–69.

Kołodko, Grzegorz (1999), 'Ten Years of Post-socialist Transition Lessons for Policy Reform', World Bank, Policy Research Working Paper No. 2095, Washington DC.

Kornai, János (1997), 'The Political Economy of the Hungarian Stabilization and Austerity Program', in Mario I. Blejer and Marko Škreb (eds), *Macroeconomic Stabilization in Transition Economies*, Cambridge: Cambridge University Press, pp. 172–203.

Krishock, Dan (2001), 'Debt restructuring angers fund managers', *Pensions International* (35), 9–10.

Krishock, Dan (2002a), 'Argentina: Outlook uncertain for 2003', *Pensions International* (46), 9–10.

Krishock, Dan (2002b), 'Worries for Argentinean funds', *Pensions International* (36), 10–11.

Krueger, Anne O. (1993), 'Virtuous and Vicious Circles in Economic Development', *American Economic Review – Papers and Proceedings*, **83** (2), 351–5.

La República (2000), 'Chávez quiere sistema de AFAPs en Venezuela. El presidente venezolano destacó funcionamiento de la seguridad social en Uruguay', *La República* (Montevideo), 4 August, 30.

Labadie, Gaston J., Agustín Canzani and Luis Costa Bonino (1995), *Aspectos políticos y sociales de la reforma de la seguridad social*, Montevideo, mimeo.

Lacurcia, Hugo (1991), 'El sistema de pensiones en el Uruguay', in Andras Uthoff and Raquel Szalachman (eds), *Sistema de Pensiones en América Latina. Diagnóstico y alternativas de reforma*, vol. 2, Santiago de Chile: CEPAL and PNUD, pp. 119–94.

Landau, Luis (1997), *Poland Country Assistance Review: Partnership in a Transition Economy*, Washington DC: World Bank.

Larrazábal Antezana, Erick and Víctor Hugo De La Barra Muñoz (1997), *Capitalización y Pensiones: Análisis y Reflexiones sobre los Modelos de Reforma*, La Paz: Sociedad de Análisis de Políticas Públicas.

Lavigne, Marie (1995), *The Economics of Transition – from Socialist Economy to Market Economy*, London: Macmillan.

Lessenich, Stephan (2000), 'The Southern Image Reversed: The Dynamics of "Transformation Dynamics" in East Central Europe', *East Central Europe*, **27** (1), 21–35.

Lewicka, Ewa, Bogusław Koc, Zbigniew Kruszyński and Jerzy Ptaszyński (1996), 'Projekt NSZZ "Solidarność"', in IPiSS, Nowe Życie Gospodarcze and Klub 500 (eds), *Modele Reformy Systemu Emerytalno-Rentowego i Ścieżki Dojścia*, Warsaw: IPiSS, pp. 53–67.

'Ley No. 1 544', *Gaceta Oficial de Bolivia*, XXXIV (1824), 22 March 1994..

'Ley No. 27 617 of 18 December 2001', *El Peruano*, 1 January 2002, 214980–2.

Lindeman, David, Michał Rutkowski and Oleksiy Sluchynskyy (2000), *The Evolution of Pension Systems in Eastern Europe and Central Asia: Opportunities, Constraints, Dilemmas and Emerging Practices*, Washington DC, mimeo.

Linz, Juan J. and Alfred Stepan (1996), *Problems of Democratic Transition and Consolidation. Southern Europe, South America and Post-communist Europe*, Baltimore and London: Johns Hopkins University Press.

Lissidini, Alicia (1998), 'Los plebiscitos uruguayos durante el siglo xx: ni tan democráticos ni tan autoritarios', *Cuadernos del CLAEH*, **23** (1–2), 195–217.

Lloyd-Sherlock, Peter (1997), *Old Age and Urban Poverty in the Developing World: The Shanty Towns of Buenos Aires*, Houndmills and New York: Macmillan and St. Martin's Press.

Lo Vuolo, Rubén M. (1996), 'Reformas previsionales en América Latina: el caso argentino', *Comercio Exterior*, **46** (9), 692–702.

Lo Vuolo, Rubén M. and Alberto C. Barbeito (1998), *La nueva oscuridad de la política social: Del Estado populista al neoconservador*, Buenos Aires and Madrid: CIEPP and Miño y Dávila Editores.

Lora, Eduardo (2000), 'What Makes Reform Likely? Timing and Sequencing of Structural Reforms in Latin America', IDB, Research Department Working Paper No. 424, Washington DC.

Lorentzen, Jochen (1995), *Opening up Hungary to the World Market: External Constraints and Opportunities*, New York: St. Martin's Press.

McClintock, Cynthia (1999), 'Peru: Precarious Regimes, Authoritarian and Democratic', in Larry Diamond, Jonathan Hartlyn, Juan J. Linz and Seymour Martin Lipset (eds), *Democracy in Developing Countries: Latin America*, Boulder and London: Lynne Rienner, pp. 309–65.

McGreevey, William (1990), 'Social Security in Latin America. Issues and Options for the World Bank', World Bank, Discussion Paper No. 110, Washington DC.

Madrid, Raúl (1998), *The Determinants of Pension Reform Around the World, 1992–97*, paper prepared for the 1998 Annual Meeting of the American Political Science Association, Boston, 3–6 September, mimeo.

Madrid, Raúl (1999), *The New Logic of Social Security Reform: Politics and Pension Privatization in Latin America*, PhD Dissertation, Stanford University, mimeo.

Madrid, Raúl (2001), *Retiring the State: The Politics of Pension Privatization*, Book manuscript, University of Texas at Austin, mimeo.

Madrid, Raúl (2002), 'The Politics and Economics of Pension Privatization in Latin America', *Latin American Research Review*, 37 (2), 159–82.

Maltby, Tony (1994), *Women and Pensions in Britain and Hungary: A Cross-national and Comparative Case Study of Social Dependency*, Aldershot: Avebury.

Márquez Mosconi, Gustavo (1997), *An Assessment of the Pension System Reform in Uruguay in 1995*, Washington DC: IDB.

Marsh, Virginia (1997), 'Hungary Spreads the Pension Load – Looming Contribution Crisis is Forcing Painful Adjustment', *Financial Times*, 22 January, 2.

Matits, Ágnes (2002), *Some Practical Issues in the Hungarian Pension Reform*, paper presented at the OECD Seminar 'Practical Lessons in Pension Reform: Sharing the Experiences of Transition and OECD Countries', Warsaw, 27–28 May, mimeo.

Menem, Carlos Saúl (1997), 'Discurso del Señor Presidente de la Nación', in CAFJP (ed.), *Jubilación privada, certidumbre social y crecimiento económico. Primera convención de la Cámara de Administradoras de Fondos de Jubilaciones y Pensiones*, Buenos Aires: CAFJP, pp. 13–17.

Mercado Lora, Marcelo (1994), 'La Transformación del Sistema de Pensiones en Bolivia', in SAFP (ed.), *Sistema Privado de Pensiones: Hacia una Política Previsional*, Lima: SAFP, pp. 1–22.

Mercado Lora, Marcelo (1998), 'La reforma del sistema de pensiones de la seguridad social', in Juan Carlos Chávez Corrales (ed.), *Las reformas estructurales en Bolivia*, La Paz: Fundación Milenio, pp. 125–80.

Merrien, François-Xavier (2001), 'The World Bank's new social policies: pensions', *International Social Science Journal*, **53** (170), 537–50.

Mesa-Lago, Carmelo (1973), 'La estratificación de la seguridad social y el efecto de desigualdad en América Latina: El caso peruano', *Estudios Andinos*, **III** (2), S. 17–48.

Mesa-Lago, Carmelo (1978), *Social Security in Latin America: Pressure Groups, Stratification, and Inequality*, Pittsburgh: University of Pittsburgh Press.

Mesa-Lago, Carmelo (1989), *Ascent to Bankruptcy: Financing Social Security in Latin America*, Pittsburgh: University of Pittsburgh Press.

Mesa-Lago, Carmelo (1991a), 'Portfolio Performance of Selected Social Security Institutes in Latin America', World Bank, Discussion Paper No. 139, Washington DC.

Mesa-Lago, Carmelo (1991b), 'Social Security and Prospects for Equity in Latin America', World Bank, Discussion Paper No. 140, Washington DC.

Mesa-Lago, Carmelo (1996), 'Pension System Reforms in Latin America: The Position of the International Organizations', *CEPAL Review* (60), 73–98.

Mesa-Lago, Carmelo (1997a), 'Die Reform der Renten in Lateinamerika und die Position der internationalen Organisationen', *Zeitschrift für ausländisches und internationales Arbeits- und Sozialrecht*, **11** (3), 161–274.

Mesa-Lago, Carmelo (1997b), 'Social Welfare Reform in the Context of Economic-Political Liberalization: Latin American Cases', *World Development*, **25** (4), 497–517.

Mesa-Lago, Carmelo (1998), 'The Reform of Social Security Pensions in Latin America: Public, Private, Mixed and Parallel Systems', in Franz Ruland (ed.), *Verfassung, Theorie und Praxis des Sozialstaats. Festschrift für Hans F. Zacher zum 70. Geburtstag*, Heidelberg: Müller, pp. 609–33.

Mesa-Lago, Carmelo (1999), 'Política y reforma de la seguridad social en América Latina', *Nueva Sociedad* (160), 133–50.

Mesa-Lago, Carmelo (2000), 'Estudio comparativo de los costos fiscales en la transicion de ocho reformas de pensiones en America Latina', CEPAL, Serie Financiamiento del Desarrollo No. 93, Santiago de Chile.

Mesa-Lago, Carmelo (2001), 'Structural reform of social security pensions in Latin America: Models, characteristics, results and conclusions', *International Social Security Review*, **54** (4), 67–92.

Mesa-Lago, Carmelo (2002), 'Myth and Reality of Pension Reform: The Latin American Evidence', *World Development*, **30** (8), 1309–21.

Mesa-Lago, Carmelo and Alberto Arenas de Mesa (1997), 'Fünfzehn Jahre nach der Privatisierung des Rentensystems in Chile: Evaluation, Lehre und zukünftige Aufgaben', *Deutsche Rentenversicherung* (7), 405–27.

Mesa-Lago, Carmelo and Fabio Bertranou (1998), *Manual de Economía de la Seguridad Social*, Montevideo: CLAEH.

Mesa-Lago, Carmelo and Katharina Müller (2002), 'The Politics of Pension Reform in Latin America', *Journal of Latin American Studies*, **34** (3), 687–715.

Mesa-Lago, Carmelo and Eva Maria Hohnerlein (2003), 'Testing the assumptions on the effects of the German pension reform based on Latin American and Eastern European outcomes', forthcoming in: *Journal of European Social Policy*, **13** (2).

Michailova, Snejina (1997), 'The Bulgarian Experience in the Privatization Process', *Eastern European Economics*, **35** (3), 75–92.

Miller, Jeffrey B. and Stefan Petranov (2000), 'The first wave of mass privatization in Bulgaria and its immediate aftermath', *Economics of Transition*, **8** (1), 225–50.

Minev, Duhomir (1993), 'Pension Provision in Bulgaria: Problems of Reform in the Context of the Transition to a Market Economy', in Iskra Beleva et al., *Bulgaria and the European Community: The Transformation of the Labour Market and Social Policy. A View Towards Europe*, Sofia: Ivan D. Danov Publishing Company, pp. 107–25.

Ministarstvo Financija (1997), *Reforma hrvatskog mirovinskog sustava i prikaz međunarodnih iskustava*, Zagreb: Ministarstvo Financija Republike Hrvatske.

Ministerio de Capitalización (1997), *Capitalización: El Modelo Boliviano de Reforma Económica y Social*, La Paz, CD-ROM.

Ministerio de Trabajo y Seguridad Social (1993), *Origen y tratamiento de las deudas del SNPS con los beneficiarios: 1980–1993*, Buenos Aires: PRONATASS.

Ministry of Finance (1994), 'Act on the Voluntary Mutual Benefit Funds', Public Finance in Hungary No. 128, Budapest.

Ministry of Finance (1997), *Pension Reform*, Budapest, mimeo.

Ministry of Labour and Social Policy (2000), *Poland 2000 – Basic Statistical Data on Social Policy*, Warsaw: Ministry of Labour and Social Policy.

Ministry of Labour and Social Welfare (1994), *White Paper: Social Security in the Republic of Bulgaria – A Strategy for Reform*, Sofia, mimeo.

Ministry of Labour and Social Welfare (1998), *Act on Pension Insurance. Published in the Oficial Gazette No. 102/98 of 29 July 1998. Translation of October 1998*, Zagreb, mimeo.

Ministry of Welfare and Ministry of Finance (1996), *Proposal for a Compositely Financed Pension System and Conditions of the Introduction of System*, Report discussed on 9 May by the Government and accepted as the ground of further work, Budapest, mimeo.

MNR and MRTK (1993), *Bolivia: El Plan de Todos – Sintesis*, La Paz, mimeo.

Mora, Marek (1999), *The Political Economy of Pension Reforms: The Case of Latin America*, Washington DC, mimeo.

Morales, Juan Antonio (1995), 'Bolivia and the Slowdown of the Reform Process', World Bank, PSD Occasional Paper No. 7, Washington DC.

Morales, Juan Antonio and Napoleón Pacheco (1999), 'El Retorno de los Liberales', in Fernando Campero Prudencio (ed.), *Bolivia en el Siglo XX. La Formación de la Bolivia Contemporánea*, La Paz: Harvard Club de Bolivia, pp. 155–92.

Movimiento Libertad (1989), *Bases para el Plan de Gobierno*, Aporte del Movimiento Libertad al Plan de Gobierno del Frente Democrático, Lima, mimeo.

Müller, Katharina (1993), *Peru 1985–90: Wirtschaftspolitik im Kontext von Heterodoxie und Populismus*, Münster and Hamburg: Lit.

Müller, Katharina (1998), 'Shall We Forget the Latin American Precedents?', *Transition*, 9 (5), 29.

Müller, Katharina (1999), *The Political Economy of Pension Reform in Central-Eastern Europe*, Cheltenham and Northampton MA: Edward Elgar.

Müller, Katharina (2000a), 'Altern in der Dritten Welt', in Joachim Betz and Stefan Brüne (eds), *Jahrbuch Dritte Welt 2001*, Munich: C.H. Beck, pp. 32–46.

Müller, Katharina (2000b), 'Pension Privatization in Latin America', *Journal of International Development* (12), 2000, 507–18.

Müller, Katharina (2000c), 'Reforma previdenciária no Leste Europeu: atores, estruturas e paradigmas', *Planejamento e Políticas Públicas* (22), 145–72.

Müller, Katharina (2001a), 'Conquistando el Este – Los modelos previsionales latinoamericanos en los países ex socialistas', *Socialis: Revista Latinoamericana de Políticas Sociales* (4), 39–52.

Müller, Katharina (2001b), 'Der peruanische Neoliberalismus: Eine kritische Analyse', in Rafael Sevilla and David Sobrevilla (eds), *Peru – Land des Versprechens?*, Bad Honnef: Horlemann, pp. 230–48.

Müller, Katharina (2001c), 'Die Privatisierung der bolivianischen Alterssicherung – eine Zwischenbilanz', in Rafael Sevilla and Ariel Benavides (eds), *Bolivien – das verkannte Land?*, Bad Honnef: Horlemann, pp. 230–45.

Müller, Katharina (2001d), 'The political economy of pension reform in eastern Europe', *International Social Security Review*, 54 (2–3), 57–79.

Müller, Katharina (2002a), 'Between State and Market: Czech and Slovene Pension Reform in Comparison', in Elaine Fultz (ed.), *Pension Reform in Central and Eastern Europe*, vol. 2: Restructuring of Public Pension Schemes: Case Studies of the Czech Republic and Slovenia, Budapest: ILO–CEET, pp. 113–46.

Müller, Katharina (2002b), *La economía política de las reformas previsionales en Europa Centro-Oriental*, Madrid and Buenos Aires: Miño y Dávila Editores and CIEPP.

Müller, Katharina (2002c), 'Pension Reform Paths in Central-Eastern Europe and the Former Soviet Union', *Social Policy and Administration*, 36 (2), 156–75.

Müller, Katharina (2002d), 'Public–Private Interaction in Structural Pension Reform', in OECD (ed.), *Regulating Private Pension Schemes: Trends and Challenges*, Private Pension Series No. 4, Paris: OECD, pp. 105–16.

Müller, Katharina (2002e), 'Transformation als Peripherisierung', *INITIAL. Zeitschrift für sozialwissenschaftlichen Diskurs*, 13 (3), 17–26.

Müller, Katharina (2003a), *Armut und Sozialpolitik in den zentralasiatischen Transformationsländern*, Bonn: German Development Institute.

Müller, Katharina (2003b), 'Las reformas de pensiones en América Latina y Europa Oriental: contexto, conceptos, experiencias prácticas y enseñanzas', forthcoming in: Klaus Bodemer (ed.), *Políticas públicas, inclusión social y ciudadanía*, Caracas: Editorial Nueva Sociedad.

Müller, Katharina (2003c), 'The Making of Pension Privatization in Latin America and Eastern Europe', forthcoming in: Robert Holzmann, Mitchell Orenstein and Michał Rutkowski (eds), *Pension Reform in Europe: Process and Progress*, Washington DC: World Bank.

Müller&Asociados (1997), 'Reforma de Pensiones: El Sistema de Capitalización Individual', Müller&Asociados, Informe Confidencial No. 103, La Paz.

Murillo, M. Victoria (1997), 'La adaptación del sindicalismo argentino a las reformas de mercado en la primera presidencia de Menem', *Desarrollo Económico*, **37** (147), 419–46.

Murillo, M. Victoria (2000), 'From Populism to Neoliberalism. Labor Unions and Market Reforms in Latin America', *World Politics*, **52** (2), 135–74.

Nahum, Benjamín (1999), *Breve historia del Uruguay independiente*, Montevideo: Ediciones de la Banda Oriental.

Naím, Moisés (2000), 'Fads and fashion in economic reforms: Washington Consensus or Washington Confusion?', *Third World Quarterly*, **21** (3), 505–28.

Neikov, Ivan (2000), 'The Pension System Must Be Part of the Economy', *BASPIC Newsletter* (1), 2.

Nelson, Joan M. (1994), 'Panel Discussion', in John Williamson (ed.), *The Political Economy of Policy Reform*, Washington DC: Institute for International Economics, pp. 472–7.

Nelson, Joan M. (2000), *External Models, International Influence, and the Politics of Social Sector Reforms*, paper prepared for the Woodrow Wilson Center Conference 'Learning from Foreign Models in Latin American Policy Reform', Washington DC, 14 September, mimeo.

Nelson, Joan M. (2001), 'The Politics of Pension and Health-care Reforms in Hungary and Poland', in János Kornai, Stephen Haggard and Robert R. Kaufman (eds), *Reforming the State: Fiscal and Welfare Reform in Post-socialist Countries*, Cambridge: Cambridge University Press, pp. 235–66.

Neves Mujica, Javier (1993), 'Sistema Nacional de Pensiones y Sistema Privado de Pensiones: Opción Diabólica', *Thémis: Revista de Derecho* (25), 7–10.

Ney, Steven (2000), 'Are You Sitting Comfortably ... Then We'll Begin: Three Gripping Policy Stories About Pension Reform', *Innovation: The European Journal of Social Sciences*, **13** (4), 341–71.

Nikolov, Nikolai (2000), 'The Funds of Individuals Insured in Unlicensed Pension Insurance Companies are Guaranteed', *BASPIC Newsletter* (4), 3.

Nikolov, Nikolai (2001), 'Pension Companies and Funds – Current Stage and Possible Trends', in Pension Reform Project (ed.), *The Bulgarian Pension Model – One Year after the Start*, Sofia: USAID, pp. 18–19.

Nowotny, Thomas (1997), 'Transition from Communism and the Spectre of Latin-Americanisation', *East European Quarterly*, **XXXI** (1), 69–91.

Noya, Nelson, Adrián Fernández Poncet and Silvia Laens (1999), 'Efectos económicos de la reforma', in Nelson Noya (ed.), *La reforma de la seguridad social en Uruguay*, Montevideo: CINVE, pp. 8–55.

Noya, Nelson and Silvia Laens (2000), 'Efectos fiscales de la reforma de la seguridad social en Uruguay', CEPAL, Serie Financiamiento del Desarrollo No. 101, Santiago de Chile.

NSSI (2000), *Republic of Bulgaria – Statistical Reference Book: Demography, Economy and Social Insurance 1980–1999*, Sofia: National Social Security Institute.

O'Neil Trowbridge, Shannon (2001), *The Role of Ideas in Neoliberal Economic Reform: The Case of Argentina*, paper prepared for the 2001 Meeting of the Latin American Studies Association, Washington DC, 6–8 September, mimeo.

OECD (2000a), *OECD Economic Survey Hungary*, Paris: OECD.

OECD (2000b), *OECD Economic Survey Poland*, Paris: OECD.

Office of the Government Plenipotentiary for Social Security Reform (1997), *Security Through Diversity – Reform of the Pension System in Poland*, Warsaw, mimeo.

Oláh, Péter and Béla Finczicziki (2001), 'Gov't promises pension reform', *Budapest Business Journal*, **9** (21), 1, 22.

Olivares, David (1996a), 'Balance y comentario de las exposiciones presentadas desde la perspectiva de los trabajadores', in ILDIS (ed.), *La administración privada de los Fondos de Pensiones: Perspectiva desde el sector laboral*, La Paz: ILDIS, pp. 83–92.

Olivares, David (1996b), 'Seguridad social colectiva, no capitalización individual', in CEDLA (ed.), *Capitalización de YPFB, reforma de la seguridad social, uso de los recursos de los Bolivianos*, La Paz: CEDLA, pp. 139–44.

ONP (2001), *Información sobre Bonos de Reconocimiento*, Oficina de Normalización Previsional, Lima: http://www.onp.gob.pe/nuestrosservicios/bono/.

Orenstein, Mitchell (2000), 'How Politics and Institutions Affect Pension Reform in Three Postcommunist Countries', World Bank, Policy Research Working Paper No. 2310, Washington DC.

Orszag, Peter R. and Joseph E. Stiglitz (2001), 'Rethinking Pension Reform: Ten Myths About Social Security Systems', in Robert Holzmann and Joseph E. Stiglitz (eds), *New Ideas about Old Age Security: Toward Sustainable Pension Systems in the 21st Century*, Washington DC: World Bank, pp. 17–62.

Ortíz de Zevallos, Gabriel, Hugo Eyzaguirre, Rosa Maria Palacios and Pierina Pollarolo (1999), *La economía política de las reformas institucionales en el Perú: los casos de educación, salud y pensiones*, IDB, Documento de Trabajo R-348, Washington DC.

Ott, Katarina (ed.) (2000), *A Citizen's Guide to the Budget*, Zagreb: Institut za javne financije.

Ott, Katarina, Marina Kesner-Škreb, Anto Bajo, Predrag Bejaković and Zoran Bubaš (2000), 'Public Sector Economics: The state of affairs, problems, and possible solutions', *IJF Newsletter* (4), 1–32.

Palacios, Robert and Roberto Rocha (1998), 'The Hungarian Pension System in Transition', in Lajos Bokros and Jean-Jacques Déthier (eds), *Public Finance Reform during the Transition: The Experience of Hungary*, Washington DC: World Bank, pp. 177–219.

Palacios, Robert, Michał Rutkowski and Xiaoqing Yu (1999), *Pension Reforms in Transition Economies*, Washington DC, mimeo.

Papadópulos, Jorge (1992), *Seguridad social y política en el Uruguay: Orígenes, evolución y mediación de intereses en la restauración democrática*, Montevideo: CIESU.

Papadópulos, Jorge (1996), 'Political Stalemate and the Crisis of Social Security in Latin America: The Case of Uruguay', in James Midgley and Martin B. Tracy (eds), *Challenges to Social Security: An International Exploration*, Westport and London: Auburn House, pp. 35–47.

Papadópulos, Jorge (1998), 'The Pension System in Uruguay: A Delayed Reform', in María Amparo Cruz-Saco Oyague and Carmelo Mesa-Lago (eds), *Do Options Exist? The Reform of Pension and Health Care Systems in Latin America*, Pittsburgh: University of Pittsburgh Press, pp. 150–164.

Papadópulos, Jorge (2001), *Politics and Ideas in Policymaking: Reforming Pension Systems in Comparative Perspective: The Cases of Uruguay and Chile*, paper prepared for the 2001 Meeting of the Latin American Studies Association, Washington DC, 6–8 September, mimeo.

Párniczky, Tibor (2000), *The Pension Reforms of CEECs and the Hungarian Pension System*, paper prepared for the OECD Forum on Private Pensions, Prague, 3–7 April, mimeo.

Pastor, Manuel and Carol Wise (2001), 'From Poster Child to Basket Case', *Foreign Affairs*, **80** (6), 60–72.

Pavković, Aleksandar (2000), *The Fragmentation of Yugoslavia: Nationalism and War in the Balkans*, Houndmills et al.: Macmillan.

Peev, Evgeni (ed.) (1999), *Separation of Ownership and Control in Southeast Europe. A Comparison of Bulgaria, Romania and Albania, 1990–96*, Sofia: Kota.

Peirce, Margaret Hollis (ed.) (1997), *Capitalization: A Bolivian Model of Social and Economic Reform*, Miami: North South Center.

Pension Reform Project (ed.) (2000), *The Bulgarian Pension Model*, Sofia: USAID.

Pension Reform Project (ed.) (2001), *The Bulgarian Pension Model – One Year after the Start*, Sofia: USAID.

Pensions International, various issues: http://www.pensionsinternational.co.uk.

Pérez B., Martín (2000), *Circuito político de una política pública: reforma al sistema de pensiones en Bolivia*, La Paz, mimeo.

Perraudin, William and Thierry Pujol (1994), 'Framework for the Analysis of Pension and Unemployment Benefit Reform in Poland', *IMF Staff Papers*, **41** (4), 643–74.

Pierson, Paul (1993), 'When Effect Becomes Cause: "Policy Feedback" and Political Change', *World Politics*, **45** (4), 595–628.

Pierson, Paul (1994), *Dismantling the Welfare State? Reagan, Thatcher, and the Politics of Retrenchment*, Cambridge: Cambridge University Press.

Pierson, Paul (2000), 'Increasing Returns, Path Dependence, and the Study of Politics', *American Political Science Review*, **94** (2), 251–67.

Pierson, Paul (2001), 'Coping with Permanent Austerity. Welfare State Restructuring in Affluent Democracies', in Paul Pierson (ed.), *The New Politics of the Welfare State*, Oxford and New York: Oxford University Press, pp. 410–56.

Pierson, Paul and R. Kent Weaver (1993), 'Imposing Losses in Pension Policy', in R. Kent Weaver and Bert A. Rockman (eds), *Do Institutions Matter? Government Capabilities in the United States and Abroad*, Washington DC: The Brookings Institution, pp. 110–50.

Piñera, José (1991), *El cascabel al gato: La batalla por la Reforma Previsional*, Santiago de Chile: Zig-Zag.

Piñera, José (1996), *Bez obawy o przyszłość*, Warsaw: Centrum im. Adama Smitha and Fundacja im. Hugona Kollątaja.

Piñera, José (1997), 'Transformacija čileanskog mirovinskog sustava', in Ministarstvo Financija (ed.), *Reforma hrvatskog mirovinskog sustava i prikaz međunarodnih iskustava*, Zagreb: Ministarstvo Financija Republike Hrvatske, pp. 33–9.

Piñera, José (2000), 'A Chilean Model for Russia', *Foreign Affairs*, **79** (5), 62–73.

Piñera, José (2001), 'Puterea muncitorilor: privatizarea sistemului de asigurari sociale in Chile', *Cato Letter* (10): http://www.pensionreform.org/europe.html.

Polackova Brixi, Hana, Anita Papp and Allen Schick (1999), 'Fiscal Risks and the Quality of Fiscal Adjustment in Hungary', World Bank, Policy Research Working Paper No. 2176, Washington DC.

Polackova Brixi, Hana, Sergei Shatalov and Leila Zlaoui (2000), 'Managing Fiscal Risk in Bulgaria', World Bank, Policy Research Working Paper No. 2282, Washington DC.

Porzecanski, Arturo C. (1978), 'The Case of Uruguay', in Carmelo Mesa-Lago, *Social Security in Latin America: Pressure Groups, Stratification, and Inequality*, Pittsburgh: University of Pittsburgh Press, pp. 70–112.

Pospischil, Anton (1984), *Das System der sozialen Sicherung in Jugoslawien*, Munich: Profil.

Posrkača, Dragan (1989), 'Old-age Retirement Pension and Disability Insurance, 1984–1988', *Yugoslav Survey*, **30** (3), 129–38.

Posrkača, Dragomir (1985), 'Old-age and Invalidity Insurance, 1980–1984', *Yugoslav Survey*, **26** (4), 111–20.

Potočnjak, Željko (2000), *Establishing New Funded Pensions in Croatia*, presentation at the ICM Conference 'Pensions in Central & Eastern Europe', Budapest, 21–22 March, mimeo.

PRONATASS (1992), *Planificación Social*, Buenos Aires: Programa Nacional de Asistencia Técnica para la Administración de los Servicios Sociales.

Przeworski, Adam (1991), *Democracy and the Market: Political and Economic Reforms in Eastern Europe and Latin America*, Cambridge: Cambridge University Press.

Przeworski, Adam et al. (1995), *Sustainable Democracy*, Cambridge: Cambridge University Press.

Puljiz, Vlado (1999), 'Crisis and reform of the pension system in Croatia', *South-East Europe Review*, **2** (4), 9–17.

Queisser, Monika (1993), *Vom Umlage- zum Kapitaldeckungsverfahren: Die chilenische Rentenreform als Modell für Entwicklungsländer?*, Munich: Weltforum.

Queisser, Monika (1997), 'Pension Reform and Private Pension Funds in Peru and Colombia', World Bank, Policy Research Working Paper No. 1853, Washington DC.

Ramos Olivera, Julio (1999), *Reforma de la previsión social – piedra angular del gobierno de coalición*, Montevideo, mimeo.

Ramos Sánchez, Pablo (1998), 'Manipulación de las expectativas en el proceso de capitalización', *Dinámica Económica*, **5** (7), 26–39.

Reed, John (2001), 'Poland: Equity culture survives missing premiums', *Financial Times*, 25 June: http//:globalarchive.ft.co.uk.

Representación de los Trabajadores en el Banco de Previsión Social (ed.) (1997), *La seguridad social en el Uruguay de hoy: Una visión social*, Montevideo: La República.

Republika Hrvatska (2000), *Statistički Ljetopis 2000*, Zagreb: Državni Zavod za Statistiku.

Rismondo, Mihovil (1997), 'Pension insurance system in the Republic of Croatia: a need for an urgent reform', in Nevenka Čučković (ed.), *Pension System Reform in Croatia*, Zagreb: IMO, Friedrich-Ebert-Stiftung and ICEG, pp. 9–20.

Robles, Juan (1993), 'AFP: ¿Medias verdades o medias mentiras?', *Actualidad Económica*, **XV** (145), 6–9.

Rocha, Roberto (1996), 'The Hungarian Public must be Better Informed about the Available Options', *Transition*, **7** (1), 14–15.

Rocha, Roberto and Dimitri Vittas (2001), 'Pension Reform in Hungary: A Preliminary Assessment', World Bank, Policy Research Working Paper No. 2631, Washington DC.

Rodrik, Dani (1993), 'The Positive Economics of Policy Reform', *American Economic Review – Papers and Proceedings*, **83** (2), 356–61.

Rodrik, Dani (1994), 'Comment', in John Williamson (ed.), *The Political Economy of Policy Reform*, Washington DC: Institute for International Economics, pp. 212–15.

Rodrik, Dani (1996), 'Understanding Economic Policy Reform', *Journal of Economic Literature*, **XXXIV** (March), 9–41.

Rodrik, Dani (1998), 'Promises, Promises: Credible Policy Reform via Signalling', in Federico Sturzenegger and Mariano Tommasi (eds), *The Political Economy of Reform*, Cambridge, MA and London: MIT Press, pp. 307–27.

Rofman, Rafael (2000), 'The pension system in Argentina six years after the reform', World Bank, SP Discussion Paper No. 0015, Washington DC.

Roggero Villena, Mario (1993), *Escoja Usted: Lo que todos deben saber sobre el Sistema Privado de Pensiones*, Lima: Tarea.

Rojas, Jorge (1998), 'La rentabilidad del Sistema Privado de Pensiones en el Perú: 1993–1997', PUC, Departamento de Economía, Documento de Trabajo No. 160, Lima.

Roldós, Jorge E. and Luis Viana Martorell (1992), *Reforma de la seguridad social: Hacia un sistema de capitalización*, Montevideo, mimeo.

Rospigliosi, Fernando (2001), 'Die peruanische Presse unter Beschuß', in Rafael Sevilla and David Sobrevilla (eds), *Peru – Land des Versprechens?*, Bad Honnef: Horlemann, pp. 269–88.

Ross, Fiona (2000), 'Beyond Left and Right': The New Partisan Politics of Welfare, *Governance: An International Journal of Policy and Administration*, **13** (2), 155–83.

Rossi, Alejandro (1999), *Reforma previsional ¿cómo y porqué?*, Buenos Aires, mimeo.

Rutkowski, Michał (1998), 'A New Generation of Pension Reforms Conquers the East – A Taxonomy in Transition Economies', *Transition*, **9** (4), 16–19.

Rutkowski, Michał (2001), 'Restoring hope, rewarding work: pension reforms in post-communist economies', in Lucjan T. Orlowski (ed.), *Transition and Growth in Post-Communist Countries*, Cheltenham and Northampton MA: Edward Elgar, pp. 243–69.

Rymsza, Marek (1998), 'Reforma ubezpieczeń społecznych w Polsce – Uwagi o pracach w Sejmie nad ustawą o systemie ubezpieczeń społecznych', *Przegląd Ubezpieczeń Społecznych*, **32** (10), 3–6.

Sachs, Jeffrey (1994), 'Life in the Economic Emergency Room', in John Williamson (ed.), *The Political Economy of Policy Reform*, Washington DC: Institute for International Economics, pp. 503–23.

SAFJP (2001), *El Régimen de Capitalización a siete años de la Reforma Previsional*, Buenos Aires: Superintendencia de Administradoras de Fondos de Jubilaciones y Pensiones.

Saldain, Rodolfo (1995), *Reforma jubilatoria: el nuevo modelo previsional. Ley 16.713 de 3 de Setiembre de 1995*, Montevideo: Fundación de Cultura Universitaria.

Saldain, Rodolfo (1999), *Evolución de la seguridad social uruguaya (1985–1999)*, Montevideo, mimeo.

Sánchez de Lozada, Gonzalo (1993), *El Plan de Todos: Mensaje de Goni a los bolivianos*, 4 April, La Paz, mimeo.

Sánchez de Lozada, Gonzalo and Victor Hugo Cárdenas (1993), *Bolivia: El Plan de Todos*, La Paz, May, mimeo.

Schamis, Hector E. (1999), 'Distributional Coalitions and the Politics of Economic Reform in Latin America', *World Politics*, **51** (2), 236–68.

Schmähl, Winfried (1999), 'Pension Reforms in Germany: Major Topics, Decisions and Developments', in Katharina Müller, Andreas Ryll and Hans-Jürgen Wagener (eds), *Transformation of Social Security: Pensions in Central-Eastern Europe*, Heidelberg: Physica, pp. 91–120.

Schmähl, Winfried and Sabine Horstmann (eds) (2002), *Transformation of Pension Systems in Central and Eastern Europe*, Cheltenham and Northampton MA: Edward Elgar.

Schrooten, Mechthild, Timothy M. Smeeding and Gert G. Wagner (1999), 'Distributional and Fiscal Consequences of Social Security Reforms in Central-Eastern Europe', in Katharina Müller, Andreas Ryll and Hans-Jürgen Wagener (eds), *Transformation of Social Security: Pensions in Central-Eastern Europe*, Heidelberg: Physica, pp. 275–89.

Schulthess, Walter E. (1988), *El sistema boliviano de seguridad social: Pautas para su reforma*, La Paz: UDAPE Ediciones.

Schulthess, Walter and Gustavo Demarco (1993), *Argentina: Evolución del Sistema Nacional de Previsión Social y propuesta de reforma*, Santiago de Chile: CEPAL and PNUD.

Schulthess, Walter and Gustavo Demarco (1995), 'Budowa drugiego filaru systemu emerytalno-rentowego w Argentynie', in IPiSS and Institute for East West Studies (eds), *Tworzenie prywatnych funduszy emerytalnych w Polsce*, IPiSS Zeszyt 1(401), Warsaw: IPiSS, pp. 193–233.

Schulthess, Walter and Gustavo Demarco (2000), 'El financiamiento del régimen previsional público en Argentina después de la reforma', CEPAL, Serie Política Fiscal No. 111, Santiago de Chile.

Schwarz, Anita M. (1998), 'Comment', in Martin Feldstein (ed.), *Privatizing Social Security*, Chicago and London: The University of Chicago Press, pp. 207–11.

Schwarz, Anita and Asli Demirguc-Kunt (1999), *Taking Stock of Pension Reforms Around the World*, Washington DC, mimeo.

Shopov, Georgi (1993), 'The Social Safety Net: Determining Factors of the Reform', *Economic Thought*, **VIII**, 59–70.

Silva, Patricio (1999), 'The new political order in Latin America: towards technocratic democracies?', in Robert N. Gwynne and Cristóbal Kay (eds), *Latin America Transformed: Globalization and Modernity*, London et al.: Arnold, pp. 51–65.

Simonovits, András (1997), 'The Case of Hungary', in Mária Augusztinovics et al., *Pension Systems and Reforms – Britain, Hungary, Italy, Poland, Sweden*, Phare ACE Research Project P95-2139-R, Final Report, Budapest, mimeo, pp. 51–77.

Simonovits, András (1999), 'The New Hungarian Pension System and Its Problems', in Katharina Müller, Andreas Ryll and Hans-Jürgen Wagener (eds), *Transformation of Social Security: Pensions in Central-Eastern Europe*, Heidelberg: Physica, pp. 211–30.

Simonovits, András (2000), 'Partial Privatization of a Pension System: Lessons From Hungary', *Journal of International Development* (12), 519–29.

Simonovits, András (2002), *Hungarian pension system: the permanent reform*, Budapest, mimeo.

Škember, Ante (2000), 'Kriza i reforma mirovinskog sustava na tri oslonca', *Financijska teorija i praksa*, **XXIV** (3), 439–54.

Slodky, Javier (1988), *La reforma del sistema previsional argentino*, Buenos Aires: Ministerio de Trabajo y Seguridad Social and Fundación Friedrich Ebert.

SNP and INASEP (1996), *Diagnóstico de las inversiones de los fondos complementarios (Gestiones 1993, 1994 y 1995)*, La Paz, mimeo.

Sosenko, Barbara (1995), 'Transformations in the System of Social Insurance in Poland During the Years 1990–93', UCEMET, Working Paper No. 19, Cracow.

Sottoli, Susana (1998), 'La política de reformas de la seguridad social en América Latina en los años noventa: estilos de gestión, actores, conflictos', *Ibero-Amerikanisches Archiv*, **24** (1–2), 139–63.

SPVS (2000), 'Boletines de Pensiones', Superintendencia de Pensiones, Valores y Seguros, Julio–Diciembre 1999, La Paz, CD-ROM.

Srinivasan, Thirukodikaval N. (2000), 'The Washington Consensus a Decade Later: Ideology and the Art and Science of Policy Advice', *The World Bank Research Observer*, **15** (2), 265–70.

Stallings, Barbara (1994), 'Discussion', in John Williamson (ed.), *The Political Economy of Policy Reform*, Washington DC: Institute for International Economics, p. 46.

Stanchev, Krassen (2001), 'Bulgaria', in Thanos Veremis and Daniel Daianu (eds), *Balkan Reconstruction*, London and Portland: Frank Cass, pp. 140–57.

Stanchev, Krassen and George Stoev (1999), 'Pension Reform Models in Latin America and Central and Eastern Europe', *Institute for Market Economics – Newsletter*, **5** (2), 1–4.

Stanovnik, Tine (2002), 'The Political Economy of Pension Reform in Slovenia', in Elaine Fultz (ed.), *Pension Reform in Central and Eastern Europe*, vol. 2: Restructuring of Public Pension Schemes: Case Studies of the Czech Republic and Slovenia. Budapest: ILO–CEET, pp. 19–73.

Stiglitz, Joseph E. (1998), 'An Agenda for Development in the Twenty-first Century', in Boris Pleskovic and Joseph E. Stiglitz (eds), *Annual World Bank Conference on Development Economics 1997*, Washington DC: World Bank, pp. 17–31.

Stiglitz, Joseph E. (2000), 'Reflections on the Theory and Practice of Reform', in Anne O. Krueger (ed.), *Economic Policy Reform: The Second Stage*, Chicago and London: The University of Chicago Press, pp. 551–84.

Stokes, Susan (1996), 'Peru: The Rupture of Democratic Rule', in Jorge I. Domínguez and Abraham F. Lowenthal (eds), *Constructing Democratic Governance: Latin America and the Caribbean in the 1990s*, Baltimore and London: Johns Hopkins University Press, pp. 58–71.

Sturzenegger, Federico and Mariano Tommasi (1998), 'Introduction', in Federico Sturzenegger and Mariano Tommasi (eds), *The Political Economy of Reform*, Cambridge MA and London: MIT Press, pp. 1–33.

Świątkowski, Andrzej (1993), 'History of Social Security in Poland', *Yearbook of Polish Labour Law and Social Policy*, **4**, 193–208.

Szczerbiak, Aleks (2001), 'Polish politics in the new millenium', in George Blazyca and Ryszard Rapacki (eds), *Poland into the New Millennium*, Cheltenham and Northampton MA: Edward Elgar, pp. 91–104.

Széman, Zsuzsa (1995), 'The Role of NGOs in Social Welfare Services in Hungary', in Victor A. Pestoff (ed.), *Reforming Social Services in Central and Eastern Europe: An Eleven Nation Overview*, Cracow: Cracow Academy of Economics and Friedrich-Ebert.Stiftung, pp. 323–47.

Tebeyan, Dikran (2000), 'Employer Obligations in the Pension Reforms', in Pension Reform Project (ed.), *The Bulgarian Pension Model*, Sofia: USAID, pp. 24–5.

Tecco Miyano, Raúl (2000), *Seguro Social: un desafío estratégico para la sociedad civil*, Lima: IDEGES.

Thomas, John W. and Merilee S. Grindle (1990), 'After the Decision: Implementing Policy Reforms in Developing Countries', *World Development*, **18** (8), 1163–81.

Tilkidjiev, Nikolai (2001), 'The King as a Prime-Minister: Peculiarity of the Bulgarian Case or a Lesson to Post-communist Transformations', FIT, Discussion Paper No. 12/01, Frankfurt/Oder.

Tommasi, Mariano (2002), *Crisis, Political Institutions, and Policy Reform: It is not the Policy, it is the Polity, Stupid*, paper prepared for the Annual World Bank Conference on Development Economics, Oslo, 24–26 June, mimeo.

Tommasi, Mariano and Andrés Velasco (1996), 'Where Are We in the Political Economy of Reform?' *Journal of Policy Reform*, **1**, 187–238.

Topiński, Wojciech and Marian Wiśniewski (1991), *Pensions in Poland – Proposals for Reform*, Warsaw, mimeo.

Torre, Juan Carlos (1998), *El proceso político de las reformas económicas en América Latina*, Buenos Aires et al.: Paidós.

Torre, Juan Carlos and Pablo Gerchunoff (1999), 'La economía política de las reformas institucionales en Argentina. Los casos de la política de privatización de Entel, la reforma de la seguridad social y la reforma laboral', IDB, Documento de Trabajo R-349, Washington DC.

Touraine, Alain (1989), *América Latina – Política y sociedad*, Madrid: Espasa-Calpe.

Toye, John (1994), 'Comment', in John Williamson (ed.), *The Political Economy of Policy Reform*, Washington DC: Institute for International Economics, pp. 35–43.

Transparency International (2001), *Press Release: The 2001 Corruption Perceptions Index*: http://www.transparency.org/cpi/2001/cpi2001.html.

Troev, Theodor (2001), 'Bulgaria – Savers begin to think about their retirement', *Financial Times*, 20 November: http//:globalarchive.ft.co.uk.

UDAPE (2000), 'Bolivia: Prospectiva Económica y Social 2000–2010', PNUD, Cuaderno de Futuro No. 10, La Paz.

Ulgenerk, Esen and Leila Zlaoui (2000), *From Transition to Accession: Developing Stable and Competitive Financial Markets in Bulgaria*, Washington DC: World Bank.

UNDESA et al. (2000), *Assessment of the Impact of Pension Reform on the Risk Population Group: Final Report*, Sofia: UNDESA et al.

UNDP (2001), *Human Development Report 2001: Making New Technologies Work for Human Development*, New York: UNDP.

Uthoff, Andras (2001), 'La reforma del sistema de pensiones en Chile: desafíos pendientes', CEPAL, Serie Financiamiento del Desarrollo No. 112, Santiago de Chile.

Valentić, Nikica (1997), 'Preparation and Implementation of a Credible Stabilization Program in the Republic of Croatia', in Mario I. Blejer and Marko Škreb (eds), *Macroeconomic Stabilization in Transition Economies*, Cambridge: Cambridge University Press, pp. 204–11.

Vargas del Carpio, Oscar (1996), *Pasión y Muerte de la Seguridad Social en Bolivia*, La Paz: Editorial Aguirre.

Vargas Llosa, Mario (1989), *Acción para el cambio: El programa de gobierno del Frente Democrático*, presentation at the XXVII Annual Conference of Executives, Lima, December, mimeo.

Vargas Llosa, Mario (1992), 'América Latina y la opción liberal', in Barry B. Levine (ed.), *El desafío neoliberal: El fin del tercermundismo en América Latina*, Bogotá: Grupo Editorial Norma, pp. 17–35.

Vera Mendez, Tabaré (1999), 'La Reforma de la Seguridad Social en el Uruguay', *Estudios de la Seguridad Social* (86), 21–47.

Verdera V., Francisco (1996), 'Seguridad social y pobreza en Perú, una aproximación', in CIEDLA (ed.), *La seguridad social en América Latina: Seis experiencias diferentes*, Buenos Aires: CIEDLA, pp. 312–403.

Verdera V., Francisco (2000), 'La población en edad avanzada en el Perú: situación actual, perspectivas y políticas', in Felipe Portocarrero S. (ed.), *Políticas sociales en el Perú: Nuevos aportes*, Lima: Red para el desarrollo de las Ciencias Sociales en el Perú, pp. 283–320.

Vittas, Dimitri (1996), 'Private Pension Funds in Hungary', World Bank, Policy Research Working Paper No. 1638, Washington DC.

Vittas, Dimitri (1997), 'The Argentine Pension Reform and Its Relevance for Eastern Europe', World Bank, Policy Research Working Paper No. 1819, Washington DC.

Wagener, Hans-Jürgen (1997), 'Transformation als historisches Phänomen', *Jahrbuch für Wirtschaftsgeschichte* (2), 179–91.

Waisman, Carlos H. (1999), 'Argentina: Capitalism and Democracy', in Larry Diamond, Jonathan Hartlyn, Juan J. Linz and Seymour Martin Lipset (eds), *Democracy in Developing Countries: Latin America*, Boulder and London: Lynne Rienner, pp. 71–129.

Walker, Eduardo and Fernando Lefort (2002), 'Pension Reform and Capital Markets: Are There Any (Hard) Links?', World Bank, SP Discussion Paper No. 0201, Washington DC.

Weaver, R. Kent (1986), 'The Politics of Blame Avoidance', *Journal of Public Policy*, 6 (October–December), 371–98.

Weaver, R. Kent (1998), 'Insights from Social Security Reform Abroad', in R. Douglas Arnold, Michael J. Graetz and Alicia H. Munnell (eds), *Framing the Social Security Debate: Values, Politics, and Economics*, Washington DC: National Academy of Social Insurance, pp. 183–229.

Webb, Richard and Graciela Fernández Baca (2000), *Perú en Números 2000 – Anuario Estadístico*, Lima: Cuánto S.A.

Weyland, Kurt (2001), *Learning from Foreign Models in Latin American Policy Reform*, paper prepared for the Annual Meeting of the American Political Science Association, San Francisco, 30 August–2 September, mimeo.

Whitehead, Laurence (1990), 'Political Explanations of Macroeconomic Management: A Survey', *World Development*, 18 (8), 1133–46.

Whitehead, Laurence (1997), 'Beyond Neo-liberalism: Bolivia's Capitalization as a Route to Universal Entitlements and Substantive Citizenship Rights?', in Margaret Hollis Peirce (ed.), *Capitalization: A Bolivian Model of Social and Economic Reform*, Miami: North South Center, pp. 71–95.

Wilczyński, Wacław (1996), 'Uczymy się od Chilijczyków!', in José Piñera, *Bez obawy o przyszłość*, Warsaw: Centrum im. Adama Smitha and Fundacja im. Hugona Kollątaja, pp. 5–7.

Williamson, John (ed.) (1990), *Latin American Adjustment: How Much Has Happened?*, Washington DC: Institute for International Economics.

Williamson, John (1994), 'In Search of a Manual for Technopols', in John Williamson (ed.), *The Political Economy of Policy Reform*, Washington DC: Institute for International Economics, pp. 9–28.

Williamson, John (2000), 'What Should the World Bank Think about the Washington Consensus?', *The World Bank Research Observer*, **15** (2), 251–64.

Williamson, John and Stephan Haggard (1994), 'The Political Conditions for Economic Reform', in John Williamson (ed.), *The Political Economy of Policy Reform*, Washington DC: Institute for International Economics, pp. 525–96.

Withers-Green, Philip (2001), 'Zurich pays $19m for BBVA's stake in Futuro de Bolivia', *Pension International* (30), 12.

Withers-Green, Philip (2003), 'Bolivia: New law endangers private pension system', *Pensions International* (47), 11–12.

World Bank (1989), *Financial Systems and Development: World Development Report 1989*, Washington DC: World Bank.

World Bank (1991), *Bulgaria – Crisis and Transition to a Market Economy*, vol. II: Sectoral Analyses, Washington DC: World Bank.

World Bank (1992a), *Hungary – Reform of Social Policy and Expenditures*, Washington DC: World Bank.

World Bank (1992b), *Report and recommendation of the President of the IBRD to the Executive Directors on a proposed Financial Sector Adjustment Loan in an amount equivalent to US$400 million to the Republic of Peru*, Washington DC, mimeo.

World Bank (1993a), *Argentina: From Insolvency to Growth*, Washington DC: World Bank.

World Bank (1993b), *Poland – Income Support and the Social Safety Net during the Transition*, Washington DC: World Bank.

World Bank (1994a), *Averting the Old Age Crisis. Policies to Protect the Old and Promote Growth*, Washington DC: Oxford University Press.

World Bank (1994b), 'Bulgaria – Public Finance Reforms in the Transition', World Bank, Report No. 12273-BUL, Washington DC.

World Bank (1994c), 'Peru – Public Expenditure Review', World Bank, Report No. 13190-PE, Washington DC.

World Bank (1994d), *Poland – Policies for Growth with Equity*, Washington DC: World Bank.

World Bank (1995a), *Hungary – Structural Reforms for Sustainable Growth*, Washington DC: World Bank.

World Bank (1995b), 'Technical Annex – Financial Markets and Pension Reform Technical Assistance Project', World Bank, Report No. T-6412-BO, Washington DC.

World Bank (1996a), 'Argentina – Country Assistance Review', World Bank, Report No. 15844, Washington DC.

World Bank (1996b), *From Plan to Market: World Development Report 1996*, Washington DC: Oxford University Press.

World Bank (1996c), 'Republic of Bulgaria – Social Insurance Administration Project', World Bank, Staff Appraisal Report No. 15531-BUL, Washington DC.

World Bank (1996d), 'Uruguay – Country Economic Memorandum', World Bank, Report No. 14263-UR, Washington DC.

World Bank (1997a), 'Croatia – Beyond Stablization', World Bank, Report No. 17261-HR, Washington DC.

World Bank (1997b), 'Poland – Country Economic Memorandum: Reform and Growth on the Road to the EU', World Bank, Report No. 16858-POL, Washington DC.

World Bank (1997c), *The State in a Changing World: World Development Report 1997*, Washington DC: Oxford University Press.

World Bank (1998), 'Memorandum of the President of the IBRD and the IFC to the Executive Directors on a Country Assistance Strategy of the World Bank Group for the Republic of Bolivia', World Bank, Report No. 17890-BO, Washington DC.

World Bank (1999a), *Hungary – On the Road to the European Union*, Washington DC: World Bank.

World Bank (1999b), *Memorandum of the President of the IBRD and the IFC to the Executive Directors on a Country Assistance Strategy of the World Bank Group for the Republic of Croatia*, Washington DC, mimeo.

World Bank (1999c), *Poland – Country Assistance Strategy: Progress Report*, Washington DC: World Bank.

World Bank (1999d), *Report and recommendation of the President of the IBRD to the Executive Directors on a proposed Loan in an amount of US$300 million to the Republic of Peru for a second Financial Sector Adjustment Loan*, Washington DC, mimeo.

World Bank (2000a), *Balancing Protection and Opportunity: A Strategy for Social Protection in Transition Economies*, Washington DC: World Bank.

World Bank (2000b), 'Bolivia: Country Assistance Evaluation', World Bank, Report No. 21412, Washington DC.

World Bank (2000c), *Croatia – A Policy Agenda for Reform and Growth*, vol. 1, Washington DC: World Bank.

World Bank (2000d), 'Croatia – Pension System Investment Project', World Bank, Report No. PID9384, Washington DC.

World Bank (2000e), 'Uruguay: Country Assistance Evaluation', World Bank, Report No. 21353, Washington DC.

World Bank (2001a), *Bulgaria – The Dual Challenge of Transition and Accession*, Washington DC: World Bank.

World Bank (2001b), *Pensions Online – Knowledge and Information: Statistics*, Washington DC: http://www.worldbank.org/pensions.

World Bank (2001c), *World Development Indicators database: Data by Topic*, Washington DC: http://www.worldbank.org/data/databytopic/class.htm.

Zabala, Ricardo (1995), 'Fundusze emerytalne w Chile', in IPiSS and Institute for East West Studies (eds), *Tworzenie prywatnych funduszy emerytalnych w Polsce*, Warsaw: IPiSS, pp. 184–92.

Zdunić, Stjepan (1997), 'Pension System Reform in Croatia', in Nevenka Čučković (ed.), *Pension System Reform in Croatia*, Zagreb: IMO, Friedrich-Ebert-Stiftung and ICEG, pp. 65–70.

Zorić, Damir (1997), 'Opening of the Workshop', in Nevenka Čučković (ed.), *Pension System Reform in Croatia*, Zagreb: IMO, Friedrich-Ebert-Stiftung and ICEG, pp. 6–7.

Zrinščak, Siniša (2000), *Croatia*, presentation at the ILO Seminar on Pension Reform in Central and Eastern Europe, Prague, 12–14 April, mimeo.

Żukowski, Maciej (1994), 'Pensions Policy in Poland after 1945: Between "Bismarck" and "Beveridge" Traditions', in John Hills, John Ditch and Howard Glennerster (eds), *Beveridge and Social Security – An International Retrospective*, Oxford: Clarendon Press, pp. 154–70.

Żukowski, Maciej (1996), 'Das Alterssicherungssystem in Polen – Geschichte, gegenwärtige Lage, Umgestaltung', *Zeitschrift für internationales Arbeits- und Sozialrecht*, **10** (2), 97–200.

Żukowski, Maciej (1997), *Wielostopniowe systemy zabezpieczenia emerytalnego w Unii Europejskiej i w Polsce: Między państwem a rynkiem*, Poznań: Wydawnictwo Akademii Ekonomicznej.

Żukowski, Maciej (1999), 'The New Polish Pension Laws', in Katharina Müller, Andreas Ryll and Hans-Jürgen Wagener (eds), *Transformation of Social Security: Pensions in Central-Eastern Europe*, Heidelberg: Physica, pp. 159–72.

Index

actor 3, 12, 13–16, 26, 41, 60, 81, 85,
90, 102, 111, 120–3, 125, 133,
134
actors
collective ~ 133
constellation of ~ 15, 80, 125
domestic ~ 13, 102, 111
external ~ 3, 12, 41, 127
individual ~ 41, 60, 85, 102, 133
political ~ 13, 26, 120–3
AFAPs *see* pension funds
AFJPs *see* pension funds
AFPs *see* pension funds
agenda
policy ~ 8, 12, 13, 15, 28, 32, 34,
40, 46, 60, 80, 84, 90, 96, 102,
107, 111, 112, 127, 130
setter 120
-shifting 8, 12, 13, 80, 102, 112,
127
Andean region 2, 3, 43–71
Anušic, Zoran 97, 102, 113, 121
APRA *see* political parties, Peruvian
Argentina 2, 10, 16. 19, 20–21, 22,
23, 24, 25–32, 37, 39, 42, 90, 113,
117, 118, 119, 120, 121, 122, 123,
124, 125, 126, 127, 128, 129, 131,
132, 135
AWS *see* political parties, Polish

Bączkowski, Andrzej 85, 86, 87, 90,
121
Banzer, Hugo 58
Barreto de Oliveira, Francisco 37
Batlle, Jorge 34
Batlle y Ordóñez, José 33
Batllismo 33, 40
Belka, Marek 86

benefit calculation *see* pension
formula
Beveridge, William 117
Beveridgean model 75
Bismarck, Otto von 117
Bismarckian
faction 27, 32, 41, 60, 122
model 1, 13, 15, 19, 65, 72, 75,
112, 128, 134
blame 1, 8, 40, 127, 133
Blancos see political parties,
Uruguayan
Bokros, Lajos 75, 76, 80, 121
Bolivia 2, 16, 19, 20–21, 22, 23, 24,
47, 51–62, 113, 121, 122, 124,
125, 126, 127, 128, 129, 130, 131
Bolivida 58, 60, 130
Boloña, Carlos 46, 50, 51, 61, 121
Bonosol 55, 56, 58, 59, 60, 62, 130
BSP *see* political parties, Bulgarian
Büchi, Hernán 46, 96
Bulgaria 2, 16, 66, 67, 68–9, 70, 71,
103–14, 118, 120, 121, 122, 123,
124, 125, 126, 127, 129, 130, 131

capital markets 14, 16, 24, 31, 51, 57,
78, 80, 95, 97, 101, 102, 108, 118,
120, 123
capitalisation 54–5, 56, 58, 60, 61,
62, 130
Cavallo, Domingo 26, 27, 32, 42, 121
central bank 13, 27, 39, 62, 113
CGT *see* trade unions, Argentine
Chile 1, 16, 19, 20–21, 22, 23, 24,
27, 28, 29, 30, 31, 32, 34, 35, 37,
42, 45, 46, 47, 50, 51, 53, 56, 59,
70, 75, 90, 92, 96, 97, 101, 106,
113, 117, 118, 119, 120, 129, 132
COB *see* trade unions, Bolivian